# Object-Oriented Programming
## Using SOM and DSOM

# Object-Oriented Programming Using SOM and DSOM

**Christina Lau**

**VNR** VAN NOSTRAND REINHOLD
An International Thomson Publishing Company

New York • London • Bonn • Boston • Detroit • Madrid • Melbourne • Mexico City
Paris • Singapore • Tokyo • Toronto • Albany NY • Belmont CA • Cincinnati OH

Library of Congress Catalog Card Number 94-20906
ISBN 0-442-01948-3



I(T)P Van Nostrand Reinhold, an International Thomson Publishing company.
ITP logo is a trademark under license.

Printed in the United States of America

Van Nostrand Reinhold
115 Fifth Avenue
New York, NY  10003

ITP Germany
Königswinterer Strasse 418
53227 Bonn
Germany

International Thomson Publishing
Berkshire House
168-173 High Holborn
London WC1V 7AA
England

International Thomson Publishing Asia
221 Henderson Road
#05–10 Henderson Building
Singapore 0315

Thomas Nelson Australia
102 Dodds Street
South Melbourne, Victoria 3205
Australia

International Thomson Publishing Japan
Hirakawacho Kyowa Building, 3F
2-2-1 Hirakawa-cho, Chiyoda-ku
Tokyo 102
Japan

Nelson Canada
1120 Birchmount Road
Scarborough, Ontario
M1K 5G4, Canada

RRDHB   16 15 14 13 12 11 10 9 8 7 6 5 4 3 2 1

OS/2 Accredited logo is a trademark of IBM Corp. and is used by Van Nostrand Reinhold under license. Object-Oriented Programming Using SOM and DSOM is independently published by Van Nostrand Reinhold. IBM Corp. is not responsible in any way for the contents of this publication.

Van Nostrand Reinhold is an accredited member of the IBM Independent Vendor League.

Library of Congress Cataloging in Publication Data

Lau, Christina.
    Object-Oriented Programming Using SOM and DSOM / Christina Lau
        p.   cm.
    Includes bibliographical references and index.
    ISBN 0-442-01948-3
    1. Object-oriented programming (Computer science)   2. Computer
software—Development   I. Title.
QA76.64.L37   1994
005.26—dc20                                          94-20906
                                                          CIP

# Contents

# Foreword

---

When the System Object Model (SOM) was first introduced by IBM in OS/2 2.0, it was immediately recognized as a major leap forward by the software engineering community. Finally, the barriers to the pervasive adoption of object technology were being removed.

SOM solves a number of very practical problems that developers of object libraries face:

- How to allow their classes to be distributed and subclassed in binary form
- How to allow their classes to be used, including full subclassability, across languages
- How to provide for subsequent updating (such as bug fixes or enhancements) of their libraries without requiring applications that use those libraries to be recompiled

Since its initial introduction on OS/2, SOM has evolved and been enhanced to satisfy the requirements of its rapidly growing user community. SOM is now fully compliant with the Object Management Group's Common Object Request Broker Architecture Standard. Implementations of SOM span multiple platforms including OS/2, Windows 3.1, AIX, and Macintosh System 7. Work is underway to provide SOM bindings from SmallTalk and COBOL.

And SOM is now much more than an advanced object model and runtime engine. The distributed SOM framework enables the development of distributed object applications. The persistence framework allows the mapping of persistent object applications. The replication framework facilitates the development of applications employing replicated objects that automatically communicate changes in state to their replicas on the network. Over the course of the next year, numerous object services built on SOM will become available including naming, events, security, transactions, and concurrency control.

As with any emerging technology, there are paradigm shifts that the user must traverse in order to benefit most from the technology. It is very helpful to have a competent guide for this transition. Christina Lau is eminently qualified to write on SOM. She has developed applications using SOM on multiple platforms in both stand-alone and client-server environments. She is recognized across IBM as an important resource for her understanding of SOM and its implementation.

I am very excited about the opportunities that the SOM technology brings to the component software industry. This book is the perfect complement to that technology. It will make your interaction and growth with the SOM technology as productive as possible.

*Cliff Reeves*
*Austin, Texas*

# Preface

This book is for people interested in learning IBM's System Object Model (SOM).
It is the result of my experiences with using SOM to build various applications.
The SOMobjects Developer Toolkit comes with a huge volume of documentation.
However, first time users generally find it difficult to locate the information they
need to begin using SOM effectively. This book is my attempt to provide specific
information on some of the most commonly asked questions. It does not attempt
to replace the SOM documentation, and does not use every feature of SOM. However, this book provides a lot of working examples that will help you to start
using SOM to design and implement your applications.

This book assumes you have some knowledge of C and C++, and some basic
understanding of object-oriented programming. If you are an experienced object-
oriented programmer, you can jump into the examples provided in this book and
become a productive SOM programmer in a very short time. If you are new to
object-oriented programming, this book will help you understand some of the
problems with existing object-oriented languages, and provide you with solutions
to these problems.

## HISTORY ON SOM

IBM first introduced the System Object Model with Version 2.0 of OS/2. It provides a language-neutral environment for building object-oriented class libraries. SOM objects are said to be language neutral because they can be
implemented in one programming language, and used by programs written in
another language. SOM objects also maintain full backward binary compatibility, classes implemented in SOM can undergo structural changes without requiring recompilation of client code. This makes it easier for users to install new
releases of class libraries.

The most significant application built on SOM is the OS/2 Workplace Shell. The Workplace Shell is implemented as a set of classes that are subclassed from SOM base classes. The full backward binary compatibility of SOM is clearly demonstrated by the Workplace Shell with the new release of SOM. A user can install a new release of SOM without affecting any existing Workplace Shell objects. There is no need to recompile, or relink, any of your existing Workplace Shell applications.

The second release of SOM was introduced in June 1993. This release was a major step up from SOM Version 1.0, and is available on both AIX/6000 and OS/2. SOM Version 2.0 has also been announced for the Windows environment, and will be generally available in the summer of 1994. The most important additions in this release were:

1. C++ bindings that allow you to implement and invoke your classes in C++.
2. The Distributed, Persistence, Replication and Emitter Frameworks.
3. CORBA compliance, SOM classes are now described in CORBA's Interface Definition Language (IDL) instead of OIDL.
4. Support for multiple inheritance.
5. Interface Repository for run-time typing information.

## HOW THIS BOOK IS ORGANIZED

This book is organized as follows:

- Chapter 1, Introduction, gives an overview of SOM.
- Chapter 2, Hello World in SOM, shows you the basic steps that are involved in creating a SOM object.
- Chapter 3, Understanding the Basics, examines the SOM system, the concepts of classes, metaclasses, inheritance, and method-resolution.
- Chapter 4, A Complement to C++, discusses how SOM complements C++, by providing some of the dynamic characteristics that are not available in C++.
- Chapter 5, Distributing Your Objects, examines the Distributed SOM Framework. Here we begin our journey to build an application that works with distributed, persistent and replicated objects.
- Chapter 6, Making Your Objects Persistent, examines the Persistence SOM Framework. We continue with the example we began in Chapter 5 and add persistence to the objects we created.
- Chapter 7, Using Replicated Objects, examines the Replication SOM Framework. We continue with our example and make replicas of our objects. We also implement an event notification system that uses the Replication Framework to broadcast changes on objects.
- Chapter 8, Working with the Interface Repository, discusses the database that SOM uses to maintain information about its classes.
- Chapter 9, Writing Your Own Emitter, examines the Emitter Framework. We build a report emitter using the Emitter Framework.
- Chapter 10, Future Directions, concludes the book and discusses some of the on-going work and the future directions of SOM.

# Acknowledgments

I want to thank Harm Sluiman for his enthusiasm and encouragement throughout the writing process.

Ashok Malhotra and Andy Martin read the entire manuscript and provided numerous suggestions and insights. I am deeply grateful for their contribution and personal commitment to reviewing the book in a very short period of time.

Bart Jacob, Harm Sluiman, Marc Smith and Hendra Suwanda also reviewed part of the manuscript and provided invaluable comments. Their suggestions have made this a better book.

I appreciate the support of the many people at IBM. Bob Orfali, Gail Ostrow, and Roger Sessions, especially, have encouraged and supported the publishing activity.

I must thank Ron Holt for so generously lending me his ThinkPad. It sped up the writing process.

Dianne Littwin and her staff at VNR were great to work with and very responsive to my urgent desire to get this book to market.

Finally, a special thanks to the SOM team for creating this superb product.

# 1

# Introduction

---



## 1.1  WHAT IS SOM?

SOM stands for System Object Model. It is a new model for developing and packaging object-oriented software. SOM offers different benefits to different people:

- To those who build and distribute class libraries: SOM can save the users of the class libraries from recompiling their source code every time there is a new release of the class library.
- To those who would like to adopt object technology but want to use a more familiar language, such as C or COBOL, for their development: SOM offers language bindings that let you implement your classes in a variety of languages.
- To those who want to build distributed applications: the *Distributed SOM Framework* provides transparent access to objects that are distributed across address spaces on different machines.
- To those who are interested in saving objects: the *Persistence SOM Framework* allows you to store objects in a persistent store, such as a file system or a relational database, and then restore the objects at a later time.
- To those who are interested in providing workgroup solutions: the *Replication SOM Framework* allows you to replicate your objects across different address spaces and handles the propagation of updates to all replicated copies of an object.
- To the compiler vendors who would like to supply SOM bindings for their compilers: the *Emitter Framework* allows you to parse an interface definition so that you can use the returned information to produce your own language emitters, without having to write your own IDL compiler.

## 1.2    WHY SOM?

SOM was developed to promote better software reuse. The original SOM architects discovered that although object-oriented programming promises great reuse potential, in reality, this was quite difficult. One of the problems is that different languages have different programming models. Classes developed in one language cannot be easily used in another language. For example, a class library developed in C++ cannot be easily used by a Smalltalk program, and a OOCOBOL program cannot easily use a Smalltalk class. This situation is even worse in C++, where classes built with different C++ compilers are often incompatible with one another.

SOM solves this problem by providing a language-neutral object model. Using SOM, classes can be developed in one language, and used in another language. SOM supports the common object-oriented concepts, such as classes, abstraction, and inheritance. This makes it possible for programmers who use procedural languages to also design and implement in an object-oriented fashion.

Since SOM is language neutral, you will find that some language-specific features are not supported in SOM. For example, SOM does not support C++ templates; however, you do not have to use SOM in your entire application. You can implement some objects as C++ objects and some objects as SOM objects. You can use C++, Smalltalk, or other languages to implement your internal objects and use SOM only when you want the functions to be accessed by different languages.

SOM also allows you to distribute class libraries as dynamic link libraries, without requiring recompilation of application source code. For libraries that are developed in procedure-based language, maintaining upward binary compatibility is normally not a problem. However, for libraries that are developed in object-oriented languages such as C++, structural changes in a class interface, such as when new methods are added, will require recompilation of client programs. This can present a serious problem, because recompilation might not be possible in cases when the source code is not available.

## 1.3    SOM ARCHITECTURE

Figure 1.1 shows the architecture of SOM. The *Language Neutral Object Interface Definition* defines the interface to an object. An interface contains only the information that the client of the object must know in order to use the object. The internal details, or the implementation of the object, are not included in the interface. The interface is described in a formal language called the *Interface Definition Language* (IDL), which is independent of other programming languages.

The SOM compiler compiles the interface definition to produce language-specific bindings. A language binding maps an IDL concept to a specific language construct. For example, an IDL inheritance specification might be mapped

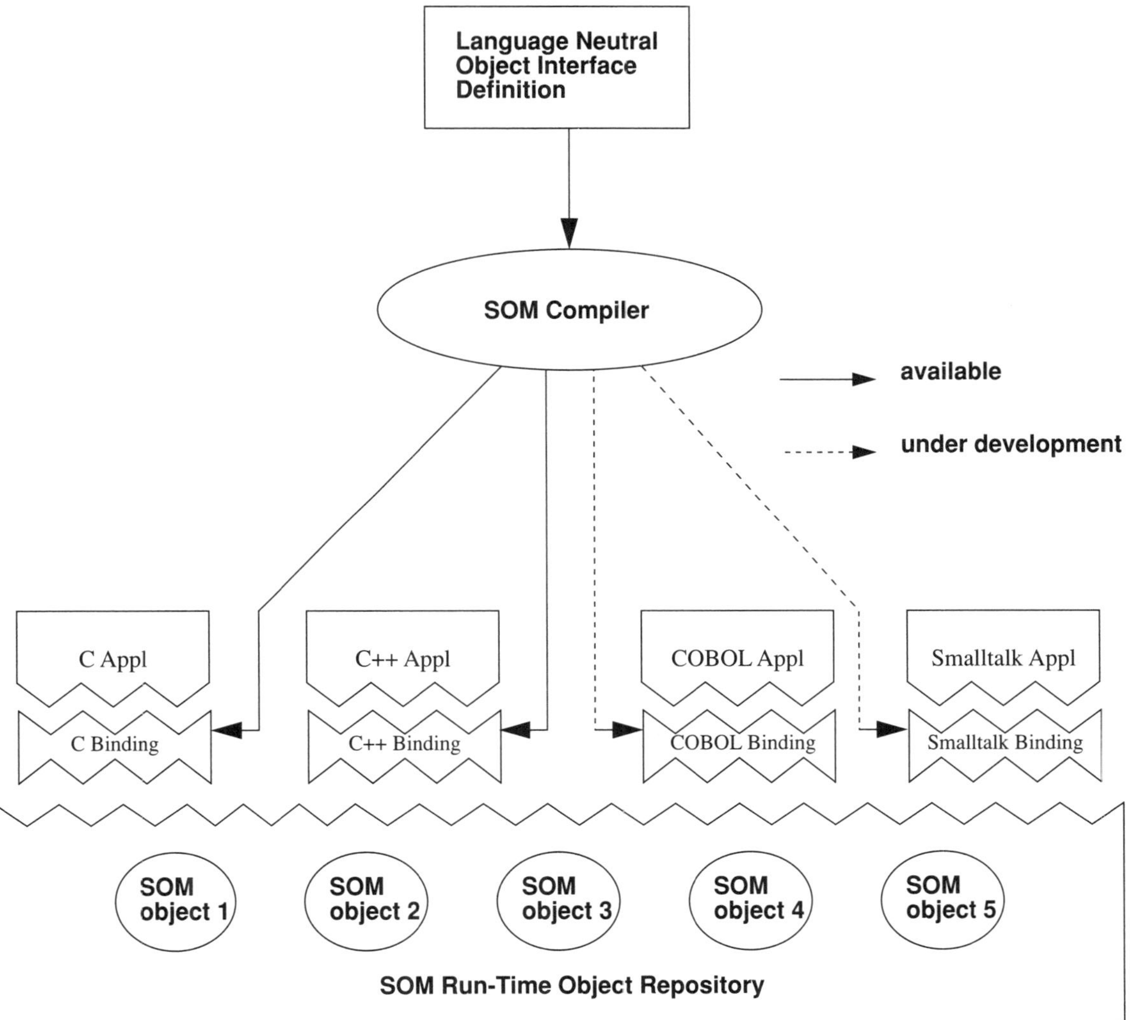


**Figure 1.1** The SOM architecture

directly onto an inheritance construct in a language that supports inheritance, or to a procedure declaration in a language that has no notion of inheritance.

The boundary between the language specific bindings to the SOM objects indicates that a client can use any of the supported languages to invoke a SOM object, regardless of the language in which the SOM object is implemented. The protocol between the language bindings and the SOM objects is based on simple procedure calls. For each language binding, the SOM compiler generates the appropriate application programming interfaces (APIs) to the SOM objects.

The SOM Run-Time Object Repository provides functions for creating objects and invoking methods on the objects. It also maintains a registry of all classes in the current process, and assists in the dynamic loading and unloading of classes. We will explore this in more detail in Chapter 3.

## 1.4    SOM COMPONENTS

SOM has now gone well beyond the initial objective of providing a common object model for different languages and maintaining upward binary compatibility of class libraries. In release 2.0, SOM introduced a number of additional components that help programmers develop object-oriented applications. Figure 1.2 shows all the components in SOM. A description of each component follows.

### 1.4.1    SOM Run-Time Kernel

The SOM run-time kernel provides a set of functions for creating objects and invoking methods on them. Other SOM components are built on the run-time kernel.

### 1.4.2    Distributed SOM

Distributed SOM (DSOM) is a framework that supports access to objects in a distributed application. An application can use DSOM to access objects in other processes, even on different machines.

### 1.4.3    Persistence SOM

Persistence SOM (PSOM) is a framework that supports storing and restoring of objects. An application can use PSOM to preserve the state of an object beyond the existence of the process that creates the object.

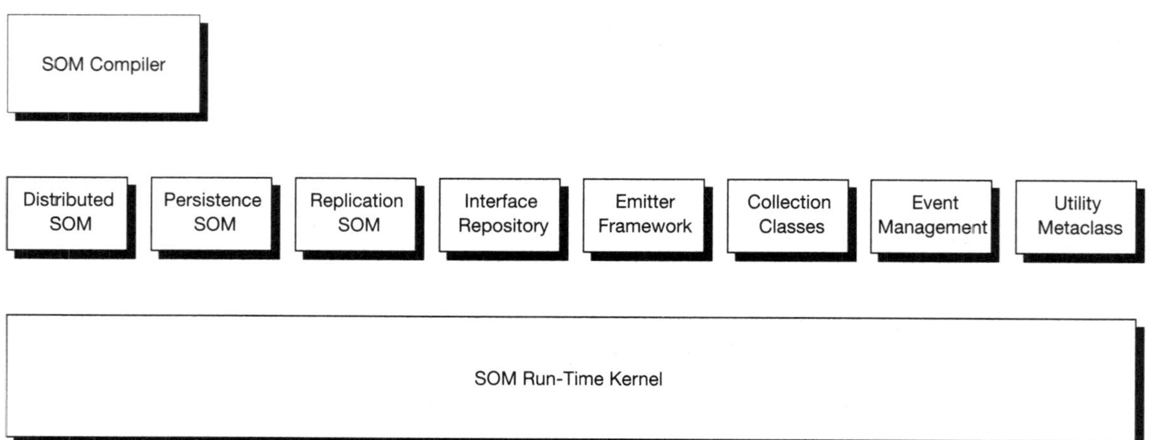


**Figure 1.2** The SOM components

### 1.4.4   Replication SOM

Replication SOM (RSOM) is a framework that allows a replica (copy) of an object to exist in multiple address spaces while maintaining a single-copy image. Updates to any copy are propagated immediately to all other copies. An application can use RSOM to instantaneously share common data objects.

### 1.4.5   Interface Repository

The Interface Repository is a database that contains all the information in an interface definition. An application can use the Interface Repository, at run-time, to find all the information that is stored in the IDL description of an object.

### 1.4.6   Emitter Framework

The Emitter Framework is a collection of classes that assist users who would like to provide language specific bindings or other more general emitters such as documentation for IDL. It off-loads the burden of having to write IDL parsers for these programmers. It also provides a template facility for specifying the output format.

### 1.4.7   Collection Classes

The Collection Classes are a large group of classes provided for the programmer's convenience. They implement most of the frequently used data structures such as lists, sets, queues, stacks, hash table, and dictionaries. These classes originated from a company named Taligent and were first implemented in C++. Taligent is jointly owned by IBM, Apple and Hewlett-Packard. Its mission is to create a new desktop environment that is object-based from the ground up. These classes have been made into SOM classes for use with the SOM Toolkit.

### 1.4.8   Event Management

The Event Management Framework is a central facility for registering all events of an application. It provides a way to group application events and to process all events in a single event-processing loop. This is useful for interactive applications that need to process background events, such as messages arriving from a remote process. This framework is particularly useful in a single-threaded environment, as it allows an application to recognize and process all events in a single main loop.

### 1.4.9   Utility Metaclass

The Utility Metaclass provides a facility that guarantees the creation of only one instance of a class.

### 1.4.10  SOM Compiler

The SOM compiler is a tool that helps programmers build classes where the interface is separated from the implementation. The SOM compiler reads an interface definition, then generates the bindings and implementation skeleton for a class.

## 1.5  SOM, OMG, AND CORBA

The Object Management Group (OMG) is a consortium that was formed in 1989 with the purpose of creating industry standards for commercially available object-oriented systems by focusing on Distributed Applications, Distributed Services, and Common Facilities. Its mission is to define a set of standard interfaces for inter-operable software components. The first specification defined is an Object Request Broker (ORB). It provides the mechanisms by which objects transparently make, and receive, requests and responses. In so doing, the ORB provides inter-operability between applications on different machines in heterogeneous distributed environments and seamlessly interconnects multiple object systems.

In September 1991, OMG selected a standard interface for the ORB. This interface is called the *Common Object Request Broker Architecture (CORBA)*. It is a joint proposal of Digital Equipment Corporation, Hewlett-Packard Company, HyperDesk Corporation, NCR Corporation, Object Design Inc., and SunSoft Corporation. The most important feature of the CORBA specification is its Interface Definition Language (IDL). The IDL language is used to describe the interfaces that client objects call and object implementation provides.

So why is this important? It is important because Distributed SOM is an ORB and complies with the CORBA specification. Therefore, a lot of the interfaces of SOM and DSOM are determined by the CORBA specification. DSOM is built on top of SOM in order to take advantage of the language neutral and the upward binary compatibility capabilities. However, it is important to realize that the implementation of DSOM does not need to be surfaced to the application.

Some of the mappings from the SOM and DSOM implementation to the CORBA specification are given below:

- Interface Definition Language
  CORBA defines IDL as the language for defining object interfaces. The SOM compiler compiles standard CORBA IDL.
- C Language Mapping
  CORBA defines the mapping of method interface definitions to C language procedure prototypes. The SOM compiler generates the same mappings for C bindings.
- Dynamic Invocation Interface
  CORBA defines a *Dynamic Invocation Interface* (DII) that allows the dynamic construction of object invocations. A request to an object using the DII has the same semantics as a request through a stub routine to the object. SOM supports invocation on an object using the DII.

- Interface Repository
  CORBA defines an *Interface Repository* (IR) that provides persistent storage for interface definitions. The information stored in the Interface Repository may be used by the ORB to perform requests. CORBA also defines operations for retrieving information from the Interface Repository.
     SOM includes an *Interface Repository emitter* that can be used to create or update an Interface Repository. SOM also provides a *Repository* class for accessing the Interface Repository.
- ORB Programming Interfaces
  CORBA defines an interface that goes directly to the ORB. The ORB interface defines operations for converting object references to strings, and converting strings to object references. The ORB interface also defines operations for creating lists and determines the default context used in the Dynamic Invocation Interface. DSOM provides an *ORB* class that implements these specifications.

There are many aspects of the CORBA specification. We have highlighted some of them here. Readers interested in more detail should refer to the CORBA specification and the SOMobjects Developer Toolkit User's Guide.


## 1.6    A FIRST LOOK AT IDL

IDL, as defined by CORBA, is a declarative language that is used to describe the interface of an object. An interface is a description of a set of possible operations that a client may request of an object. An IDL specification can include the following elements:

1. Constant declarations
2. Type declarations
   This can include basic types (e.g., short, long, float, and double), constructed types (e.g., structures and discriminated unions), and template types (e.g., sequences and strings) .
3. Attribute declarations
   An attribute is modeled as a pair of accessor functions, one to get the value of the attribute, the other to set the value of the attribute.
4. Operation (method) declarations
   An operation is used to define the services provided by an object. It has a signature that consists of:

   - Parameters that are required for the operation
   - Results of the operation
   - Exceptions that may be raised by the operation
   - Contextual information that may affect the request
   - Execution semantics of the request

5. Exception declarations
   This allows the declaration of data structures that can be used to return exception conditions.

**6.** Module declarations
A module is used to scope IDL identifiers.

IDL also allows the specification of interface inheritance. One interface can be derived from another interface. The derived interface can define new elements, as well as redefine any of the attributes, operations, and types of the base interface.

The following is an example of an IDL. The name of the interface is *Book,* and it is derived from the *Document* interface. A client of a *Book* object can invoke the get or set operation on the attribute *title*. A client of a *Book* object can also invoke the *print* method.

```
interface Book: Document
{
        attribute string title;
        long print(in short pageNum);
};
```

## 1.7    SOM IDL, CORBA IDL, AND OIDL

SOM IDL is an extension of the CORBA IDL. There are two main extensions:

**1.** Implementation statement
A SOM IDL may contain an implementation statement that specifies implementation information about a class. Implementation information may include things like the version number of the class, the name of the dynamic library in which the class resides, etc. Since the implementation statement is specific to SOM IDL, it should be proceded by an *#ifdef __SOMIDL__* directive and followed by an *#endif* directive. The following shows an example of a SOM IDL:

```
interface Book : Document
{
        attribute string title;
        long print(in short pageNum);
        #ifdef __SOMIDL__
        implementation
        {
            dllname = "document.dll";
        };
        #endif
};
```

Any statements that are defined in the implementation section are not CORBA and therefore will not be understood by other IDL compilers. The details of the allowable constructs in the implementation section will be described in different sections throughout the book.

2. Support of pointer types

In addition to supporting the base CORBA types, SOM IDL also permits the use of pointer types. Pointer types allow the construction of more complex data types and are also supported by the predecessor, Object Interface Definition Language (OIDL). However, the use of pointer types for new interfaces should be avoided, where possible, to ensure the maximum portability of the IDL definitions.

OIDL is the SOM Object Interface Definition Language in release 1.0. It was defined prior to the CORBA specification. When IDL was defined by CORBA, SOM quickly moved to support the standardized language. The SOM Toolkit supplies a program, **ctoi**, to assist users in converting interface definitions that are written in OIDL to IDL.

There are a number of reasons why OIDL users should convert to IDL. IDL offers multiple inheritance, exception handling, and type checking that are not available in OIDL. More importantly, however, the frameworks that were added in release 2.0, such as DSOM, require the use of IDL. Users who do not want to convert their OIDL descriptions to IDL can continue to use the SOM compiler to generate binding files from OIDL descriptions.

Throughout this book, we will be using SOM IDL. When we use the term IDL, we mean SOM IDL unless otherwise specified.

## 1.8    LANGUAGE BINDINGS

While IDL defines the interface to an object, client programs that use the object are not written in IDL. Instead, they are written in languages where language bindings have been defined. Figure 1.1 showed the different language bindings. The C and C++ language bindings are currently available from IBM and are shipped with the SOM Toolkit.

### 1.8.1    C Language Binding Syntax

Let's take a look at the syntax that a C client would use to invoke the *print* method on a *Book* object whose IDL is shown in the previous section. We will assume that a pointer to the *Book* object is stored in the variable *mybook* and not worry about how to obtain a pointer to this object for now. The following shows the C fragment that invokes the *print* method.

```
_print(mybook, ev, 10);
```

At first glance, this statement might look somewhat bizarre. Why is the name of the method preceded with an underscore, and why are there three arguments, as opposed to one argument, defined in the IDL specification? The following paragraphs will explain.

The underscore before the method name is actually a short form representation. It has a long form which follows:

```
Book_print(mybook, ev, 10);
```

The long form is defined by the C Language Mapping in CORBA. The name of a method is qualified with the interface name to provide the correct scoping. The SOM C bindings simply provide a convenient short-form macro that is also compatible with release 1.0. The long-form macro is always generated in the C binding files and can be used instead of the short form. If you want better code portability to other vendors' platforms that support CORBA, stick with the long form. In addition, if there is any ambiguity that may arise if a client uses two interfaces introducing the same method name, the long form should be used.

In order to invoke a method on an object, the object must be specified in the statement. Since C is a procedural language, it does not have the notion of an object. Therefore, a natural way of including an object will be as an argument in the call. This is what the CORBA specification defines and what the SOM C binding implements.

The second argument, *ev,* is a pointer to the **Environment** data structure that is defined by CORBA. It is used to pass exception information between the caller, and the called, method. The **Environment** structure is discussed in more detail in Section 3.14 on page 60. The C Language Mapping in CORBA designates the second parameter of an operation to be a pointer to the **Environment** structure and this is what the SOM C binding implements.

The third argument, *10,* is the page number parameter for the *print* method.

The following summarizes the argument syntax, when using the SOM C language bindings.

1. An invocation to a method defined in IDL requires at least two arguments. The first one is a pointer to the object that responds to the method. The second one is a pointer to the **Environment** structure.
2. If the IDL specification of the method includes a context specification, then a **Context** parameter must be specified immediately after the **Environment** pointer argument. Otherwise, this parameter is not needed as shown in this example. See Section 3.15 on page 63 for a detailed discussion on context. Note that none of the SOM supplied methods require context arguments.
3. The remaining arguments correspond to the parameters specified in the IDL.

For compatibility with the SOM 1.0 C bindings, there is one final exception to the argument rules. This is when the OIDL call style is defined in the IDL specification. OIDL does not support the **Environment** and the **Context** parameters. Therefore there will no **Environment** and **Context** parameters when the call style is OIDL. The call style is specified in the implementation section of the IDL using the *callstyle* modifier. If you use *callstyle=oidl,* then the method will not include the **Environment** and the **Context** parameters.

### 1.8.2   C++ Language Binding Syntax

Now, let's look at the syntax for a C++ client. The following shows the C++ fragment for invoking the *print* method on the object *mybook*.

```
mybook->print(ev, 10);
```

This syntax resembles the normal C++ invocation syntax. An invocation to a method defined in IDL requires at least one argument for the **Environment** structure, except when OIDL style is used. If the method includes a context specification, a **Context** parameter must be specified after the **Environment** argument. This is followed by the remaining arguments from the method declaration.

Note that the CORBA 1.1 specification does not include a C++ Language Mapping. However, OMG is in the process of standardizing a C++ Language Mapping for CORBA 2.0. Future releases of SOM are expected to comply with the C++ Language Mapping.

## 1.9   GETTING STARTED

To run the programs described in this book, you need to have the following products installed:

- OS/2 2.1
- C Set++ 2.1
- OS/2 2.1 Developer's Toolkit
- SOMobjects Developer Toolkit Version 2.0 for OS/2
- TCP/IP Version 2.0 (optional)

All the programs in this book are written using the SOM 2.0 Toolkit for OS/2 and the IBM C Set++ 2.1 products. The source code for the programs can be found on the utilities disk in the back of this book so that you can make modifications. If you are interested in using SOM on AIX or Windows, you can still use most of the material in this book. In particular, all of the SOM objects are portable. The exceptions are the Graphical User Interface (GUI) code, which uses Presentation Manager primitives, and the makefiles. You can consult the SOMobjects Developer User's Guide for details on how to create makefiles for AIX and Windows. TCP/IP is only required for the Replication SOM example. You can run all the other examples without TCP/IP installed.

### 1.9.1   Environment Setup

After you install the SOMobjects Toolkit, you need to decide whether you want to program using C++ or C. If you want to program using C++, run the **somxh** command to generate the C++ binding files for the classes supplied with the SOMobjects Toolkit.

If you want to program using C, there are two forms of C bindings. You will need to select one. The first form is the strict CORBA-compliant form, in which * is not exposed in object references. The second form is compatible with the OIDL in SOM 1.0, where * is visible in object references. For example, to declare an instance of class *Foo*, you would code either

```
        Foo afoo;                        /* CORBA-compliant form */
   or
        Foo *afoo;                       /* OIDL-compatible form */
```

As the name suggests, the CORBA-compliant form allows clients to access your objects using the CORBA C Language Mapping. This might be more appropriate if your objects intend to be ported to other platforms that support the CORBA standard. The OIDL-compatible form might be more suitable if you plan to move your C to C++ implementations at some future point, because the C++ implementations use * in the object references.

If you choose the CORBA-compliant form, then run the **somcorba** command to generate the C binding files.

If you choose the OIDL-compatible form, then run the **somstars** command to generate the C binding files. Also, you need to set the environment variable SMADDSTAR:

```
        set SMADDSTAR=1
```

You might want to use both C++ and C bindings in your application development. In this case, you will need to run **somxh** and either **somcorba**, or **somstars**.

However, if you want to switch between the two C coding styles, you will need to re-run the appropriate command, set, or remove, the SMADDSTAR variable, and then manually convert all the C code that you have written to the other style. This can be a tedious process, so it is advisable to stick to one C coding style.

If you are a new SOM user, then it is recommended that you use **somcorba** for C and **somxh** for C++.

## 1.9.2    Conventions Used in this Book

All the samples that are built in this book will use IDL. The call style will be the CORBA style. Therefore, all the methods will require an **Environment** argument. We will not use any OIDL.

You will notice that some of the SOM methods do not require an **Environment** argument. This is because they have to be compatabile with the previous release of SOM.

Most of the implementation will be done using the C++ bindings. The are two reasons for this choice:

**1.** The C++ syntax is clearer.

2. All the examples in the SOM manuals are presented in C. Therefore, to be a valuable reference for programmers, I have chosen to use C++ so that programmers can compare the two.

Occasionally, I use C to illustrate the language neutral aspect of SOM. In this case, I will use the CORBA-compliant C bindings.

# 2

# Hello World in SOM

In this chapter, we are going to create our first SOM object. This SOM object will print "Hello World". This exercise has two purposes:

1. To introduce you to the steps that are required to develop a SOM object
2. To demonstrate the language inter-operability provided by SOM

## 2.1  SOME BASIC TERMINOLOGY

Many definitions of objects and object related terms can be found in different publications and literature. For the purpose of this book, we will use the following terminology:

- An *object* is an encapsulated entity that provides one or more services that can be requested by a client. A *SOM object* is a run-time entity with a specific set of methods and instance variables. The methods can be called by a client program, and the instance variables are used by the object to store its state.
- An *interface* describes the information that the client of an object must know in order to use the object. An object interface is described using SOM IDL.
- A *class* defines the implementation of an object. Every SOM object is an instance of a single SOM class.
- *Inheritance* is the technique for developing or deriving new classes from existing classes. The original class is called the *base* class or the *parent* class. The derived class is called a *child* class or a *subclass*.

Some of the meanings behind these definitions may not be very clear at this point. Do not worry about this. In this and the next two chapters, the meanings of these terms will become clearer as we step through the features and design of SOM.

## 2.2    GAME PLAN

We mentioned in Chapter 1 that a SOM class can be implemented in one programming language then used in another programming language through the use of language bindings. We will demonstrate this capability in the remaining sections of this chapter. Specifically, we will implement the SOM *Hello* class in C++ and show how two clients, one written in C and the other written in C++, can invoke a method on a *Hello* object. This is shown in Figure 2.1.

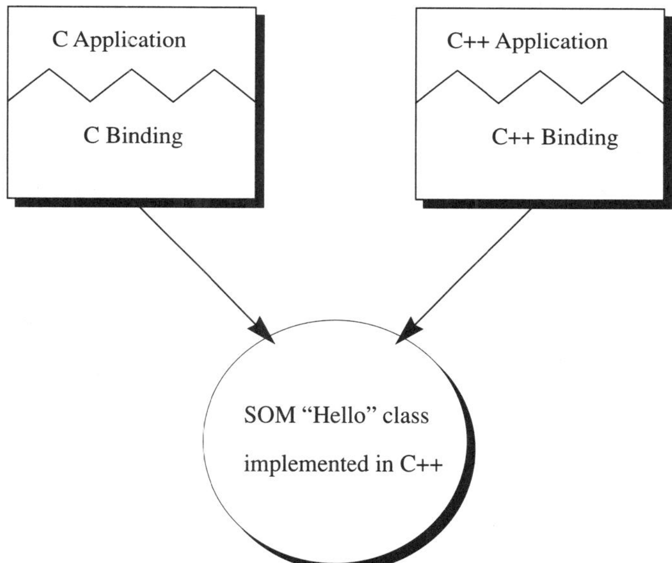


**Figure 2.1** Client usage of a class is not dependent on the implementation language

## 2.3    DEVELOPMENT STEPS

The development of a SOM class involves the following steps.

1. Define the interface for the object by creating an IDL source file. This file must have a .idl extension.
2. Run the SOM compiler on the .idl file to produce binding files and an implementation template.
3. Customize the implementation by adding code to the implementation template.

**4.** Create a client program that uses the class.

**5.** Compile and link the client program with the class implementation.

**6.** Execute the client program.

We will go through each of these steps in our implementation of the *Hello* class. The *Hello* class has one method, *printHello*. When a client invokes the *printHello* method, it will print out the string "Hello World from SOM!".

## 2.4    DEFINE HELLO INTERFACE

The first step is to define the interface for the *Hello* object. This interface is defined in *hello.idl* whose listing is given in Figure 2.2.

In the following paragraphs, we examine the *hello.idl* source file.

### 2.4.1    Include Section

The first line, *#include <somobj.idl>*, tells the SOM compiler where to find the interface definition (.idl files) for this class's parent classes. Our *Hello* class is derived from the *SOMObject* class whose IDL is defined in *somobj.idl*.

*SOMObject* is the root class for all SOM classes. Every SOM class must be derived from *SOMObject* or from some other class that is derived from *SOMObject*. We will discuss *SOMObject* in Chapter 3.

```
#include <somobj.idl>
interface Hello : SOMObject
{
    attribute string msg;

    void printHello();

    #ifdef __SOMIDL__
    implementation
    {
       releaseorder : _get_msg, _set_msg,
                    printHello;
    };
    #endif
};
```

**Figure 2.2** The Hello IDL

### 2.4.2    Interface Statement

The *interface* statement specifies the name of the interface and the inheritance hierarchy of the interface. In SOM, objects are implemented using classes, and therefore the name of the interface is used as the name of the class. The inheritance specification in the *interface* statement represents the parent class names.

### 2.4.3    Attribute Section

The *attribute* section defines the attributes for an interface. Each attribute must be of a valid IDL type.

Attributes are *instance variables* for which *get* and *set* methods will automatically be defined. These *get* and *set* methods can be used directly by a client program. In our *Hello* class, declaring the attribute *msg* causes SOM to generate the following methods:

```
string      _get_msg();
void        _set_msg(in string msg);
```

In SOM, there is another way of declaring instance variables. You can declare instance variables in the implementation section of the SOM IDL. This is discussed in Section 3.5 on page 32.

### 2.4.4    Method (Operation) Section

The *method (operation)* section defines the interface for each method that is introduced by this interface. Our *Hello* class contains one method, *printHello,* which prints the message string.

### 2.4.5    Implementation Section

The *implementation* section defines the implementation information for the *Hello* class. The *releaseorder* statement specifies the order in which the SOM compiler will place the class's methods in the data structures that it builds to represent the class.

The *releaseorder* must include every method name introduced by the class, including the *get* and *set* methods that are automatically generated for each attribute. When the class is first created, the order of the method names on the list is unimportant. Once the class has client programs, the method names on the list must not be reordered. If a method is removed from the class, the method name must not be removed from the list. If new methods are added to the class in a future release, the new methods must be added to the end of the list.

The *releaseorder* is the key to maintaining backward binary compatibility of your class. By following the rules described here, you can avoid recompilation of client programs when your class changes. This topic will be discussed in more detail in Chapter 4, A Complement to C++.


## 2.5    SOM COMPILE HELLO.IDL

After you have defined the interface, the next step is to run the *hello.idl* source file through the SOM compiler to generate the binding files and an implementation template. At this point, you need to decide in what language you would like to implement your class. Earlier, we said that we will implement our *Hello* class in C++. For the purpose of illustration, we will show the SOM compile steps for both C++ and C implementations.


### 2.5.1    Implementing the Class in C++

To implement your *Hello* class in C++, you need to generate a *C++ usage binding* file (*hello.xh*), a *C++ implementation binding* file (*hello.xih*) and a *C++ implementation template* file (*hello.cpp*).

The *C++ usage binding* file is a header file that is to be included in any C++ client programs that use the class. It is also included by the *C++ implementation binding* file. The *C++ usage binding* file contains, among other things, a class wrapper that looks like the code shown in Figure 2.3.

This may look odd, but you can see how a C++ client can now use the C++ notation to invoke a SOM object by including the *C++ usage binding* file. Thanks to the language binding, programmers do not need to know the underlying SOM APIs, and never need to look at the generated binding files.

The *C++ implementation binding* file is a header file that is included in the *C++ implementation template* file. It contains macros for accessing the class's instance variables, invoking parent methods, etc.

The *C++ implementation template* is a source file that contains stub procedures for each new, and overridden, method in the class. Their bodies are to be filled in by the class implementor.

To generate these files, run the SOM compiler using the **sc** command as follows:

```
sc -sxh hello.idl              (generates usage binding: hello.xh)
sc -sxih hello.idl             (generates implementation binding: hello.xih)
sc -sxc hello.idl              (generates implementation template: hello.cpp)
```

Or you can use:

```
sc -sxh;xih;xc hello.idl
```

as a quicker variation.

```
class Hello : public SOMObject
{
    public:

    void *operator new(size_t size)
    {
      SOM_IgnoreWarning(size);
       if (!HelloClassData.classObject)
       HelloNewClass(Hello_MajorVersion,Hello_MinorVersion);
      return (void *)
      ((somTD_SOMClass_somNew)
      somresolve_((SOMObject *)((void*)(HelloClassData.classObject)),
      SOMClassClassData.somNew))
      ((SOMClass *)((void*)(HelloClassData.classObject)));
    }

    void operator delete(void * obj)
    {
      ((SOMObject *)obj)->somFree();
    }

    /* public method: _get_msg */
    string _get_msg(Environment *ev)
    {
      return SOM_Resolve(this,Hello,_get_msg)
      (this,ev);
    }

    /* public method: _set_msg */
    void _set_msg(Environment *ev, string msg)
    {
      SOM_Resolve(this,Hello,_set_msg)
      (this,ev,msg);
    }

    /* public method: printHello */
    void printHello(Environment *ev)
    {
      SOM_Resolve(this,Hello,printHello)
      (this,ev);
    }
}
```

**Figure 2.3** Excerpt from the Hello C++ usage binding file

### 2.5.2    Implementing the Class in C

To implement your *Hello* class in C, you need to generate a *C usage binding* file (*hello.h*), a *C implementation binding* file (*hello.ih*), and a *C implementation template* file (*hello.c*).

The *C usage binding* file is a header file that must be included in all C client programs that use the class. It is also included by the *C implementation binding* file. Similar to the *C++ usage binding* file, the *C usage binding* file includes macros to invoke the SOM APIs. A fragment that shows the *printHello* method is given below, in Figure 2.4. Note that this is close to, but not exactly, what is generated.

The *C implementation binding* file is a header file that is included in the *C implementation template* file. It contains macros for accessing the class's instance variables, invoking parent methods, etc.

The *C implementation template* is a source file that contains stub procedures for each new and overridden method in the class. Their bodies are to be filled in by the class implementor.

To generate these files, run the SOM compiler using the **sc** command as follows:

```
sc -sh hello.idl            (generates usage binding: hello.h)
sc -sih hello.idl           (generates implementation binding: hello.ih)
sc -sc hello.idl            (generates implementation template: hello.c)
```

Or you can use:

```
sc -sh;ih;c hello.idl
```

as a quicker variation.

```
/*
 * New Method: printHello
 */
typedef void SOMLINK somTP_Hello_printHello(Hello somSelf, Environment *ev);
#pragma linkage(somTP_Hello_printHello, system)
typedef somTP_Hello_printHello *somTD_Hello_printHello;
#define Hello_printHello(somSelf,ev) \
        (SOM_Resolve(somSelf, Hello, printHello) \
        (somSelf,ev))
#define _printHello Hello_printHello
```

**Figure 2.4** Excerpt from the Hello C usage binding file

## 2.6    CUSTOMIZE THE printHello METHOD

The next step is to add code to the implementation template. The *C++ implementation template* that is generated from the last step is shown in Figure 2.5.

The terms *SOM_Scope* and *SOMLINK* appear in the prototype of all stub procedures and represent internal information for SOM. For each method procedure, the first parameter is always *somSelf,* which is a pointer to the target object. In this example, *somSelf* is a pointer to the *Hello* object. The second parameter is always *ev* (unless the call style is OIDL), which is a pointer to an **Environment** structure that can be used to return error information.

The first statement in the stub procedure initializes a local variable, *somThis,* to point to the structure representing the instance variables introduced by this class. Note that if the class introduces no instance variables, this line will be commented out.

The second statement, *HelloMethodDebug,* is a macro that will produce a message every time the method is entered, if debugging is turned on. Debugging can be turned on by setting the **SOM_TraceLevel** global variable to a non-zero value.

To invoke another method that is introduced in this class, you can use the notation:

somSelf->*<methodName>* (*args*)

where *args* are the arguments to the method.

```
/*
 * This file was generated by the SOM Compiler and Emitter Framework.
 * Generated using:
 * SOM Emitter emitxtm: somc/smmain.c
 */


#define Hello_Class_Source
#include <hello.xih>


SOM_Scope void SOMLINK printHello(Hello *somSelf, Environment *ev)
{
    HelloData *somThis = HelloGetData(somSelf);
    HelloMethodDebug("Hello","printHello");
}
```

**Figure 2.5** The Hello C++ implementation template file

To access an attribute that is introduced in this class, you can use the notation:

somThis->*<attributeName>*

We will now add code (see Figure 2.6) to the *printHello* method. This method prints out the contents of the *msg* attribute.

## 2.7    CREATE CLIENT PROGRAM

We now write two client programs, one in C and one in C++. Both programs will create an instance of the *Hello* class and then invoke the *printHello* method.

### 2.7.1    C Client Program

A client program that is written in C and uses the *C usage binding* is shown in Figure 2.7.

Recall that a pointer to an **Environment** structure is required for every method call. There are several ways to allocate this structure. One way, as shown here, is to use the function **somGetGlobalEnvironment**. Section 3.14 on page 60 describes the other ways of allocating this structure and shows how one can set and get values from the **Environment** structure.

*HelloNew()* is a macro that is defined in *hello.h*. It is used for creating an instance of the *Hello* class. For programmers that use the *C usage binding*, SOM provides the *<className>***New**() macro for creating instances of the class *<class-Name>*.

The *_set_msg* method is invoked to set the *msg* attribute in the *Hello* class. Notice that the *_set_msg* method begins with an underscore. Therefore, following the C method calling convention, to invoke the *_set_msg* method, two leading underscores are required. This is true for all the *get* and *set* methods that are generated for each attribute in a SOM class.

The *printHello* method is then invoked to print out the *msg* attribute.

When the client is finished with the *myHello* object, it should be freed by invoking the **somFree** function.

```
SOM_Scope void SOMLINK printHello(Hello *somSelf, Environment *ev)
{
    HelloData *somThis = HelloGetData(somSelf);
    HelloMethodDebug("Hello","printHello");


    cout << somThis->msg << "\n";
}
```

**Figure 2.6** Customize the printHello method

```
#include <hello.h>

main()
{
        Hello myhello;
        Environment *ev;

        ev = somGetGlobalEnvironment();
        myHello = HelloNew();

        __set_msg( myHello, ev, "Hello World from SOM!");
        _printHello(myHello, ev);

        _somFree(myHello);
}
```

**Figure 2.7** A C client program that uses the Hello class

## 2.7.2    C++ Client Program

A client program that is written in C++ and uses the *C++ usage binding* is shown below (Figure 2.8):

```
#include <hello.xh>

main()
{
        Hello *myhello;
        Environment *ev;

        ev = somGetGlobalEnvironment();
        myHello = new Hello;

        myHello->_set_msg( ev, "Hello World from SOM!");
        myHello->printHello(ev);

        delete myHello;
}
```

**Figure 2.8** A C++ client program that uses the Hello class

Similar to the C client, the **somGetGlobalEnvironment** function is called to allocate an **Environment** structure.

SOM recognizes the standard C++ *new* operator. Therefore, the *new* operator can be used to create an object of the specified class.

The *_set_msg* method is invoked to set the *msg* attribute in the *Hello* class. The *printHello* method is then invoked to print out the *msg* attribute.

When the client is finished with the *myHello* object, it should be freed by invoking the *delete* operator.

## 2.8    COMPILE AND LINK

We have written the C++ code that implements the *Hello* class, and we have created two sample client programs. We are ready to compile and link the client programs with the class implementation to produce two executables. The SOM run-time must be linked in by including the *somtk.lib*.

The makefile that is used to create the class and the client programs are listed in Figure 2.9. Invoke NMAKE to build the executables.

## 2.9    EXECUTE THE PROGRAM

Finally, we are ready to say "Hello World from SOM". Type:

    > chello

Hello World from SOM!

Type:

    > cpphello

Hello World from SOM!

## 2.10   SUMMARY

Language bindings allow SOM objects to be used by different programming languages. They hide the SOM APIs from the programmers and allow the programmers to use SOM objects in the most natural notation. When other language bindings, such as Smalltalk, become available, a C++ program can use or subclass the SOM objects developed in Smalltalk as if they are C++ objects. Similarly, SOM objects developed in other languages can appear as Smalltalk objects, and the Smalltalk browser can be used to browse these objects.

Figures 2.10 and 2.11 summarize the SOM development process when using C++ or C.

```
.SUFFIXES:
.SUFFIXES: .cpp .obj .idl .xih .xh .c .h

all: cHello.exe cppHello.exe

.cpp.obj:
        icc -I. /c+ $<
.c.obj:
        icc -I. /c+ $<

.idl.xh:
        sc -sxh $*.idl
.idl.xih:
        sc -sxih $*.idl
.idl.cpp:
        sc -sxc $*.idl
.idl.h:
        sc -sh $*.idl
# Link cHello
cHello.exe: hello.obj cMain.obj
        icc -Fe"cHello.exe" hello.obj cMain.obj somtk.lib

 # Link cppHello
cppHello.exe: hello.obj cppMain.obj
        icc -Fe"cppHello.exe" hello.obj cppMain.obj somtk.lib

# Compile Hello SOM class
hello.obj : hello.cpp hello.xih hello.xh hello.idl

# Compile C client
cMain.obj : cMain.c hello.h

# Compile C++ client
cppMain.obj : cppMain.cpp hello.xh
```

**Figure 2.9** The Hello class Makefile

So what happens if you have added code to the implementation template and then decide to change the interface definition file (the .idl file)? You will need to re-run the SOM compiler to regenerate the binding files and the implementation template. What happens to the existing code? Will it be overwritten?

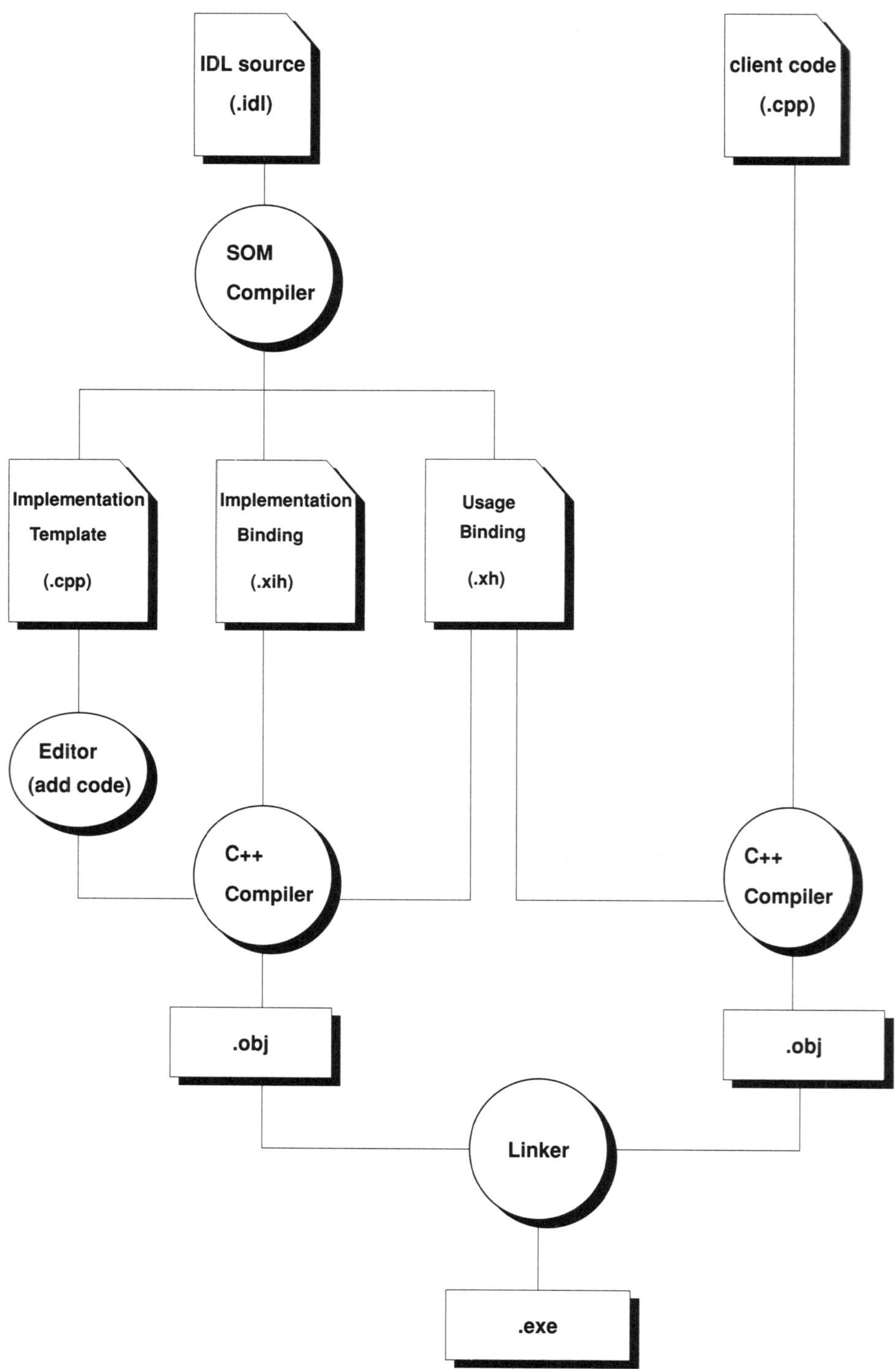


**Figure 2.10** The SOM development process using C++

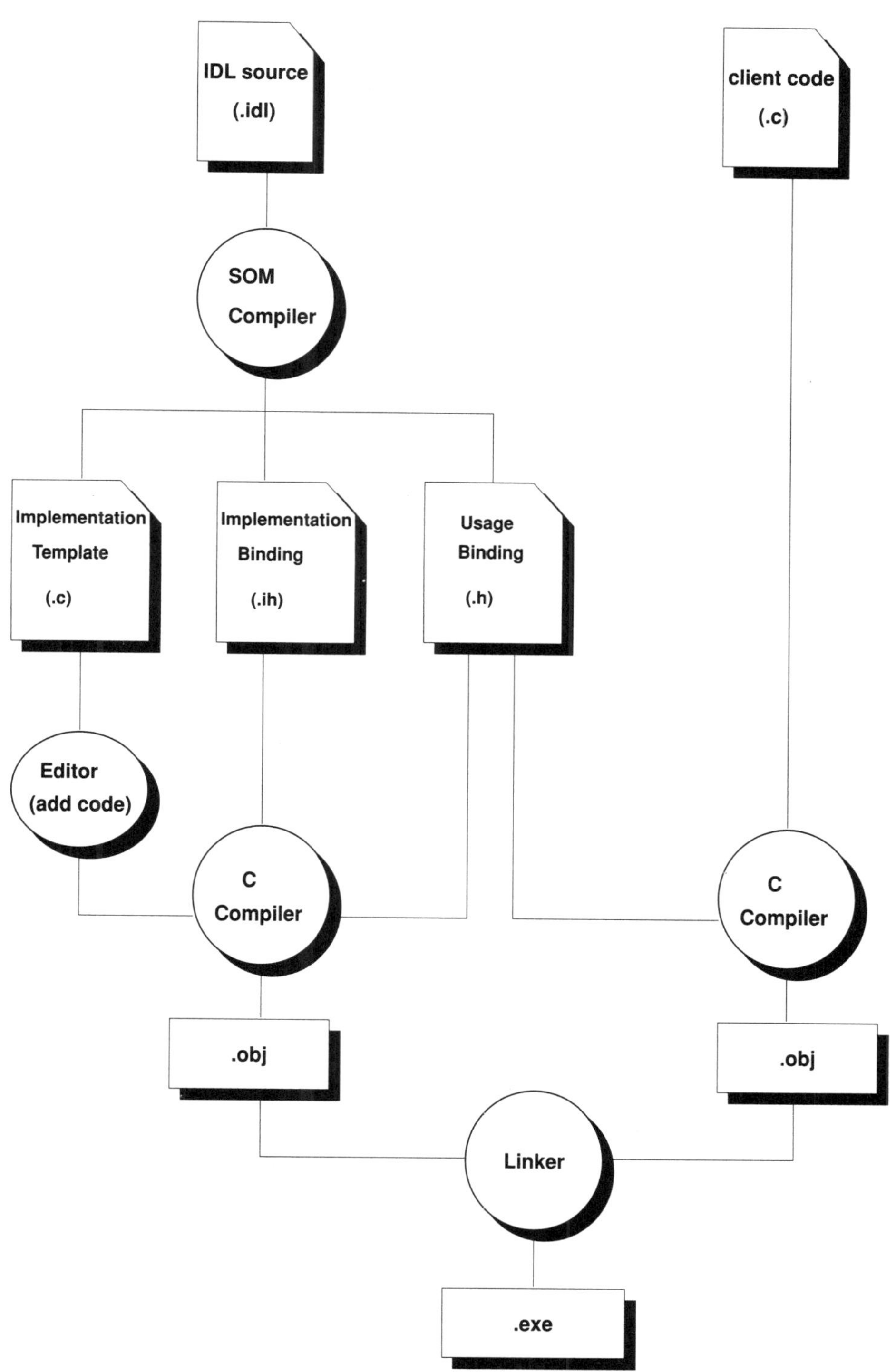


**Figure 2.11** The SOM development process using C

The SOM compiler is smart enough to recognize that an implementation file already exists, and it will not regenerate a new one. Instead, the SOM compiler will make updates to the existing file. New methods will be added, and changes to any existing prototypes will be reflected. These updates will not delete any existing code.

# 3

# Understanding the Basics

We covered the development and use of a SOM object in the last chapter. In this chapter, we will look at the SOM kernel. We will discuss the concepts and the terminologies that make up the SOM run-time environment. We will examine the SOM inheritance model and the options it provides for method resolution. A good understanding of these fundamental concepts will help you when you write your SOM programs.

## 3.1 SOMObject, THE ROOT OF ALL SOM CLASSES

In SOM, an *object* is a run-time entity with a specific set of *instance methods* and *instance variables*. The methods can be called by a client program, and the variables store data that is specific to the object. This model is similar to most object-oriented languages.

*SOMObject* is the root class for all SOM classes. All SOM classes must be subclasses of *SOMObject* or of some other class derived from *SOMObject*. *SOMObject* introduces a number of methods that define the behavior common to all SOM objects. *SOMObject* has no instance variables. Therefore, inheriting from *SOMObject* does not increase the size of the objects.

*SOMObject* provides the **somInit** and the **somUninit** methods. The **somInit** method is called on every object as it is created in order to initialize the object. The **somUninit** method performs the inverse of **somInit**. These methods are typically overridden by subclasses that have instance variables, so they can be initialized and uninitialized.

*SOMObject* also provides a number of methods for obtaining information about an object at run-time. For example, you can use these methods to find the class name of an object, the size of an object or determine whether an object is an instance of a specific class. We will see a usage example in Section 4.4 on page 85.

*SOMObject* also provides methods for performing *dispatch-function resolution*, a topic that will be discussed later in this chapter.

## 3.2    SOMClass, THE ROOT OF ALL SOM METACLASSES

A SOM class defines the implementation of a SOM object. Every SOM object is an instance of a SOM class. In contrast to object-oriented languages such as C++, SOM classes are also represented as objects at run-time. Classes can have their own variables and methods. These objects are called *class objects*. Their variables are called *class variables* (to distinguish them from *instance variables*), and their methods are called *class methods* (to distinguish them from *instance methods*).

Just like an object is an instance of a class, a *class object* is an instance of another class, called a *metaclass*.

A *class* defines *instance methods* to which its *objects* respond. A *metaclass* defines *class methods* to which a *class object* responds. Class methods perform class-related operations such as creating new instances of a class, maintaining a count of the number of instances of the class, and other operations of a supervisory nature.

*SOMClass* is the root class for all SOM metaclasses. All SOM metaclasses must be subclasses of *SOMClass* or of some other class derived from *SOMClass*. *SOMClass* introduces a number of methods that define the behavior common to all SOM class objects. The default metaclass for every class is *SOMClass*.

*SOMClass* provides the **somNew** method for creating a new instance of a class. When you invoke *<className>New()* in C or *new <className>* in C++ to create an instance of *<className>*, the bindings invoke **somNew** on the specified class. The **somNew** method allocates space for the new class object. It then calls **somInit** to initialize the newly created object and returns a pointer to it.

*SOMClass* also provides a number of methods for obtaining infomation about a class at run-time. For example, you can use these methods to find the methods the class supports, its relationships with other classes, or its version number. As we will see later in this book, SOM's implementation of classes as objects gives us a lot of flexibility at run-time.

## 3.3    SOM KERNEL CLASSES

The SOM kernel is made up of three classes: *SOMObject, SOMClass,* and *SOMClassMgr*. The relationship of these classes are shown in Figure 3.1.

*SOMClassMgr* is a special class, one instance of this class is created automatically during SOM initialization. This instance is pointed to by the global variable

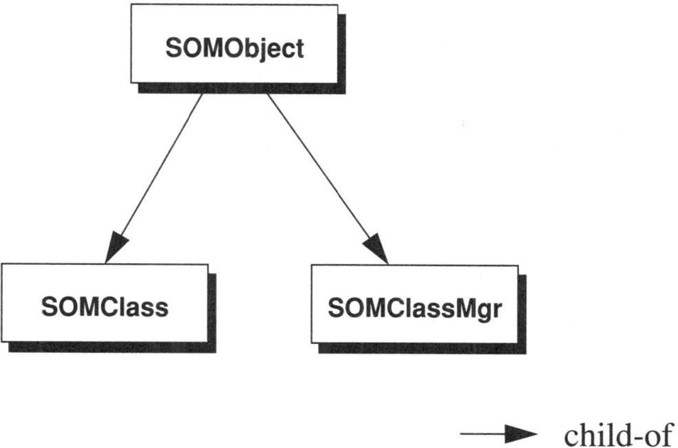



**Figure 3.1** SOM Primitive Classes

**SOMClassMgrObject**. It maintains a run-time registry for all existing classes within the current process and assists in the dynamic loading and unloading of class libraries.

You can package multiple classes into a class library. On OS/2, these libraries are known as Dynamic Linked Libraries (DLLs). *SOMClassMgr* automatically loads the DLLs when you instantiate an object of a class using the language bindings. *SOMClassMgr* also provides methods that let you dynamically load a class if you do not know at compile time which class you are going to use. This topic is discussed in Section 4.3 on page 82.

*SOMClassMgr,* however, does not automatically unload a DLL when all the instances of a class are freed. It does provide methods that allow you to unload a class and its class library. However, you have to determine when it will be safe to unload a class. A technique you can use is a *metaclass* to keep track of all the instances that are created for a class and unload the class when they are all freed. Usage examples for a metaclass are provided later on in this chapter.

## 3.4    SOM RUN-TIME ENVIRONMENT INITIALIZATION

During the initialization of the SOM run-time environment, four primitive SOM objects are automatically created. They are the class objects for *SOMObject*, *SOMClass*, and *SOMClassMgr*, plus one instance of *SOMClassMgr* pointed to by the global variable **SOMClassMgrObject**. In addition to creating these four primitive SOM objects, the initialization also sets up global variables to hold data structures that maintain the state of the environment.

So when does the initialization of the SOM run-time take place? If you are using the C or C++ bindings, the SOM run-time environment is automatically initialized the first time you create an object.

If you are using other languages, or no bindings, you need to call the **somEnvironmentNew** function to initialize the SOM run-time environment.

## 3.5    ATTRIBUTES VS. INSTANCE VARIABLES

In Section 2.4.3 on page 17, we specified that an attribute is an instance variable where the *get* and *set* methods are automatically generated. In SOM IDL, there is another way of defining an instance variable. One can define an instance variable in the *implementation* section. The syntax is identical to the ANSI C syntax for variable declarations. For example, the following declares two instance variables, $x$ and $y$:

```
#ifdef __SOMIDL__
implementation
{
    short x;
    double y;
};
#endif
```

Instance variables differ from attributes in the following ways.

1. An instance variable cannot be accessed by client programs.
2. An instance variable cannot be accessed by subclasses' methods.
3. An instance variable can only be accessed by the methods in the defining class.

Within the class that defines the instance variable, the way to access it is the same as an attribute. For example, to access the instance variable $x$, one can use the following form:

```
somThis->x;            // C++ Bindings
```

If you want the instance data to be accessed by client programs or subclasses, use an *attribute* declaration instead. How to access a parent's attribute is discussed later in this chapter.

## 3.6    PUBLIC VS. PRIVATE

By definition, everything specified in a CORBA IDL file is public. That is, an IDL describes the services that an object provides and can be invoked by a client.

What if you want to designate some methods or data as private? In SOM IDL, you can use the *#ifdef __PRIVATE__* pre-processor macro. For example, the following IDL (Figure 3.2) shows how you can specify a private method.

When you run the SOM compiler to generate the binding files and the implementation template, you need to specify the **-p** option if you want the compiler to generate bindings for both the private and public attributes and methods. For

```
    #include <somobj.idl>
    interface Foo : SOMObject
    {
       attribute short count;

    #ifdef __PRIVATE__
       void meth1();
    #endif


       void meth2();

       #ifdef __SOMIDL__
       implementation
       {
             re easeorder:  _get_count,
                            _set_count,
    #ifdef __PRIVATE__
                            meth1,
    #else
                            dummy,
    #endif
                            meth2;
       };
       #endif
    };
```

**Figure 3.2** Declaring a private method in IDL

example, the following command will generate a C++ implementation template
that provides a stub procedure for every method in the *Foo* interface.

```
sc -p -sxc foo.idl
```

How do you prevent a client from knowing about the private methods? You can
either generate a usage binding file that does not contain private information by
not specifying the **-p** option in the SOM compile command, or you can strip away
the private information from the IDL file by running a utility (called **pdl**) that is
provided with the SOM Toolkit. You then give the version that only contains public definitions to the client.

Private methods also need to be listed in the *releaseorder* in order to maintain
binary compatibility. To prevent client from knowing the name of a private

method, you can use a dummy name as a place holder in the *releaseorder* as illustrated in the above example.


## 3.7    INHERITANCE

Inheritance is the mechanism that allows you to create new classes from existing classes. The original class is called the *parent* class or the *base* class. The derived class is called a *child* class or a *subclass*. The inheritance model in SOM is summarized below and is illustrated with usage examples.

1. A subclass inherits interfaces from its parent classes: attributes (which are equivalent to a *get* and a *set* method) and methods that are available in a parent class are also available in any class that is derived either directly or indirectly from it.
2. A subclass inherits implementations from its parent classes. The implementations are the procedures that implement the methods and can be written in any supported programming language.
3. A subclass can introduce its own attributes and methods.
4. A subclass can override (redefine) the methods from their parent classes using the *override* modifier.
5. A class can disallow a method from being overridden by subclasses by using the *nooverride* modifier.
6. When you redefine (override) an inherited method, you cannot change the signature of the method.
7. A class cannot inherit from multiple parents that provide different methods of the same name.
8. A class can inherit from multiple parents that have a common ancestor. In this case, the class only inherits one copy of the same method or attribute. An ambiguity situation may arise when one of its parents overrides a method in the common ancestor class. SOM uses the *left path precedence* rule to resolve this kind of ambiguity. This topic is discussed in detail in Section 3.7.6 on page 38.


### 3.7.1    The override and nooverride Modifiers

Let's look at the following *Animal* IDL.

```
interface Animal : SOMObject
{
        attribute string name;
        void sleep();
        void habitat();

        #ifdef __SOMIDL__
        implementation
```

```
        {
          releaseorder : _get_name, _set_name, sleep, habitat;
          somInit: override;                    // Override inherited method somInit
          sleep: nooverride;
        };
        #endif
    };
```

The *Animal* class overrides the method **somInit** from its parent class *SOMObject*. It specifies that the *sleep* method cannot be overridden by subclasses, since all animals must sleep.

### 3.7.2    How to Invoke a Parent's Method

A subclass invokes a method introduced in a parent class using the same notation, as if the method is introduced by the subclass. That is, a subclass can use the form:

somSelf->*<methodName>* (*args*)

to invoke a parent's method where *args* are the arguments to the method. To access a parent's attribute, the subclass would substitute *<methodName>* with the *_get* and the *_set* methods for the attribute.

When you run the SOM compiler to generate the implementation template for the class, a stub procedure is generated for each inherited method. A default implementation is also provided for each inherited method. The default implementation invokes the parent's method.

SOM generates convenience macros in the implementation header file so that a subclass can invoke the parent's method that it is overridding. Typically, a subclass calls the parent's method and then adds additional functions to the method. The macro has the following syntax:

*<className>*_**parent_***<parentClassName>*_*<methodName>*

The following shows the stub procedure that is generated for the **somInit** method.

```
    SOM_Scope void SOMLINK somInit(Animal *somSelf)
    {
          AnimalData *somThis = AnimalGetData(somSelf);
          AnimalMethodDebug("Animal", "somInit");

          Animal_parent_SOMObject_somInit(somSelf);
    }
```

The *Animal_parent_SOMObject_somInit* macro invokes the *SOMObject* implementation of **somInit**. If a class has multiple parents, the SOM compiler will generate a macro for each of them.

### 3.7.3    Trying to Override a Method that Has nooverride Modifier

If a subclass attempts to override a method that has a *nooverride* modifier, the SOM compiler produces an error. Let's look at the following *Cat* IDL:

```
#include <animal.idl>
interface Cat : Animal
{
    void meow();

    #ifdef __SOMIDL__
    implementation
    {
       releaseorder: meow;
       sleep: override;
    };
    #endif
};
```

When you compile the *Cat* IDL, the compiler produces the following error:

> "cat.idl", line 15: error: "sleep", cannot override "nooverride" methods.

### 3.7.4    Overriding an Attribute

Let's modify the *Cat* IDL to fix the *sleep* problem. We also want to override the *name* attribute. The new error-free *Cat* IDL is shown below:

```
#include <animal.idl>
interface Cat : Animal
{
    void meow();

    #ifdef __SOMIDL__
    implementation
    {
       releaseorder: meow;
       _set_name: override;
       _get_name: override;
    };
    #endif
};
```

When you override an attribute, you are actually redefining the pair of accessor methods on the attribute. It is illegal IDL syntax to specify *name: override*. The compiler will produce an error because it assumes you are trying to re-define a method called *name*, which is not present in the base *Animal* class. (Recall how an attribute is short-hand for a *_get* and a *_set* method.)

### 3.7.5   Ambiguity with Multiple Inheritance

It is illegal IDL to inherit from two interfaces with the same method name. Let's look at the following example.

We add a new class *Pet*. The *Pet* IDL is shown below. It introduces two methods *habitat* and *owner*.

```
#include <somobj.idl>
interface Pet : SOMObject
{
    void habitat();
    void owner();
    #ifdef __SOMIDL__
    implementation
    {
        releaseorder: habitat, owner;
    };
    #endif
};
```

We modified our *Cat* IDL so that it inherits from both *Animal* and *Pet*. The new *Cat* IDL is shown below:

```
#include <animal.idl>
#include <pet.idl>

interface Cat : Animal, Pet
{
    void meow();

    #ifdef __SOMIDL__
    implementation
    {
        releaseorder: meow;
    };
    #endif
};
```

When we compile the *Cat* IDL, the compiler produces the following error:

> "cat.idl", line 5: error: "habitat" ambiguous: introduced by "Animal" and "Pet".

### 3.7.6    Left Path Precedence Rule

If a class inherits from multiple parents that have a common ancestor, the class only inherits one copy of the same method. However, an ambiguous situation can arise when one of its parents overrides a method in the common ancestor class. Which implementation should this class inherit? Should it inherit the implementation from the common ancestor class or should it inherit the implementation from the class that overrides the method? Consider the inheritance diagram in Figure 3.3.

The *LivingThings* class defines a method *breath*, implemented by procedure *proc1*. The *Animal* and the *Pet* class are derived from the *LivingThings* class. The *Pet* class overrides the implementation of the *breath* method with *proc4*. The class *Cat* is derived from both the *Animal* and the *Pet* class. Which implementation of the *breath* method does the *Cat* class inherit?

SOM resolves this ambiguity by using the *left path precedence* rule: the procedure that is used for the method is the one that is on the leftmost path. The

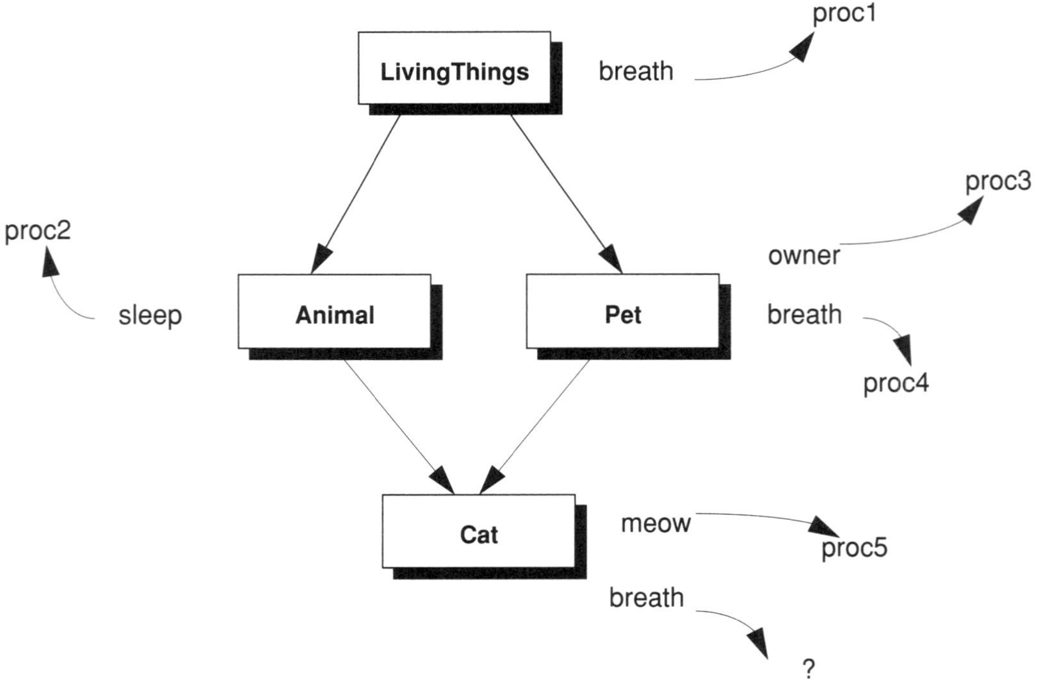


**Figure 3.3** Common parents in multiple inheritance

ordering is determined by the position of the parent classes in the IDL specification. In our example, assuming that the IDL for the *Cat* class lists the parent *Animal* before *Pet*, *Cat* inherits the implementation of the *breath* method defined by the class *LivingThings* instead of the class *Pet*.

A conceptual diagram that shows the *method table* for *Cat* is shown in Figure 3.4. A method table is a table of pointers to the procedures that implement the methods that an object supports. This table is built by the class of the object. The *breath* method in the *Cat* class is implemented using *proc1* instead of *proc4*, since the *Animal* class is the leftmost ancestor of *Cat*, from which the method *breath* is inherited.

## 3.8   PARENT CLASS VS. METACLASS

The notion of a parent class and a metaclass and their respective inheritance hierarchy can be confusing. Any given class in SOM has *one or more parent classes and one metaclass*. A metaclass has its own inheritance hierarchy that is independent of the class inheritance hierarchy. Consider the example in Figure 3.5.

Here the parent class of *Animal* is *SOMObject*. This means that *Animal* inherits all the instance methods and the instance variables from *SOMObject*. An instance of *Animal* can invoke any of the instance methods defined in *SOMObject* or *Animal* class.

The metaclass of *Animal* is *MetaAnimal*. *MetaAnimal* defines the class methods for the *Animal* class object to perform. The class object *Animal* is an instance of the metaclass *MetaAnimal*.

Recall that *SOMObject* is the root of all SOM classes and *SOMClass* is the root of all SOM metaclasses. Thus, two independent hierarchies are formed as denoted by the solid line. The relationships between a class and its parent

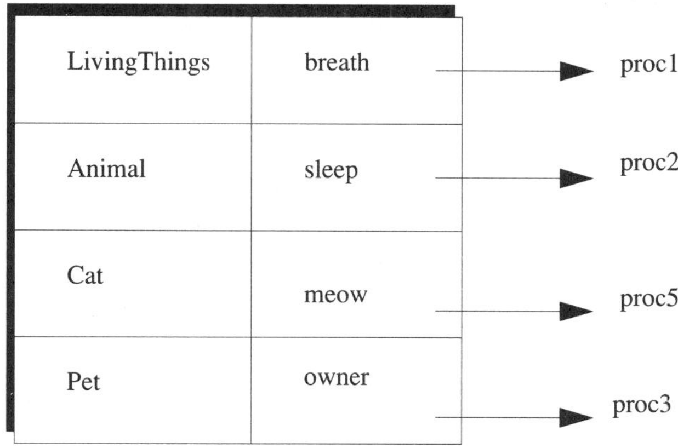


**Figure 3.4** Method table for cat

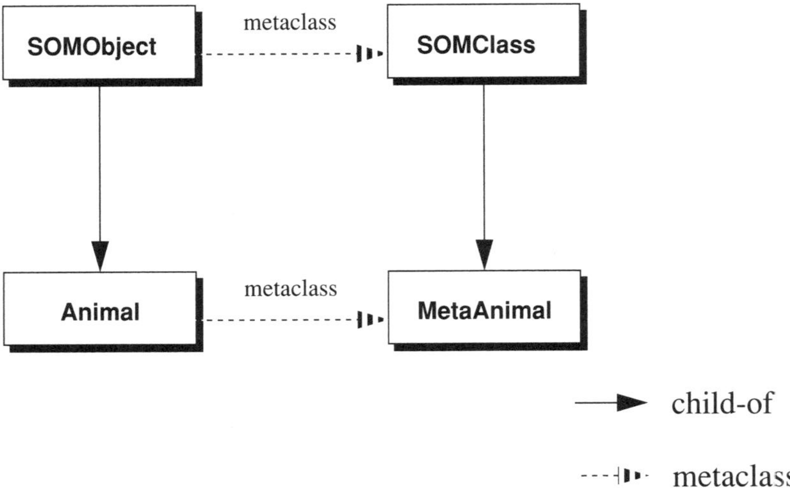


**Figure 3.5** Parent class vs. metaclass

classes, or metaclass, are defined in the IDL. If you do not specify a parent class, the default is *SOMObject*. If you do not specify a metaclass, the default is *SOMClass*.

## 3.9    METACLASS EXAMPLE

Let's look at a typical use of an explicitly defined metaclass. Recall that we use the *new* operator (or the *<className>New()* macro in C) to create an instance of a class. Unfortunately, the language bindings for both do not allow you to pass parameters. For an object that requires particular initialization values, it would be nice if one could pass these values as each object is created. Native C++ provides you with this capability. One can specify arguments in a class constructor to initialize the data members of the class.

Luckily, in SOM, one can explicitly define metaclass to handle this situation. If a class requires particular initialization values for its instance variables, it can implement a *class method* that will take input values, create an instance of the class, and initialize the instance variables to the specified input values. Instead of using *new*, a client program will call this *class method* to create an instance of the class.

The *Animal* class, whose IDL is given in Figure 3.6, illustrates this. We define the metaclass *MetaAnimal* for *Animal*. The metaclass provides the class method *createAnimal* that creates an instance of the *Animal* class and initializes the name of the animal.

The interface for *MetaAnimal* is defined in the same IDL source file. The *metaclass* modifier in the implementation section specifies the metaclass for *Animal*.

```
#include <somobj.idl>              // include SOMObject interface definition
#include <somcls.idl>              // include SOMClass interface definition

interface Animal;                  // Forward Declaration for Animal
interface MetaAnimal : SOMClass    // Metaclass for Animal
{
    // This method creates an instance of the Animal class and sets the
    // name of the animal to the input "name".
    Animal createAnimal(in string name);

    #ifdef __SOMIDL__
    implementation
    {
      releaseorder : createAnimal;
    };
    #endif
};

interface Animal : SOMObject
{
    attribute string name;

    void sleep();

    #ifdef __SOMIDL__
    implementation
    {
      releaseorder : _get_name, _set_name,
                  sleep;
      metaclass = MetaAnimal;        // Identify Animal's Metaclass
    };
    #endif
};
```

**Figure 3.6** The animal.idl file contains MetaAnimal and Animal

The implementation of *createAnimal* is given in Figure 3.7.

The **somNew** method is called to create an instance of the *Animal* class. The *_set_name* method is then invoked to set the name of the animal to the specified input value.

```
SOM_Scope Animal SOMLINK createAnimal(Animal *somSelf, Environment *ev,
                                      string name)
{
    Animal *animal;

    animal = somSelf->somNew();
    animal->_set_name(ev, name);
    return (animal);
}
```

**Figure 3.7** The createAnimal implementation


## 3.9.1    Client Usage Example

Instead of using the *new* operator, a client program will use the *createAnimal* class method to create an instance of *Animal*. Let's look at the code fragment (Figure 3.8) for creating two *Animal* objects with names *Spot* and *Lassie*.

We first invoke the *AnimalNewClass* procedure to create a new *Animal* class object. For each class, SOM generates a *<className>***NewClass** procedure in the usage binding file (.*xh* or .*h* file). This procedure creates the class object for the given class, as well as the class objects for its parent classes and metaclass. The *<className>***NewClass** procedure takes two arguments: the major version number and the minor version number of the class. The *Animal_MajorVersion* and *Animal_MinorVersion* arguments are defined in the usage binding file and refer to the version numbers of the *Animal* class at the time the usage binding file is generated.

You can specify the major and minor version number of a class by specifying the *majorversion* and *minorversion* modifiers in the implementation section of the IDL. Their defaults are zero if you do not specify them. The values for *Animal_MajorVersion* and *Animal_MinorVersion* are therefore zero, since we did not specify the modifiers in the IDL.

```
MetaAnimal     *metaAnimalClsObj;
Animal         *animal1, *animal2;

metaAnimalClsObj = AnimalNewClass(Animal_MajorVersion,
                                  Animal_MinorVersion);
animal1 = metaAnimalClsObj->createAnimal(ev, "Spot");
animal2 = metaAnimalClsObj->createAnimal(ev, "Lassie");
```

**Figure 3.8** A client that invokes the createAnimal method

If the version numbers are non-zero, then the numbers you pass to *<class-Name>***NewClass** are checked against the version numbers in the class implementation to detemine if the class is compatible with the client's expectation. If it is not compatible, an error will occur.

After the class object is created, the *createAnimal* method can be called to create an instance of *Animal* with the specified name.

Notice that when we use the *new* operator (or the *<className>New()* macro when using C), we do not have to invoke *<className>***NewClass** explicitly. This is because the *new* operator calls *<className>***NewClass** implicitly to create the class object.

## 3.10   THE SOMSingleInstance METACLASS

Sometimes it is necessary to define a class for which only one instance can be created. You may want such a class to keep track of some global information. SOM provides a *SOMSingleInstance* metaclass that allows you to do this:

```
#ifdef __SOMIDL__
implementation
{
    metaclass = SOMSingleInstance;
};
#endif
```

When you specify *SOMSingleInstance* as the metaclass, SOM will guarantee that there is only one instance of the class, no matter how many times you invoke *new* to create an instance of that class.

## 3.11   DERIVED METACLASS

A special situation can occur with metaclasses when using multiple inheritance. Consider the following interface definitions:

```
interface Animal : SOMObject
{
    ...
    #ifdef __SOMIDL__
    implementation
    {
      metaclass = MetaAnimal;          // Identify Animal's Metaclass
    };
    #endif
};
```

```
interface FlyingObject : SOMObject
{

    ...

    #ifdef __SOMIDL__
    implementation
    {
      metaclass = MetaFlyingObject;    // Identify FlyingObject's Metaclass
    };
    #endif
};


interface Robin : Animal, FlyingObject
{

    ...

};
```

The *Robin* class inherits from the *Animal* class and the *FlyingObject* class. Both the *Animal* class and the *FlyingObject* class have an explicitly defined metaclass. However, the *Robin* class does not define an explicit metaclass in its IDL. What metaclass should *Robin* have?

SOM automatically builds a *Derived Metaclass* for the *Robin* class that inherits from *MetaAnimal* and *MetaFlyingObject*. This guarantees that an instance of *Robin* class can always invoke a method on *Animal* class or *FlyingObject* class. If a *Derived Metaclass* is not built, then an error situation can occur when a *Robin* instance invokes a method from the *Animal* class that invokes a method in the *MetaAnimal* class. This hierarchy is shown in Figure 3.9.

To summarize, SOM encourages the explicit definition of named metaclasses. At the same time, SOM relieves programmers from any metaclass incompatibility problems when defining a new class. If you do not explicitly define your metaclass, SOM will automatically derive the right one for you.

## 3.12  METHOD RESOLUTION

Method Resolution is the process of determining, at run-time, which method procedure to execute in response to a method invocation. SOM provides three mechanisms for method resolution: *offset resolution, name-lookup resolution,* and *dispatch-function resolution.*

As a client, your choice of method resolution depends on how much information you have when you are writing your program. At one end of the spectrum, if you know which method you want to invoke and the name of the class at compile time, you will use offset resolution because it is the fastest. At the other end, if you do not know anything about the class or the method until run-time, you will use the dispatch-function resolution which is the slowest but also the most flexible.

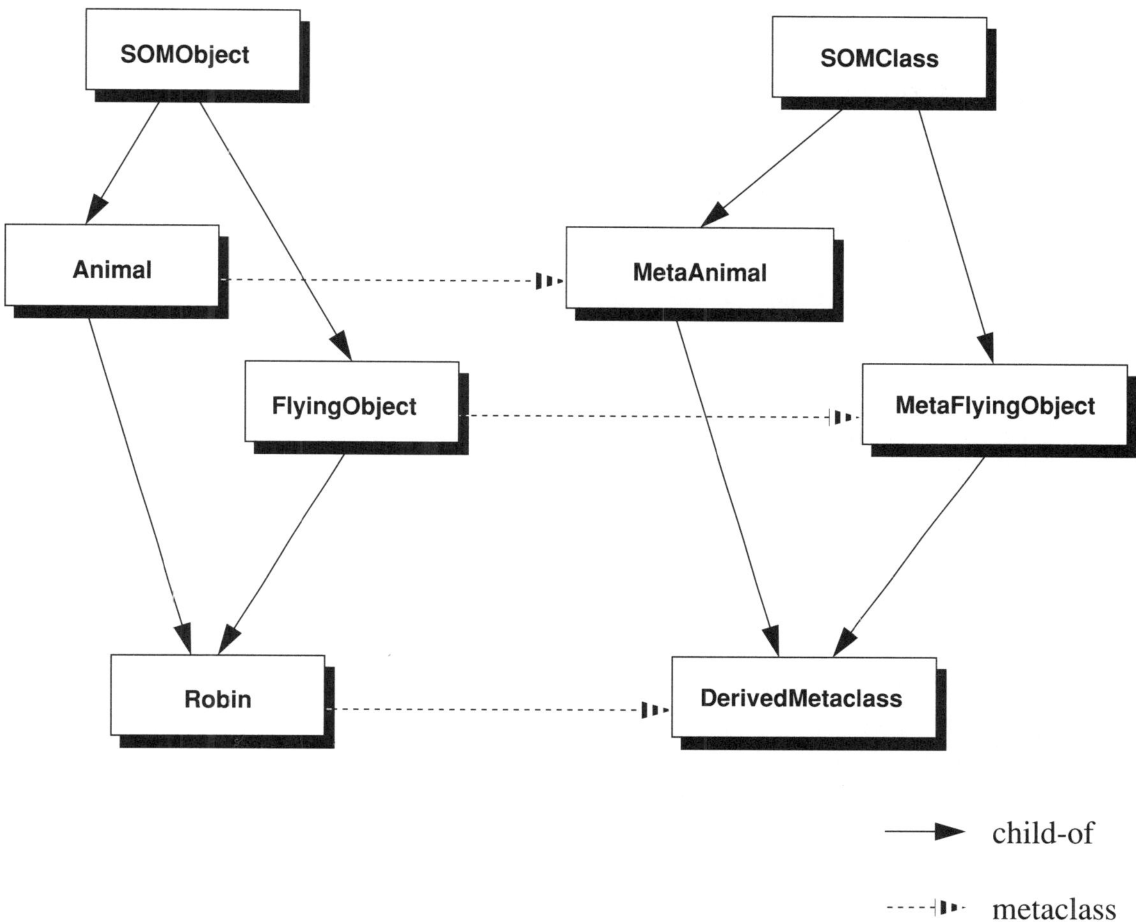


**Figure 3.9** Multiple inheritance and metaclasses

In the following sections, we will look at the three method resolution techniques and compare them. We will also show client usage in all three cases. We will use the *Car* class whose IDL is given in Figure 3.10. The *Car* class has an *instance method printCarSpec*. It also has an explicitly defined metaclass *MetaCar*. The *MetaCar* class has a *class method createCar*. The examples will also help reinforce the differences between an *object* and a *class object*.

### 3.12.1 Offset Resolution

Offset resolution is the fastest and easiest to use. It is the default way of invoking methods when using the C and C++ language bindings. When offset resolu-

```
#include <somobj.idl>
#include <somcls.idl>

interface Car;
interface MetaCar : SOMClass
{
    // This method creates an instance of Car and
    // sets the make, model and price of the car
    Car createCar(in string make, in string model, in long price);

    #ifdef __SOMIDL__
    implementation
    {
      releaseorder : createCar;
    };
    #endif
};

interface Car : SOMObject
{
    attribute string make;
    attribute string model;
    attribute long price;

    // This method prints the car specification
    void printCarSpec();

    #ifdef __SOMIDL__
    implementation
    {
      releaseorder : _set_make, _get_make,
                     _set_model, _get_model,
                     _set_price, _get_price,
                     printCarSpec;

      metaclass = MetaCar;
    };
    #endif
};
```

**Figure 3.10** The car IDL

tion is used, SOM locates the address of a method procedure from a method table. Exactly how this process is performed is explained in Section 4.1.2 on page 75.

The following constraints must be satisfied to use offset resolution:

- The name of the class must be known at compile time.
- The name of the method, and the required arguments, must be known at compile time.
- The method must be a *static method*, instead of a *dynamic method*. A static method is a method that is declared in the IDL specification of a class. A dynamic method is a method that is not declared in the IDL specification of a class but is added to the class at run-time, using the **somAddDynamic-Method**[*] in *SOMClass*. To invoke a dynamic method, you must use either name-lookup or dispatch-function resolution. A static method can be invoked using any of the method resolution techniques.

Offset resolution is nearly as fast as an ordinary procedure call. It is similar in speed to the C++ virtual function, as both of them involve looking up the address of a function from a method table.

### Client Usage

Figure 3.11 shows how a C++ client will invoke the *createCar* and the *printCarSpec* methods using offset resolution.

```
MetaCar *mcar;
Car      *car;

// Create a class object using the CarNewClass procedure
mcar = CarNewClass(0,0);

// Invoke the createCar method on the class object to create an object
car = mcar->createCar(ev, "Honda", "Prelude", 20000);

// Invoke the printCarSpec method on the object
car->printCarSpec(ev);
```

**Figure 3.11** A client program that uses offset resolution

---

[*]The `SOMAddDynamicMethod` is not documented in the Reference Manual. However, its description can be found in *somcls.idl*. It is used by interpreted system such as Object Rexx or Object Basic, where classes are constructed dynamically.

### 3.12.2  Name-Lookup Resolution

At first glance, name-lookup resolution looks strange. Name-lookup resolution requires the client to first acquire a pointer to the method procedure and then use this pointer to invoke the method.

SOM provides many ways to obtain a pointer to a method procedure. For example, any of the **somLookupMethod, somFindMethod**, **somFindMethodOK**, or **somResolveByName** can be used. These methods are invoked on a *class object* and take as an argument the **somId** for the desired method or the name for the method. The **somId** of a method can be obtained by calling the **somIdFromString** procedure and passing the method's name. In addition to returning a pointer to the method procedure, some of these methods return additional information such as whether or not the class supports the specified method.

The procedure pointer that is obtained from any of the above methods has to be typecasted so that the compiler can create the correct procedure call. This type name follows the notation **somTD_**_<className>__*<methodName>*.

To use name-lookup resolution, you must know the method arguments at compile time. The method name can be unknown at compile time since it can be supplied as a parameter to any of the look-up methods. The class name can also be unknown at compile time, as long as you can obtain a pointer to the *class object* at run-time, so that you can invoke any of the look-up methods.

Name-lookup resolution is slower than offset resolution, roughly two to three times the cost of an ordinary procedure call.

### Client Usage

Figure 3.12 shows the equivalent code for invoking the *createCar* and the *printCarSpec* methods using name-lookup resolution.

The **somLookupMethod** is used to find the address of the procedure that implements the method on the receiver class. Notice that we invoke the **somLookupMethod** on the _*MetaCar* and the _*Car* class objects. Where do these class objects come from?

If you look at the *usage binding* file for the *Car* IDL, you will see the following definitions:

```
#define _MetaCar      MetaCarClassData.classObject
#define _Car          CarClassData.classObject
```

_*MetaCar* points to the *MetaCar* class object and _*Car* points to the *Car* class object. But where do these data structures come from, and how do they get initialized? We will examine this topic in Chapter 4.

Comparing the syntax for offset resolution versus name-lookup resolution, it might not be clear why anyone would want to use name-lookup resolution. One obvious use of name-lookup resolution is when you do not know which method to invoke until run-time. However, the usefulness of name-lookup resolution goes beyond that.

```
MetaCar                                *mcar;
Car                                    *car;
somTD_MetaCar_createCar                metaCarMethodPtr;
somTD_Car_printCarSpec                 carMethodPtr;


// Create a class object using the CarNewClass procedure
 mcar = CarNewClass(0,0);


// To invoke class method createCar, first get a pointer to the method procedure.
 metaCarMethodPtr = (somTD_MetaCar_createCar)
                _MetaCar->somLookupMethod( somIdFromString("createCar"));


// Invoke the createCar method by using the pointer and passing the right arguments.
 car = metaCarMethodPtr(mcar, ev, "Honda", "Prelude", 20000);


 // To invoke instance method printCarSpec, first get the pointer to the method procedure.
carMethodPtr = (somTD_Car_printCarSpec)
               _Car->somLookupMethod( somIdFromString("printCarSpec"));
// Invoke the printCarSpec method using the pointer and passing the right arguments.
carMethodPtr(car,ev);
```

**Figure 3.12** A client program that uses name-lookup resolution

Name-lookup resolution allows clients to write generic code, when abstract base classes are used in a class hierarchy. An abstract base class defines a set of base methods where subclasses can subsequently redefine. Since the name and the signature of the methods are the same, it is sufficient for the client to only include the usage bindings for the base class, and use name-lookup resolution to invoke the methods in the subclass. The following example illustrates this.

Assuming we have two classes, *AmericanCar* and *BritishCar* that are derived from *Car*. Both of them redefine the methods in the *Car* class. A client program can write a generic procedure to invoke the *printCarSpec* method as shown in Figure 3.13.

Based on the type of the *targetObj*, the corresponding *printCarSpec* method will be invoked. Note that the client does not have to include the usage binding files for the *AmericanCar* and the *BritishCar* class. The typedef from the base class is sufficient. In addition, if new subclasses are added in the future, the same piece of generic code can still be used to invoke the *printCarSpec* methods from the new subclasses.

```
#include "car.xh"
generic(Car *targetObj)
{
      somTD_Car_printCarSpec carMethodPtr;


      //***********************************************************************
      // Get a pointer to the method produce that implements the
      // printCarSpec method on the "targetObj".
      //***********************************************************************
      carMethodPtr = (somTD_Car_printCarSpec) somResolveByName( targetObj, "printCarSpec");


      //*********************************************************************************************
      // Invoke the printCarSpec method by using the pointer and passing the right arguments.
      //*********************************************************************************************
      carMethodPtr(targetObj,ev);

}
```

**Figure 3.13** Writing generic code with name-lookup resolution

As an added convenience, the SOM compiler generates macros for name-lookup resolution, if you specify that a method is to be invoked using name-lookup resolution, by using the *namelookup* modifier in the IDL. The macro has the following syntax:

**lookup_**<*methodName*> (*receiver, args*)

The *receiver* is a pointer to the object and *args* are arguments to the method.

For example, suppose you add the following to the implementation section of the *Car* IDL:

```
#ifdef __SOMIDL__
 implementation
 {
      printCarSpec: namelookup;
 }
```

Then, a client can write a much simpler procedure to invoke the *printCarSpec* method, as illustrated in Figure 3.14.

```
generic2(Car *targetObj)
{

  //***********************************************************************
  // Convenience macro if namelookup modifier is defined in IDL
  //***********************************************************************
  lookup_printCarSpec(targetObj, ev);

}
```

**Figure 3.14** Writing generic code with convenience macros

### 3.12.3  Dispatch-Function Resolution

Dispatch-function resolution provides you with the maximum flexibility to determine, at run-time, what method you want to invoke. The class name, method name, and the list of arguments can all be determined at run-time.

The *SOMObject* class provides the **somDispatch** method that can be used to perform dispatch-function resolution. The arguments for the method are given below:

```
boolean somDispatch ( retValue,        // Return value
                      somId,           // method Id
                      argList);        // variable argument list
```

The parameter *retValue* is a pointer to the result of the method that is being invoked. The parameter *somId* identifies the method to be invoked. Recall that the **somId** of a method can be obtained by calling the **somIdFromString** procedure and passing the method's name. The parameter *argList* is a variable argument list that contains the arguments to be passed to the method. The argument list must contain all arguments for the method. That is, the first entry must include a pointer to the target object, and the second entry must include a pointer to the **Environment** structure unless the OIDL style is used. The return value is a boolean that indicates whether the method was successfully dispatched.

The *variable argument list* parameter requires special discussion. SOM allows you to declare a method that takes a variable number of arguments through a parameter of type **va_list**. Note the following when using this type.

1. The **va_list** parameter must be a final parameter, preceded by at least one other parameter.
2. You must use the parameter name *ap* when you declare a parameter of type **va_list**. Note the following example:

```
void myMethod(in short count, in va_list ap);
```

**3.** The **va_list** type is not a CORBA data type. It is not supported by DSOM. If a method requires a variable argument list, but the object also has to be accessed remotely, use a **sequence** instead. The **sequence** type is discussed in Section 3.13.2 on page 55.

**Client Usage**

Figure 3.15 shows the equivalent code for invoking the *createCar* and the *printCarSpec* methods using the dispatch-function resolution. It shows how you can use the *va_arg* macro to initialize the variable argument list.

Regardless of which method resolution technique you use, you must clearly differentiate between an *object* and a *class object*. In our examples, we first use the *CarNewClass* procedure to create a *Car class object*. We then invoke the *class method, createCar,* on the *Car class object* to create a *Car object*. We then invoke the *instance method, printCarSpec,* on the *Car object*.

We also want to recap the differences between a *class method* and an *instance method*. The *createCar* method is a *class method* that is defined in the metaclass. The *printCarSpec* method is an *instance method* that is defined in the class. To invoke a *class method*, we need a *class object* handle. To invoke an *instance method*, we need an *instance object* handle. Failing to do this will result in a run-time error when the wrong method is dispatched on a handle.

In using the *CarNewClass* procedure to create a class object, we require the usage binding file to be included in the client program. In Section 4.3 on page 82, we will show you a more dynamic way to create class objects that do not require the usage binding file.

## 3.13   SOM DATA TYPES

SOM supports all the type declarations in the CORBA IDL. It also includes some types that are specific to SOM. Table 3.1 provides a summary of the list of data types. The more complicated types are described in the following sections.

### 3.13.1   String Type

The default implementation of the *set* method for an attribute does a shallow copy of the value that is passed. This means that the attribute value will disappear when the client program frees its memory. For an attribute of type **string**, this might not be appropriate since the object might want to retain a copy of the string value after the *set* method is invoked. Should the object desire such a behavior, the class implementor can specify the *noset* modifier and implement the *set* method manually. The *Employee* class, whose IDL is given in Figure 3.16, illustrates this situation.

The *Employee* class specifies the *noset* modifier for the name attribute. This causes the SOM compiler to generate a *_set_name* stub procedure for the attribute.

The *_set_name* method allocates memory for the name using **SOMMalloc** and then performs a string copy to store the name. The **somInit** method is redefined

```c
    MetaCar        *mcar;
    Car            *car;
    va_list        startArg, arg, arg2;
    long           total;

    // Create a class object using the CarNewClass procedure.
    mcar = CarNewClass(0,0);


    //************************************************************
    // Allocate space for createCar argumets.
    //************************************************************
    total = strlen("Honda")+1 + strlen("Prelude")+1 +
            sizeof(long) + sizeof(MetaCar*) + sizeof(Environment*);
    arg = (char*) SOMMalloc(total);
    startArg = arg;                    // remember the beginning of the argument list.


    //************************************************************
    // Push the arguments into the va_list.
    //************************************************************
    va_arg(arg, MetaCar*) = mcar;
    va_arg(arg, Environment*) = ev;
    va_arg(arg, string) = "Honda";
    va_arg(arg, string) = "Prelude";
    va_arg(arg, long) = 20000;

    // Invoke the createCar method on the class object
    mcar->SOMObject_somDispatch( (somToken*)&car,
                                 somIdFromString("createCar"),
                                 startArg);


    //************************************************************
    // Allocate space for printCarSpec arguments.
    //************************************************************
    arg2 = (char*) SOMMalloc(8);
    startArg = arg2;                   // remember the beginning of the argument list


    //************************************************************
    // Push the arguments into the va_list.
    //************************************************************
    va_arg(arg2, Car*) = car;
    va_arg(arg2, Environment*) = ev;.

    // Invoke the printCarSpec method on the instance object.
    car->SOMObject_somDispatch((somToken*)0,
                               somIdFromString("printCarSpec"),
                               startArg);
```

**Figure 3.15** A client program that uses dispatch-function resolution

**Table 3.1**  Summary of IDL/SOM Type

| IDL/SOM Type | Description | IDL Usage Examples |
|---|---|---|
| short | range: $-2^{15} .. 2^{15}-1$ | attribute short x; |
| long | range: $-2^{31} .. 2^{31}-1$ | attribute long x; |
| unsigned short | range: $0 .. 2^{16}-1$ | attribute unsigned short x; |
| unsigned long | range: $0 .. 2^{32}-1$ | attribute unsigned long x; |
| float | single-precision floating point | attribute float x; |
| double | double-precision floating point | attribute double x; |
| char | an 8-bit quantity | attribute char x; |
| boolean | values: TRUE or FALSE | attribute boolean x; |
| octet | an 8-bit quantity | attribute octet x; |
| any | Use to specify any IDL type. | attribute any x; |
| struct | The same as a C struct. | struct Point {<br>    short x;<br>    short y;<br>};<br>attribute Point aPoint; |
| union | Discriminated union, a cross between C union and switch. | union swType switch (long) {<br>    case 1: long x;<br>    case 2: float y;<br>    default: char z;<br>};<br>attribute swType foo; |
| enum | An ordered list of identifiers. | enum Fruit {apple,orange};<br><br>attribute Fruit aFruit; |
| sequence | Defines a sequence of types. The syntax is:<br><br>sequence<type, size><br><br>where type is any valid IDL type, and size is an optional number that specifies the maximum size of the sequence. | attribute sequence<short> shortseq;<br><br>attribute sequence<Table,10> tablist; |
| string | Defines a sequence of char. The syntax is:<br><br>string<size><br><br>where size is an optional number that specifies the maximum size of the string. | attribute string name;<br><br>attribute string<20> address; |
| arrays | Defines fixed-size, multi-dimensional arrays. Note that an attribute cannot be declared as an explicit array.<br><br>For example, the following IDL syntax is invalid:<br><br>attribute long myarray[10]; | typedef long longArrayType[10];<br><br>attribute longArrayType myarray; |
| Object types | The name of an interface can be used as a type in IDL. | attribute Animal dog; |
| Pointers | Pointers are not CORBA standard but are supported by the SOM compiler. | attribute Animal *dog; |

```
    #include <somobj.idl>

    interface Employee: SOMObject
    {
      attribute string name;

      #ifdef __SOMIDL__
      implementation
      {
        releaseorder : _get_name, _set_name;
        name: noset;
        somInit: override;
        somUninit: override;
      };
      #endif
    };
```

**Figure 3.16** The Employee IDL

to set the name attribute to zero. Since the _set_name_ method allocates memory for the name attribute, the **somUninit** method is redefined to free that memory. The implementation for the _Employee_ class is shown in Figure 3.17.

### 3.13.2 Sequence Type

The C and C++ bindings for SOM map **sequence** onto **struct** with the following members:

```
    unsigned long          _maximum;
    unsigned long          _length;
    type                   *_buffer;
```

The _type_ is substituted by the specifed type of the **sequence**. The **_maximum** member stores the total size that is allocated for the **sequence**. The **_length** member stores the number of values actually stored in the **_buffer** member. The bindings also provide the macros **sequenceLength**, **sequenceMaximum,** and **sequenceElement** so that you can use them to access the members of the **struct**.

To refer to the **sequence** type in your C or C++ client programs, use the following notation:

```
    _IDL_SEQUENCE_type
```

where _type_ is the type of the sequence. The following example illustrates how to use **sequence** type in the class implementation, as well as from a client's perspective.

```
#define Employee_Class_Source
#include <employee.xih>


/*
 *Method from the IDL attribute statement:
 *"attribute string name"
 */
SOM_Scope void SOMLINK _set_name(Employee *somSelf, Environment *ev,
                                          string name)
{
     EmployeeData *somThis = EmployeeGetData(somSelf);
     EmployeeMethodDebug("Employee","_set_name");

     if (somThis->name)
     {
              SOMFree(somThis->name);
     }

     somThis->name = (string) SOMMalloc(strlen(name)+1);
     strcpy(somThis->name, name);
}


SOM_Scope void SOMLINK somInit(Employee *somSelf)
{
     EmployeeData *somThis = EmployeeGetData(somSelf);
     EmployeeMethodDebug("Employee","somInit");

     Employee_parent_SOMObject_somInit(somSelf);
     somThis->name = NULL;
}


SOM_Scope void SOMLINK somUninit(Employee *somSelf)
{
     EmployeeData *somThis = EmployeeGetData(somSelf);
     EmployeeMethodDebug("Employee","somUninit");

     if (somThis->name)
     {
              SOMFree(somThis->name);
     }
     Employee_parent_SOMObject_somUninit(somSelf);
}
```

**Figure 3.17** The Employee class implementation

The *Company* class IDL is given in Figure 3.18. It contains the attribute *empList* which is a **sequence** type. The *empList* is used to maintain the list of *Employee*. The *addEmployee* method adds an *Employee* object to the list.

The **somInit** method is redefined so that we can allocate storage for the *empList*. Similarly, the **somUninit** method is redefined, so that we can free that storage. The implementation of the methods are given in Figure 3.19.

A client program that uses the *Employee* and *Company* class is given in Figure 3.20. The notation _IDL_SEQUENCE_Employee refers to the sequence *empList*.

### 3.13.3  Any Type

The C and C++ bindings for SOM map **any** onto the following **struct**:

```
typedef struct any {
  TypeCode _type;
  void        *_value;
} any;
```

```
#include <somobj.idl>

interface Employee;
interface Company : SOMObject
{
      const unsigned long MAXNUM=10;

      attribute sequence<Employee,MAXNUM> empList;

      long addEmployee(in Employee entry);

      #ifdef __SOMIDL__
      implementation
      {
        releaseorder : _get_empList, _set_empList,
                    addEmployee;
        somInit: override;
        somUninit: override;
      };
      #endif
};
```

**Figure 3.18** The Company IDL

```
SOM_Scope long SOMLINK addEmployee(Company *somSelf, Environment *ev,
                                   Employee* entry)
{
    CompanyData *somThis = CompanyGetData(somSelf);
    long rc;
    CompanyMethodDebug("Company","addEmployee");

    if (sequenceLength(somThis->empList) < sequenceMaximum(somThis->empList))
    {
      sequenceElement(somThis->empList, sequenceLength(somThis->empList)) = entry;
      sequenceLength(somThis->empList)++;
      rc = 0L;
    }
    else
    {
      // reach maximum sequence boundary
      rc = -1L;
    }
    return rc;
}

SOM_Scope void SOMLINK somInit(Company *somSelf)
{
    CompanyData *somThis = CompanyGetData(somSelf);
    CompanyMethodDebug("Company","somInit");

    Company_parent_SOMObject_somInit(somSelf);
    sequenceMaximum(somThis->empList) = MAXNUM;
    sequenceLength(somThis->empList) = 0;
    somThis->empList._buffer = (Employee **) SOMMalloc(sizeof (Employee *) * MAXNUM);
}

SOM_Scope void SOMLINK somUninit(Company *somSelf)
{
    CompanyData *somThis = CompanyGetData(somSelf);
    CompanyMethodDebug("Company","somUninit");

    if (somThis->empList._buffer)
    {
      SOMFree(somThis->empList._buffer);
    }
    Company_parent_SOMObject_somUninit(somSelf);
}
```

**Figure 3.19** The Company class implementation

```
#include "employee.xh"
#include "company.xh"
#include <iostream.h>

main()
{
    Environment *ev = somGetGlobalEnvironment();
    Employee *emp1, *emp2;
    Company *comp;
    _IDL_SEQUENCE_Employee list;
    short i;

    // Create Employee Mary
    emp1 = new Employee;
    emp1->_set_name(ev, "Mary");

    // Create Employee John
    emp2 = new Employee;
    emp2->_set_name(ev, "John");

    // Add Mary and John to Company
    comp = new Company;
    comp->addEmployee(ev, emp1);
    comp->addEmployee(ev, emp2);

    // Print out all the Employee name
    list = comp->_get_empList(ev);

    for (i=0; i < sequenceLength(list); i++)
    {
      cout << sequenceElement(list,i)->_get_name(ev) << "\n";
    }
}
```

**Figure 3.20** A client program that uses Employee and Company classes

The **_type** member is a **TypeCode** that represents the type of the value. The **_value** member is a pointer to the actual value. A **TypeCode** provides the complete information about an IDL type. **TypeCode** is described in more detail in Chapter 8, and a complete list of **TypeCode**s is given in Table 8.1.

The following shows how you can assign a float to an **any** type:

```
any myany;
float val = 1.2;

myany._type = TC_float;
myany._value = &val;
printf("%f\n", *((float *) myany._value));
```

## 3.14  SOM EXCEPTIONS

An *exception* is an indication that a method request was not performed success-fully. In IDL, exceptions are implemented by passing back error information after a method call, as opposed to the "catch/throw" model in C++.

### 3.14.1  Exception Declaration

Exceptions are declared in IDL. An exception declaration begins with the key-word **exception**. It contains a list of members whose values can be accessed when the exception is raised. The syntax is similar to a **struct** definition. Indeed the C and C++ language bindings map an exception declaration to a structure construct.

To associate specific exception information for a method, a **raises** expression must be included in the method declaration in the IDL. The **raises** expression specifies which exceptions may be raised as a result of an invocation of the method. The exceptions that are specified must have been previously declared.

The *ErrorExample* class, whose IDL is given in Figure 3.21, illustatrates how to declare exceptions in IDL. The *BadCall* exception may be raised by the *execute* method. The *BadCall* exception contains two fields for suppling additional infor-mation on the exception.

CORBA also defines a list of standard exceptions that can be raised by any method call. These standard exceptions may not be listed in the **raises** state-ment. Therefore, if a method declaration does not include any **raises** statement, it means that there are no specific exceptions. However, it is still possible to receive one of the standard exceptions from the method.

### 3.14.2  Setting Exception Value

When a method detects an exception, it must call **somSetException** to set the exception value in the **Environment** structure that is passed to the method. The **somSetException** procedure requires the following arguments:

```
void somSetException(env ,              // pointer to Environment structure
                  exception_type,       // Exception Type (system/user/none)
                  exception_name,       // Exception Name
                  parms);               // Exception Structure
```

```
#include <somobj.idl>

interface ErrorExample : SOMObject
{
    enum reasonCode { OK, FATAL, INCOMPLETE };

    exception BadCall
    {
      long errorCode;
      char reason[80];
    };


    void execute() raises(BadCall);

    #ifdef __SOMIDL__
    implementation
    {
      releaseorder : execute;
    };
    #endif
};
```

**Figure 3.21** The ErrorExample IDL

The parameter *exception_type* can be either NO_EXCEPTION, USER_EXCEPTION or SYSTEM_EXCEPTION. The parameter *exception_name* is the string name of the exception.

The SOM compiler generates a string name for each expression. For example, the string name for the *BadCall* exception is *ex_ErrorExample_BadCall*. The parameter *parms* is a pointer to the exception structure which must be allocated using **SOMMalloc**.

The implementation for the *execute* method as shown in Figure 3.22 demonstrates how to set an exception value.

### 3.14.3  Getting Exception Value

We mentioned that the **Environment** structure is used for passing exception information between the caller and the called method. We have also seen how to use the **somGetGlobalEnvironment** function to obtain the global **Environment** structure. You can use a local **Environment** structure to pass exception information so that the exception raised in this call is not known to all the other objects that use the global environment structure. The **SOM_CreateLocal-**

```
#define ErrorExample_Class_Source
#include <error.xih>

SOM_Scope void SOMLINK execute(ErrorExample *somSelf, Environment *ev)
{
    /* ErrorExampleData *somThis = ErrorExampleGetData(somSelf); */
    BadCall *badRc;
    ErrorExampleMethodDebug("ErrorExample","execute");

    // Method logic ...

    //*************************************************************************
    // Demonstrate Exception Setting
    //*************************************************************************
    badRc = (BadCall *) SOMMalloc(sizeof(BadCall));       // allocate exception structure
    badRc->errorCode = ErrorExample_INCOMPLETE;    // set exception detail
    strcpy(badRc->reason, "Unexpected error");

    somSetException(ev,
                    USER_EXCEPTION,
                    ex_ErrorExample_BadCall,
                    (void *) badRc);
}
```

**Figure 3.22** ErrorExample::execute() method implementation

**Environment** or the **SOM_InitEnvironment** macros can be used to create a local environment.

After a method returns, a client program can look at the **Environment** structure to see if there was an exception. The **Environment** structure contains a **_major** field. If **_major** is not equal to NO_EXCEPTION, then an exception is raised by the call.

To retrieve the exception name and the exception value, the **somExceptionId** and the **somExceptionValue** functions must be called. Both of these functions take an **Environment** structure pointer as parameter. The **somExceptionId** function returns the exception name as a string. The **somExceptionValue** function returns a pointer to the exception structure. Based on the exception name that you obtained using **somExceptionId**, you can cast the pointer to the appropriate exception structure and retrieve the values.

If the exception is a standard exception, a generic exception structure, **StExcep,** is used to return the values. This generic exception structure has two fields: one to return a subcategory error code, and the other to return a completion status code.

Figure 3.23 shows how a client program invokes the *execute* method from the *ErrorExample* class and then checks for exception information. If there is an exception, the client obtains the exception values and then calls **somException-Free** to free the memory that is allocated for the exception structure.

## 3.15　SOM CONTEXT

CORBA defines a *context object* that contains a list of properties. Each property consists of a name and a string value associated with that name. A client can use a *context object* to store information about its environment, and the information can be propagated to a server's environment. By convention, context properties represent information about circumstances of a request that are inconvenient to pass as parameters.

SOM implements a *Context* class that can be used to create a *context object*. It also supports the passing of a **Context** parameter in a method call, when a *context expression* is present in a method declaration. Both of these specifications are defined in CORBA. The following sections provide some usage examples.

### 3.15.1　Context Declaration

To associate context information for a method, a *context expression* must be included in the method declaration in the IDL. The *context expression* specifies a list of property names that the method can use.

When a *context expression* is present in the method declaration, the method invocation requires an additional **Context** argument after the **Environment** argument. This additional argument is used to pass the *context object*. If the properties that are defined in the *context expression* are included in the *context object,* their values will be passed to the method implementation.

The *ContextExample* class, whose IDL is given in Figure 3.24, illustrates how to declare a *context expression* in IDL. A *context expression* begins with the keyword **context**. The *context expression* that is associated with the *startup* method contains two properties: *userid* and *password*.

### 3.15.2　Setting Context

To set the **Context** parameter, a client must create a *Context* object and then set those properties to be made available to the method call. The *Context* class provides the methods **set_one_value** and **set_values** for setting one or more property values in the *Context* object.

Figure 3.25 shows how a client program would create a *Context* object and then invoke the **set_one_value** to set the property *userid* to the value *chris*. The *Context* object is then passed as a parameter when the *startup* method is invoked.

```cpp
#include "error.xh"
#include <iostream.h>

main()
{
    Environment   *ev;
    ErrorExample  *ex1;
    char          *exId;
    BadCall       *bc;
    StExcep       *stExVal;

    ev = somGetGlobalEnvironment();
    ex1 = new ErrorExample;
    ex1->execute(ev);

    // Check the Environment structure for exception
    switch(ev->_major)
    {
      case SYSTEM_EXCEPTION:
                exId = somExceptionId(ev);
                stExVal = (StExcep *) somExceptionValue(ev);
                cout << "Minor Code " << stExVal->minor;
                cout << "Status " << stExVal->completed;
                somExceptionFree(ev);
                break;

      case USER_EXCEPTION:
                exId = somExceptionId(ev);
                if (strcmp(exId, ex_ErrorExample_BadCall) == 0)
                {
                    bc = (BadCall *) somExceptionValue(ev);
                    cout << bc->errorCode << "\n";
                    cout << bc->reason << "\n";
                    somExceptionFree(ev);      // Free exception memory
                }
                break;

      case NO_EXCEPTION:
                break;
    }
}
```

**Figure 3.23** A client program that uses the ErrorExample class

```
#include <somobj.idl>
interface Context;                // include SOM Context class declaration

interface ContextExample : SOMObject
{
     void startup() context(userid, password);

     #ifdef __SOMIDL__
     implementation
     {
       releaseorder : startup;
     };
     #endif
};
```

**Figure 3.24** The ContextExample IDL

```
#include <somd.xh>
#include <cntxt.xh>
#include "context.xh"

main()
{
     Environment *ev;
     ContextExample *ex1;
     Context *ctx;

     ev = somGetGlobalEnvironment();

     ctx = new Context;
     ctx->set_one_value(ev, "userid", "chris");

     ex1 = new ContextExample;
     ex1->startup(ev,ctx);
}
```

**Figure 3.25** A client program that uses the ContextExample class

### 3.15.3   Getting Context

To get the **Context** value in a method implementation, the *Context* class provides the method **get_values** that can be used to retrieve the context property value(s). The properties are returned in a list object known as a **NVList**. The **NVList** interface is also defined by CORBA. It is used for constructing parameter lists and supports operations to add and get elements from the list. **NVList** is used in the *dynamic invocation interface*, which is discussed in Section 5.9 on page 107.

Figure 3.26 shows the implementation of the *startup* method. The *startup* method invokes the **get_values** method on the **Context** parameter to retrieve the property value for the *userid* property. The result is returned in the **NVList** object *val*. The **get_item** method is then invoked on the **NVList** object to retrieve the first item. The **get_item** method returns the name of the item, the data type of the item, the value of the item, the length of the value, and a bitmask that contains flag values.

Using the client program shown in the last section, the item name will contain the string *userid,* and the item value will contain the string *chris*.

## 3.16   MODULE STATEMENT

In SOMobjects Developer Toolkit 2.0, if you want to define multiple interfaces in a single *.idl* file, then you need to use a **module** statement. If you do not use a **module** statement, and the interfaces are not a class-metaclass pair, then the SOM compiler will only generate the bindings for the last interface in the file.

However, if you install the SOMobjects Developer Toolkit CSD202 or higher, you can define as many interfaces as you want in a single *.idl* file without using a **module** statement. The SOM compiler will generate the bindings for all the interfaces. The **module** statement is simply a scoping mechanism.

Figure 3.27 shows an example of a **module** statement. The *common.idl* file contains two interfaces: *Rectangle* and *Circle*.

The usage binding that is generated by the SOM compiler forms the class name by concatenating the module name, an underscore, and the interface name. Figure 3.28 shows how the two interfaces can be accessed by a C++ client.

```
#define ContextExample_Class_Source
#include <context.xih>
#include <stdio.h>
#include <somd.xh>

SOM_Scope void SOMLINK startup(ContextExample *somSelf, Environment *ev,
                              Context *ctx)
{
  /* ContextExampleData *somThis = ContextExampleGetData(somSelf); */
  NVList *val;
  long rc;
  ContextExampleMethodDebug("ContextExample","startup");

  // Search the current context object only
  rc = ctx->get_values(ev, NULL, 0, "userid", &val);

  if (rc == 0)
  {
      Identifier name;
      TypeCode typecode;
      void *value;
      long len;
      Flags flags;

      val->get_item( ev,
                     0,                    // first item
                     &name,                // item name
                     &typecode,            // item data type
                     &value,               // item value
                     &len,                 // item value length
                     &flags);              // bitmask flag

      printf("name: %s \n", name);

      if ( TypeCode_kind(typecode,ev) == tk_string )
      {
              printf("value: %s\n", *((string *) value) );
      }
  }
  val->free(ev);
}
```

**Figure 3.26** ContextExample::startup () method implementation

```
#include <somobj.idl>

module CommonShape {
    interface Rectangle : SOMObject
    {
        void draw();

        #ifdef __SOMIDL__
        implementation
        {
            releaseorder: draw;
        };
        #endif
    };

    interface Circle : SOMObject
    {
        void draw();

        #ifdef __SOMIDL__
        implementation
        {
            releaseorder: draw;
        };
        #endif
    };
};
```

**Figure 3.27** The CommonShape module

```
#include "common.xh"

main()
{
    CommonShape_Rectangle *rect;
    CommonShape_Circle *circ;
    Environment *ev;

    ev = somGetGlobalEnvironment();

    rect = new CommonShape_Rectangle;
    circ = new CommonShape_Circle;

    rect->draw(ev);
    circ->draw(ev);
}
```

**Figure 3.28** A client program that uses the CommonShape module

# 4

# A Complement to C++

If you are asking yourself, "Why SOM instead of C++," you are not alone. This is one of the most frequently asked questions. In this chapter, we will attempt to answer this question by looking at some of the problems with C++, and how SOM solves these problems. In the process, we will introduce a few key features of SOM and show you how to use them.

## 4.1 THE NEED TO RE-COMPILE

Dynamic Link Libraries (DLLs) have become the standard way for packaging and distributing software on OS/2 and other systems. DLLs allow library functions to change without requiring the programs that use the DLLs to recompile or to relink, as long as the interface to the library functions remains unchanged. This is because the code in the DLL is not linked to the user's program until runtime. Therefore, it is possible to replace the DLL without affecting any user program.

DLLs work very well in maintaining binary compatibility, as long as the libraries are written in a procedure-based language. However, as we will see in the following example, this paradigm fails when libraries are developed in an object-oriented language like C++. The user of a C++ class has to recompile the source code whenever there are changes to the class header file. The changes can be as simple as adding an instance variable to the class, adding a method to the class, or relocating the class in the hierarchy.

Consider the following class interface:

```
class A
{
    public:
            short val1;
            long val2;

            A(short, long);
            void display();
};
```

The implementation for the class is given below:

```
#include <iostream.h>
#include "A.hpp"

A :: A(short x, long y)
 : val1(x),
   val2(y)
{}

void A :: display()
{
    cout << "The values are ";
    cout << val1 << " " << val2 << "\n";
}
```

The following client program is dynamically linked to the class.

```
#include "A.hpp"

main()
{
    A myObj(5, 100);

    myObj.display();
}
```

When you run the program, you get the following:

```
> The values are 5 100
```

Later, we modify the class slightly to introduce a new instance variable. The new class interface is given below:

```
class A
{
    public:
        short val1;
        char *val3;
        long val2;

        A(short, long);
        void display();
};
```

The interface and implementation for the class constructor and the *display* method remain unchanged. We replaced the original class DLL with this new DLL and rerun the client program again. This time we get the same output,

> The values are 5 100

but the program crashes!

So why did this happen? Let's look at the memory layout of the object before and after the change. This is shown in Figure 4.1.

With the new object layout, when the client program assigns 100 to *val2*, it was assigned to the memory location of *val3*, which is not expecting a long value. This caused the crash.

To avoid the crash, the client program must be recompiled with the new class header file, even though the change to the class does not require any code change in the client program.

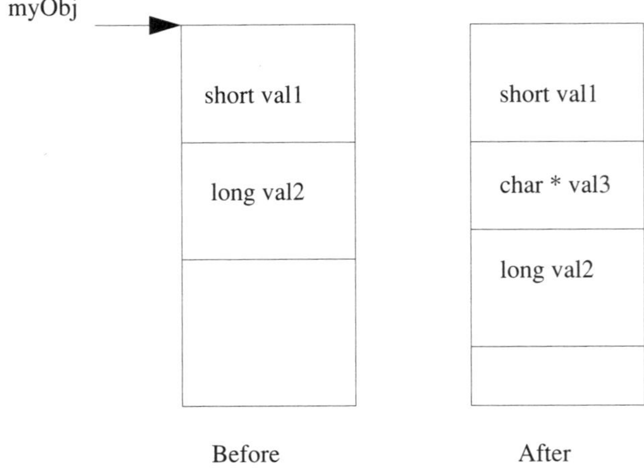


**Figure 4.1** Memory layout of the C++ object before and after the change

Although this example is trivial, and the crash can be avoided with some careful programming, it demonstrates the problem with changing class header files in C++. Imagine yourself purchasing a class library (DLL) that was developed in C++, and you have different applications using this library. Whenever there is a new release of the class library, you need to recompile all of your existing applications, because it is likely that a new release will have new header file changes. In some cases, this might not be possible, as the source code for these applications is not available. And you end up having to manage multiple releases of the same class library.

In the next section, we show how SOM resolves this problem by using the *releaseorder* modifier.

### 4.1.1    SOM Releaseorder

A major contribution of SOM is that SOM classes can undergo structural changes without requiring the client programs to recompile, if the structural changes do not require source code changes in the client programs. To accomplish this, the implementor for the class must fill in the *releaseorder* modifier for the class, following the rules described in Section 2.4.5 on page 17.

We rewrite the class interface for *A* in IDL. The instance variables *val1* and *val2* are mapped to attributes[*] in the IDL. The *_get* and the *_set* method for each attribute are added to the *releaseorder*. The IDL for *A* is shown below:

```
#include <somobj.idl>
interface A : SOMObject
{
        attribute short val1;
        attribute long val2;

        void display();

        #ifdef __SOMIDL__
        implementation
        {
          releaseorder : display,
                        _get_val1, _set_val1,
                        _get_val2, _set_val2;
        };
        #endif
};
```

---

[*]Recall that only attributes can be accessed by client programs. If you mapped *val1* and *val2* to instance variables in the implementation section, they will not be accessible to client programs.

The implementation for the class is shown below:

```
#define A_Class_Source
#include <a.xih>
#include <iostream.h>

SOM_Scope void SOMLINK display(A *somSelf, Environment *ev)
{
    AData *somThis = AGetData(somSelf);
    AMethodDebug("A","display");

    cout << "The values are ";
    cout << somThis->val1 << " " << somThis->val2 << "\n";
}
```

The class is packaged into a DLL. The details of this process are discussed in Section 4.2 on page 78. The client program is modified to use the SOM class instead of the C++ class:

```
#include "a.xh"

main()
{
    Environment *ev;
    A *myObj;

    ev = somGetGlobalEnvironment();
    myObj = new A;

    myObj->_set_val1(ev,5);
    myObj->_set_val2(ev,100);

    myObj->display(ev);
}
```

As before, when you run the program, you get:

> The values are 5 100

We now modify the class IDL to introduce a new attribute. The *get* and *set* methods for the new attribute are added to the end of the *releaseorder* list.

```
#include <somobj.idl>
interface A : SOMObject
{
    attribute short val1;
    attribute string val3;
    attribute long val2;

    void display();

    #ifdef __SOMIDL__
    implementation
    {
        releaseorder : display,
                    _get_val1, _set_val1,
                    _get_val2, _set_val2,
                    _get_val3, _set_val3;
    };
    #endif
};
```

We recompile the class implementation and replace the original DLL with the new DLL. When we rerun the client program, we get the following:

> The values are 5 100

We have changed our class definition successfully, without affecting our client program.

### 4.1.2    So What is the SOM Magic?

Simply put, the magic is based on levels of indirection. To understand how it works, we need to look at the SOM run-time data structures, and how a method is invoked.

In SOM, every class has a global data structure named *<className>***Class-Data**. This data structure is provided in the usage binding of the class. It consists of a pointer to the class object, followed by a series of "method tokens". A method token can be thought of as a value that identifies a method. There is a method token for every method that is introduced by this class. These method tokens are ordered in the same order as the method names in the *releaseorder*.

For example, the *ClassData* structure for the original class *A* looks like the following:

```
SOMEXTERN struct AClassDataStructure {
    SOMClass *classObject;
```

```
        somMToken display;
        somMToken _get_val1;
        somMToken _set_val1;
        somMToken _get_val2;
        somMToken _set_val2;
    } AClassData;
```

During the initialization of a class object (e.g., when *new <className>* is called), SOM builds the method table for the class and sets up the offset of the method tokens. A method table is a table of pointers to the procedures (body of code) that implements the methods. This is shown in Figure 4.2.

When a method is invoked, e.g., *myObj->display(ev)*, the SOM run-time performs the following steps.

1. Using the class name and the method name, constructs the method token for the specified method.
2. Using the method token, obtains a pointer to the procedure that implements the specified method.
3. Invokes the body of code using this pointer.

The **SOM_Resolve** macro performs steps one and two. If you look at the usage binding that is generated for a method in a class, you will see that this is exactly what it is doing.

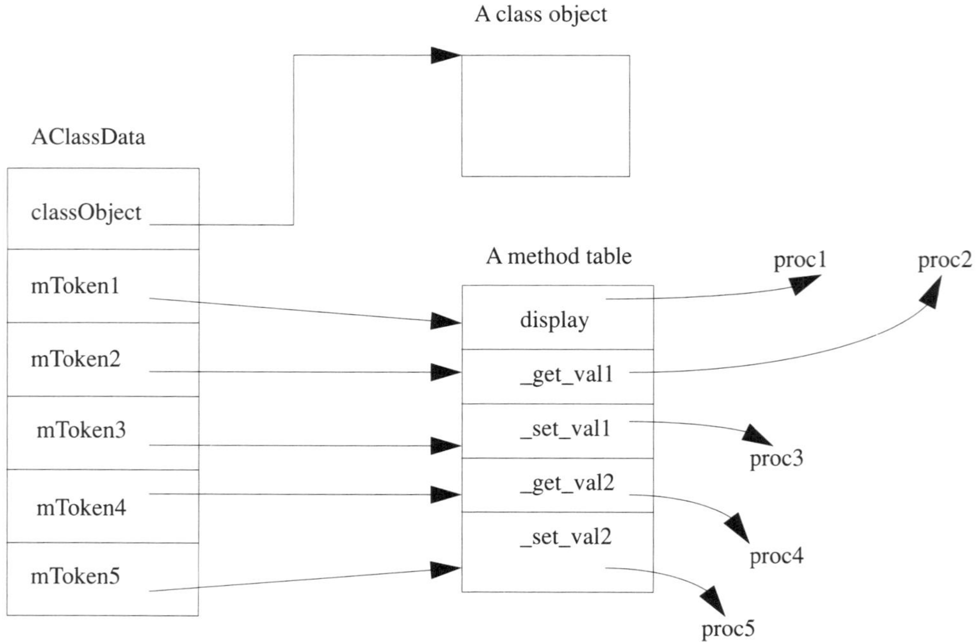


**Figure 4.2** Initializing method tokens

Now what happens when we add the attribute *val3*? Recall that we added its *_get* and *_set* methods to the end of the *releaseorder*. This causes the *AClassData* to look like the following:

```
SOMEXTERN struct AClassDataStructure {
        SOMClass *classObject;
        somMToken display;
        somMToken _get_val1;
        somMToken _set_val1;
        somMToken _get_val2;
        somMToken _set_val2;
        somMToken _get_val3;
        somMToken _set_val3;
    } AClassData;
```

This, in turn, creates the run-time picture shown in Figure 4.3.

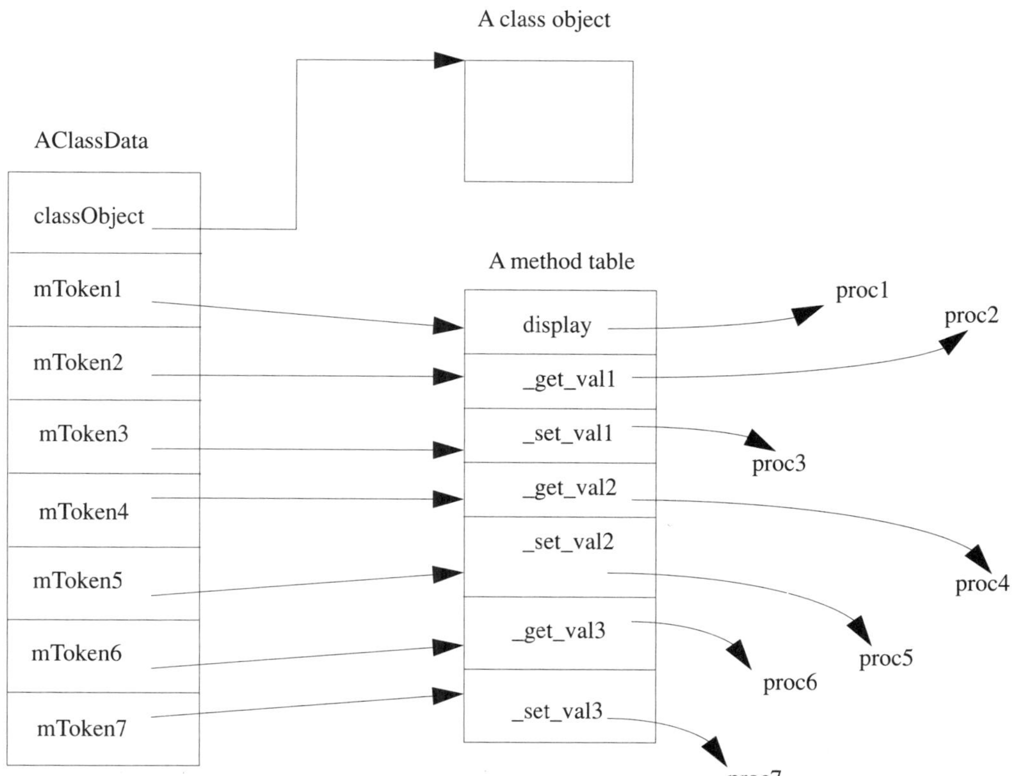


**Figure 4.3** Method tokens after val3 added with proper releaseorder

Now you can see why the client program still works after we change the class structure. Since we added the methods to the end of the *releaseorder*, the method tokens for the *_set_val1*, *_set_val2* and the *display* methods still resolve to the same procedure address. Therefore binary compatibility can be preserved.

Consider what will happen if you reorder the *releaseorder*, to the following:

```
#ifdef __SOMIDL__
implementation
{
        releaseorder : display,
                        _get_val2, _set_val2,
                        _get_val1, _set_val1,
                        _get_val3, _set_val3;
};
#endif
```

The *AClassData* will look like the following:

```
SOMEXTERN struct AClassDataStructure {
        SOMClass *classObject;
        somMToken display;
        somMToken _get_val2;
        somMToken _set_val2;
        somMToken _get_val1;
        somMToken _set_val1;
        somMToken _get_val3;
        somMToken _set_val3;
} AClassData;
```

which creates the run-time picture shown in Figure 4.4.

Because the client has not recompiled to pick up the new *AClassData*, when it invokes *_set_val1*, it will be calling the wrong procedure. It is using *mToken3* which resolves to *proc5*, instead of *proc3*. In other words, binary compatibility is broken, and the client will need to recompile the source code.

## 4.2    EXPORT ENTRY IN DLLS

To build a DLL on OS/2, you must create a module definition (.DEF) file. If you want a function to be available to programs that call the DLL, you must export the function by listing its name under the EXPORTS keyword in the .DEF file. This can become tedious if your DLL is written in C++.

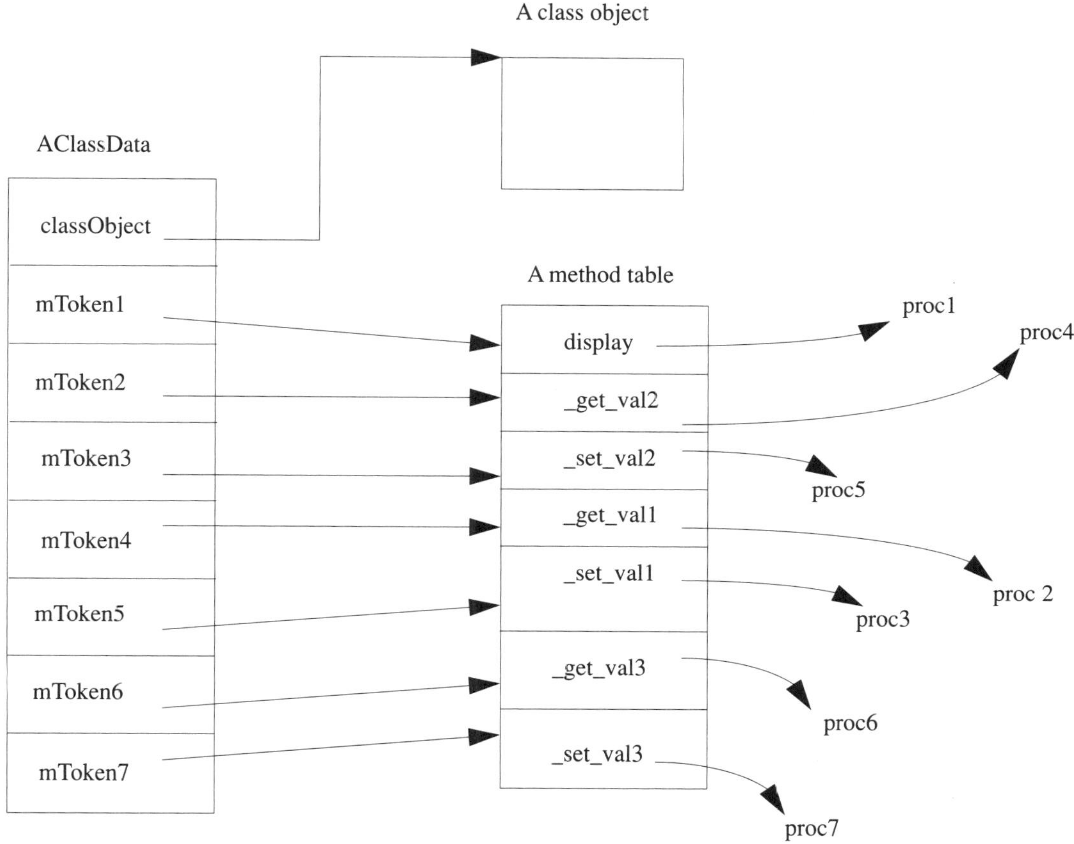



**Figure 4.4** Reorder releaseorder

First, you must list the mangled name of the function. To figure out the mangled name of the function you want to export, you need to run the utility **CPP-FILT** that comes with the C Set++ compiler. This will extract all the names from your object files. You then copy the ones you want to export into your .DEF file. Needless to say, this can be an error-prone endeavor.

Second, the number of export entries for a class may be huge, if the class contains a large number of member functions. Even private or protected member functions will need to be exported if they are used by an exported function.

By contrast, SOM requires no more than three export entries per class, and each export entry follows a naming convention. In the following, we will show you step-by-step how to build a DLL for SOM classes.

### 4.2.1    Creating a DLL for SOM Classes

In this example, we create the DLL *domestic* to contain two SOM classes: *Cat* and *Dog*.

1. For each class in the DLL, specify the DLL name in the class's IDL file. The DLL name is specified by setting the *dllname* modifier in the implementation section of the IDL. The *Cat.idl* is given below:

```
#include <somobj.idl>
interface Cat : SOMObject
{
        attribute string name;

        void display();                    // Print the string: "I am a Cat"

        #ifdef __SOMIDL__
        implementation
        {
                releaseorder : display,
                                    _get_name, _set_name;
                dllname = "domestic.dll";
        };
        #endif
};
```

2. Create a initialization function for this DLL. The initialization function is called by SOM whenever it loads a class library. It must follow the following function prototype:

```
#ifdef __IBMC__
        #pragma linkage(SOMInitModule,system)
#endif

SOMEXTERN void SOMLINK SOMInitModule(long majorVersion,
                                       long minorVersion,
                                       string className)
```

The initialization function generally invokes  *<className>***NewClass** for each class in the class library to create the class objects. The initialization function (*initfunc.cpp*) for the *Cat* and *Dog* classes in the class library *domestic* is shown below:

```
#include "cat.xh"
#include "dog.xh"

#ifdef __IBMC__
        #pragma linkage(SOMInitModule,system)
```

```
#endif

SOMEXTERN void SOMLINK SOMInitModule(long majorVersion,
                                     long minorVersion,
                                     string className)
{
        SOM_IgnoreWarning(majorVersion);
        SOM_IgnoreWarning(minorVersion);
        SOM_IgnoreWarning(className);

        CatNewClass(Cat_MajorVersion, Cat_MinorVersion);
        DogNewClass(Dog_MajorVersion, Dog_MinorVersion);
}
```

3. Compile all the implementation files for the classes and the initialization function. The C Set++ compiler requires the compiler option **/Ge-** to be specified when compiling a DLL file. For example, the following command compiles the *cat.idl* file.

```
icc /c+ /Ge- /I. cat.idl
```

4. Create a .DEF file for the DLL. This can be done in two steps. First, run the *def* emitter from the SOM compiler to generate the necessary exported symbols for each class. Second, combine the exported symbols into one .DEF file. For example, the following command generates the *cat.def* file.

```
sc -sdef cat.idl
```

The *cat.def* file is listed below:

```
; This file was generated by the SOM Compiler.
; FileName: cat.def.
; Generated using:
; SOM Precompiler somipc: somc/smemit.c
; SOM Emitter emitdef: somc/smmain.c
LIBRARY cat INITINSTANCE
DESCRIPTION 'Cat Class Library'
PROTMODE
DATA MULTIPLE NONSHARED LOADONCALL
EXPORTS
CatCClassData
CatClassData
CatNewClass
```

Notice that three export symbols are generated. This is the advantage we described earlier. Symbols *<className>***ClassData** and *<className>***CClass-Data** are external data structures referenced by the SOM bindings. The symbol *<className>***NewClass** is the name of the function used to create the class.

To produce the .DEF file for our *domestic* DLL, we combine the *cat.def* and the *dog.def* files that are generated from the *Cat* and the *Dog* IDL. We also need to include the initialization function, **SOMInitModule**, in the export list. The final *domestic.def* file is given below:

```
LIBRARY domestic INITINSTANCE
DESCRIPTION 'Domestic Animal Class Library'
PROTMODE
DATA MULTIPLE NONSHARED LOADONCALL
EXPORTS
SOMInitModule
CatCClassData
CatClassData
CatNewClass
DogCClassData
DogClassData
DogNewClass
```

**5.** Link the object files and .DEF file into a DLL. You can use **icc** to invoke the compiler and the linker. For example, you can use the following command to create *domestic.dll*.

```
icc /Fe"domestic.dll" cat.obj dog.obj initfunc.obj domestic.def os2386.lib somtk.lib
```

We will demonstrate the use of the DLL *domestic* in the next example.

## 4.3   DYNAMIC CLASS LOADING

Suppose you are building a graphical user interface (GUI) builder that supports reuseable parts. You might have a push-button control, a list-box control, or some other user-defined controls. Each of these controls are implemented as objects that exhibit different behavior. A typical user will ask the GUI builder to create controls and use them in the applications. Since not all the controls are predefined at compile time, it will be hard to use C++ to implement such a system because C++ requires the class name to be known at compile time. What we need is a system that supports the dynamic loading of classes that are unknown at compile time.

SOM provides methods that let you dynamically load a class and create a class object when the name of the class is unknown at compile time. This is possible because, in SOM, classes are objects at run-time, as opposed to C++, where classes are types, which are fixed at compile time. The *SOMClassMgr* class provides two methods for dynamically loading and creating class objects: **somFindClsInFile** and **somFindClass**.

### 4.3.1    The somFindClsInFile Method

The **somFindClsInFile** method is the more restrictive of the two. It requires the specific name of the DLL in which your class resides. The following shows the syntax for the method in C.

```
myClass = _somFindClsInFile(SOMClassMgrObject,    // global instance
                            classId,              // somId for the class
                            classMajorVersion,    // class major version number
                            classMinorVersion,    // class minor version number
                            dllname);             // DLL filename
```

The parameter *SOMClassMgrObject* is a pointer to the instance *SOMClassMgr*. There is only one instance of *SOMClassMgr*, and it is created during SOM initialization. The parameter *classId* is a **somId** that represents the name of the class. It can be obtained by passing the name of the class to the function **somIdFromString**. The parameters *classMajorVersion* and *classMinorVersion* are normally set to 0, unless you want to check against the version numbers of the class. The parameter *dllname* specifies the name of the DLL that contains the class. You must specify the complete pathname for the DLL. The DLL must also be placed in one of the directories specified on the LIBPATH statement in your *config.sys* file.

The DYNALOAD program shown in Figure 4.5 uses **somFindClsInFile** to dynamically load the DLL *domestic* that we built in the previous section. It takes the name of the class as an input parameter. If the class is created, it will invoke the *display* method on the animal to display its characteristics.

We run the program with different input.

> DYNALOAD Dog

I am a Dog

> DYNALOAD Cat

I am a Cat

> DYNALOAD Bird

Can't load class Bird

```cpp
#include <iostream.h>
#include <som.xh>
#include <somcm.xh>

main(int argc, char *argv[], char *envp[])
{
  SOMClass *myClass;
  somId classId;

  // Initialize SOM run-time environment
  somEnvironmentNew();

  classId = somIdFromString( argv[1] );
  myClass = SOMClassMgrObject->somFindClsInFile(classId,
                          0,0,
                          "C:\\BOOK\\CHAP4\\DYNALOAD\\DOMESTIC.DLL");

  if (myClass)
  {
    SOMObject *myObj;
    Environment *ev;

    ev = somGetGlobalEnvironment();
    myObj = myClass->somNew();
    myObj->somDispatch( (somToken*)0,
                        somIdFromString("display"),
                        myObj,
                        ev);
  }
  else
  {
    cout << "Can't load class " << argv[1] << "\n";
  }
}
```

**Figure 4.5** The DYNALOAD program

The DYNALOAD program illustrates how one can invoke a method, when the language bindings for a class are not available. Once the class object is created, the **somNew** method is called to create an instance of the class. The **somDispatch** method can then be called to invoke a method on the object.

### 4.3.2    The somFindClass Method

Another method that can be used to create a class object is **somFindClass**. The **somFindClass** method is similar to **somFindClsInFile**, except that you do not have to specify the DLL name. The C syntax for **somFindClass** is shown below:

```
myClass = _somFindClass(SOMClassMgrObject,      // global instance
                        classId,                // somId for the class
                        classMajorVersion,      // class major version number
                        classMinorVersion);     // class minor version number
```

There are a few things to note when using **somFindClass**. The **somFind-Class** method uses **somLocateClassFile** to obtain the name of the file that contains the class. The default implementation of **somLocateClassFile** checks the *Interface Repository* for the value of the *dllname* modifier of the class. We discussed the setting of the *dllname* modifier in Section 4.2.1 on page 79. To populate the Interface Repository, run the SOM compiler with the **-u** option. The following command shows how you can update the Interface Repository with the *Cat* and the *Dog* IDL files.

```
sc -sir -u cat.idl dog.idl
```

The Interface Repository is a database that maintains information about classes described in IDL files. It is used by the Distributed, Persistence, and Replication Framework. We will look at some of the programming interfaces in Chapter 8.

Note that if the *dllname* modifier is not specified, then **somLocateClassFile** will return the class name as the DLL name. If your class does not reside in a DLL that has the same name, then you will get an error indicating that the class is not found. Therefore, you should always explicitly set the *dllname* modifier, or follow the convention: the name of the class is the same as the name of the DLL that contains the class.

## 4.4    RUN-TIME TYPE IDENTIFICATION

Currently, C++ provides no support for determining the type of an object at run-time. The need for run-time type identification arises in an inheritance hierarchy, when methods can be supported in one derived class, but not in the others. Given a pointer to the base class, it becomes necessary to check the type of the object to make sure that one can safely invoke a particular method.

While run-time type identification can be avoided to a large extent by using virtual functions, there are cases where it is not possible. For example, a user might want to extend the function of a class by subclassing, but cannot add or modify the original class to use virtual functions, because the source code of the original class is not available. This represents a legitimate case of using run-time type identification. Indeed, one of the language extensions that has been accepted by the C++ committee is the run-time type identification proposal by Stroustrup and Lenkov.

SOM provides methods that let you query information about an object at run-time. In particular, the **somIsA** method lets you determine whether an object is an instance of a given class. You invoke **somIsA** on a target object, passing the *class object* that the target object should be tested against, as an input parameter. It returns true, if the object is an instance of the specified class, otherwise it returns false.

How do you get a pointer to a *class object* that you want to test against? We have already discussed a number of ways. One way is to invoke the *<class-Name>***NewClass** procedure, which creates and returns a pointer to the class object of the specified class. Another way is to use the **somFindClsInFile** or the **somFindClass** method, if the language bindings for the class are not available at compile time. A third way is to use the *ClassData* structure that we discussed in Section 4.1.2 on page 75.

Recall that each class has a global data structure, named *<className>***Class-Data**. This data structure contains a pointer to the *class object*, which is built during initialization. Therefore, if you have the usage bindings file for the class, you can obtain a pointer to the *class object* by specifiying *<className>***Class-Data.classObject**.

The following example illustrates the above points. Consider the following interfaces:

```
interface Employee : SOMObject
{
    short salary();
};
interface Manager : Employee
{
    short bonus();              // Manager receives bonus on top of base salary
};
interface Programmer : Employee
{
    short overtime();           // Programmer receives overtime paid
};
```

A client program, which calculates the salary for an employee, might be written as follows:

```
calcSalary(Employee *emp)
{
    SOMClass *mgrClass;
    Environment *ev = somGetGlobalEnvironment();


    //*************************************************************************************
    // Use the ClassData structure to get the pointer to the Programmer class object
    //*************************************************************************************
    if (emp->somIsA(ProgrammerClassData.classObject))
    {
        cout << "Programmer salary: " ;
        cout << (emp->salary(ev) + ( (Programmer *) emp)->overtime(ev));
    }


    //*********************************************************************
    // Create a Manager class object using ManagerNewClass
    //*********************************************************************
    mgrClass = ManagerNewClass(0,0);
    if ( emp->somIsA(mgrClass) )
    {
        cout << "Manager salary: " ;
        cout << (emp->salary(ev) + ((Manager *) emp)->bonus(ev));
    }
}
```

When *calcSalary* is called with a pointer that points to a *Programmer* object, the first **somIsA** test will be successful and the *overtime* method is called on the *Programmer* object. When *calcSalary* is called with a pointer that points to a *Manager* object, the second **somIsA** will be successful and the *bonus* method is called.

The preceding example also illustrates two different ways of getting a pointer to a class object. In the first case, the expression *ProgrammerClassData.classObject* is used. In the second case, the procedure *ManagerNewClass* is used.


## 4.5   SUMMARY

Perhaps the problems described in this chapter are not important to you. Perhaps you already have work arounds for them. The intent here is to provide you with additional options if you are trying to solve similar problems.

SOM is not intended to replace existing object-oriented languages such as C++. SOM is not a language. However, it provides additional run-time capability that can be used to supplement C++. It also provides a new technology for packaging class libraries. Your application is likely to have both SOM and C++

objects. This is encouraged as there are capabilities in C++ that are not surfaced in the C++ bindings for SOM. Some of the C++ capabilities that are not available include: passing parameters in the constructor, overloading, and class templates.

Note that the lack of C++ capabilities will be considerably alleviated when the DirectToSOM compiler becomes available. With the DirectToSOM technology, you will be able to compile your C++ objects directly into SOM objects and generate IDL from the corresponding C++ interface. Chapter 10 provides more information on this topic.

# 5

# Distributing Your Objects

Distributed SOM (DSOM) allows applicatons to access SOM objects across address spaces. There are two flavors of DSOM: Workstation DSOM and Workgroup DSOM. Using Workstation DSOM, an application can access objects in other processes, or other address spaces, in a single-machine environment. Currently, the Workstation DSOM Enabler is available for both OS/2 and AIX. The Workstation DSOM Enabler for Windows has been recently announced and will be available in the summer of 1994.

Using Workgroup DSOM, an application can access objects distributed across a network of machines. In the current release, Workgroup DSOM supports distribution across local area networks (LANs) comprising both OS/2 and AIX systems. Workgroup DSOM for Windows has also been recently announced, and this allows you to distribute your objects across networks comprising OS/2, AIX, and Windows. Future releases of DSOM may support other platforms, including large, enterprise-wide networks.

The *SOMobjects Developer Toolkit Version 2.0 for OS/2* as used in this book includes the Workstation DSOM for OS/2. The examples included on the diskette run on OS/2. However, if you install the Workgroup Enabler for OS/2 and AIX, then you will be able to move the SOM objects to AIX and access them from OS/2. This architecture is important because it allows developers to develop their distributed objects in a single-machine environment and then deploy the objects in a distributed environment by switching to the Workgroup Enabler.

## 5.1 DSOM OVERVIEW

DSOM supports transparent, remote access to distributed objects. The DSOM run-time routes requests to objects that are outside the address space of a client.

In effect, DSOM is a remote method capability. It allows a client to run methods on remote objects. Figure 5.1 shows the DSOM structure.

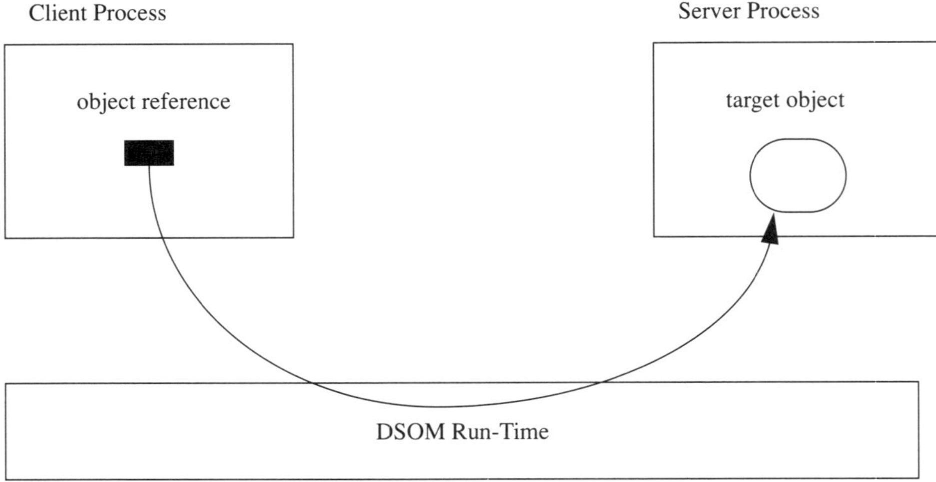


**Figure 5.1** DSOM structure

DSOM is typically used when you want to allow objects to be shared by multiple processes. In DSOM terminology, the objects exist in a DSOM server, and different clients can access the objects via the DSOM run-time. Another situation where DSOM should be used is when you want to divide your application so that a failure in one part of the application will not cause the entire application to crash. One potential example of such usage is the OS/2 Workplace Shell. By implementing the Workplace Shell as a DSOM server, the Workplace Shell can avoid crashing due to Workplace Shell application errors.

The development of a DSOM application involves the following steps.

1. Define the interface for your objects and write code to implement your objects.
2. Create a server program that executes and manages the objects you defined in step one.
3. Create a client program that accesses the objects.
4. Configure your DSOM environment.
5. Build and register your classes and your server program.
6. Run the client program.

The following sections provide details on each of the above steps.

## 5.2    DEFINE AND IMPLEMENT YOUR OBJECTS

DSOM has been designed so that it is easy for you to migrate your non-distributed objects into a distributed environment. This means that you can build a class library following the steps described in "Creating a DLL for SOM Classes" on page 79 without knowing that your class library would ever be accessed remotely. You define your class interfaces in IDL and then implement your classes. You do not need to derive your classes from any special DSOM classes.

Keep the following steps in mind when you design and implement your classes so that you will not need to make any changes to your classes when you want to use them in a distributed environment:

1. Set the *dllname* modifier in the implementation section of each class IDL to the name of the dynamic library that contains the class.
2. Avoid printing to standard output. This is because the server that is running your objects might not have a display.
3. If you are creating or deleting objects in your methods, you might need to determine whether the objects you are creating are local or remote. This is because the calls to create local objects are different from the calls to create remote objects.
4. If an object wants to preserve a data value that is created by a client, it must explicitly allocate memory and make a copy of it. The client copy will be freed at the end of the method call.
5. If you are passing structures with embedded pointers as parameters, you will need to manage your own pointer de-referencing. DSOM does not copy pointer values when copying the values of the structure fields.

## 5.3    SERVER PROGRAM

In DSOM, a server program is a program that manages objects. Upon a request from a client, a DSOM server will load the DLL for the class, create or locate the target object and handle the demarshalling and marshalling of requests and results. A server program has to be registered with DSOM in an *Implementation Repository*. The Implementation Repository is a database that is used by DSOM to find and activate servers, when a client invokes a method on a remote object. The mechanism to register a server program with the Implementation Repository is described in Section 5.6.2 on page 101.

A server program consists of three parts:

- A main program that provides a process for the objects in the class libraries that the server manages.
- A server object, derived from *SOMDServer* class that provides methods to manage the objects in the server process.
- One or more class libraries that provide the object implementations. Usually these libraries are built as DLLs so that they can be loaded and linked by the server program dynamically.

### 5.3.1    Using the Generic Server Program

DSOM provides a generic server program that is already compiled and linked. It can be used in many environments. The generic server simply receives requests and executes them synchronously until the server is stopped. The generic server program will find and load any DLL automatically if it has not already been loaded.

If you build your classes following the practices described above and then use the generic server program, you can very easily distribute your classes without additional programming cost.

The name of the generic server program is **somdsvr**. The path for the program is *%SOMBASE%\bin\somdsvr.exe* on OS/2.


### 5.3.2   Writing your own Server Program

Sometimes the generic server program is not sufficient for some applications. For example, an application might want a server to behave as both client and server. Such a server can respond to incoming requests, as well as access remote objects that are managed by other servers. In this case, one can write their own application specific server program. A server program must include the following functions.

1. Initialize the DSOM run-time environment.
2. Initialize the SOM Object Adaptor, *SOMOA*. The *SOMOA* handles all communications between the client and server.
3. Initialize the *ImplementationDef* object. The *ImplementationDef* object represents the implementation definition of a server. It contains attributes that describe the server's ID, server's alias, host name, classes that the server manages, etc. The *ImplementationDef* object can be retrieved from the Implementation Repository by passing the server's ID or the server's alias.
4. Indicate that the server is ready to process requests.
5. Start processing requests loop.

The code in Figure 5.2 shows an example of a server program.


## 5.4   CLIENT PROGRAM

For the most part, a client program in DSOM looks very much like a client program in SOM. The differences lie in the initialization of the run-time environment, the creation and destruction of an object, as well as the finding of existing objects or servers. A client program does not need to know where an object is located or what communication protocols are used between systems.


### 5.4.1   DSOM Initialization

First, every DSOM program must include the file *<somd.xh>* (or *<somd.h>* if you are using C bindings). This file defines the constants, global variables, and run-time interfaces that are used by DSOM. Next, the client must call the DSOM initialization function, **SOMD_Init**, to initialize the DSOM run-time environment.

```
#include <somd.xh>
#include <somoa.xh>
#include <implrep.xh>
#include <stdio.h>

int main(int argc, char **argv)
{
    Environment ev;
    long rc;

    // Initialize DSOM environment
    SOM_InitEnvironment(&ev);
    SOMD_Init(&ev);

    // Initialize SOM Object Adapter
    SOMD_SOMOAObject = new SOMOA;

    // get ImplementationDef from Implementation Repository using the input Implementation Id
    SOMD_ImplDefObject = SOMD_ImplRepObject->find_impldef(&ev, (ImplId) argv[1]);

    // Indicate that the server is ready to process requests
    SOMD_SOMOAObject->impl_is_ready(&ev, SOMD_ImplDefObject);

    // Start processing requests
    for (; ;)
    {
      // Add application specific logic
      rc = SOMD_SOMOAObject->execute_next_request(&ev, SOMD_WAIT);
      // Add application specific logic
    }
}
```

**Figure 5.2** A server program

When **SOMD_Init** is called, a run-time object, called the *DSOM Object Manager* is created. The *DSOM Object Manager* provides the services for clients to create, find, and destroy objects in the DSOM run-time environment. A pointer to this object is stored in the global variable **SOMD_ObjectMgr**.

Before the process exits, the **SOMD_Uninit** function should be called to free the DSOM resources. A typical implementation for DSOM initialization is presented below:

```
#include <somd.xh>
main()
{
   Environment *ev;

   ev = SOM_CreateLocalEnvironment();      // create and initialize an Environment structure
   SOMD_Init(ev);                          // initialize DSOM runtime

   ...
   SOMD_Uninit(ev);                        // Free DSOM resources
   SOM_DestroyLocalEnvironment(ev);        // Free Environment structure

}
```

### 5.4.2    Creation and Destruction of Remote Objects

After the DSOM environment is initialized, you can create a remote object. You can either create an object on any server that implements the class, or you can find a specific server and create an object on that server. If an object is created, DSOM returns a *proxy* to the object. A proxy is a local representation for a remote target object. A proxy inherits the target object's interface. Therefore, once you obtain a proxy, you can invoke the methods on the target object using the proxy. The operations invoked on the proxy are not executed locally, they are forwarded to the real target object for execution.

### 5.4.2.1    Using A Random Server

To create an object in an arbitrary server, a client will call the **somdNewObject** from the *DSOM Object Manager*. The following shows the syntax for the method in C.

```
myObject = _somdNewObject(SOMD_ObjectMgr,      // global instance
                          env,                 // pointer to Environment structure
                          objectClassName,     // name of the class
                          hints);              // create options(optional)
```

The parameter *SOMD_ObjectMgr* is a pointer to the DSOM Object Manager that is created during DSOM initialization. The parameter *objectClassName* is a string that represents the class name of the object. The parameter *env* is a pointer to the client's **Environment** structure. The parameter *hints* is an optional string that can be used to specify creation options.

Here is how you will use **somdNewObject** to create a remote object. Say you use the following *new* operator to create a local *Person* object:

```
person = new Person();
```

You will replace it with the following to create a remote *Person* object:

```
person = (Person *) SOMD_ObjectMgr->somdNewObject(ev, "Person", "");
```

If no object could be created, NULL is returned and an exception is raised. Otherwise, a *Person* proxy is returned in the variable *person*. From this point on, the client would use the proxy to invoke methods on the object in the same way it would if the object was local. For example, the client can invoke the *_set_name* method on the *Person* proxy:

```
person->_set_name(ev, "Mary");
```

This results in a message being sent to the server process that contains the object. The DSOM run-time at the server decodes the message and invokes the method on the target object. The result is then returned to the client process in a message. The DSOM run-time at the client decodes the message and returns the result to the caller.

### 5.4.2.2   Using A Specific Server

When a client calls **somdNewObject** to create a remote object, it places no constraints as to where the remote object is created. However, a client might want more control over the distribution of objects. In this case, the client can use the methods provided by the *DSOM Object Manager* to find specific servers for creating their objects.

A client can ask the *DSOM Object Manager* to find a server by name, by ID, or by a class it supports. Recall that a server has to be registered with DSOM in an Implementation Repository. The registration information contains, among other things, a unique server name (known as "Implementation Alias"), a unique Implementation ID, and the classes associated with the server. The *DSOM Object Manager* consults the Implementation Repository to find the requested server. If a server is found, a server proxy is returned. The client can then use the server proxy to create or destroy objects in that particular server.

To find a server by name, a client will call the **somdFindServerByName** method from the *DSOM Object Manager*. The following shows the syntax for the method in C.

```
myServer = _somdFindServerByName( SOMD_ObjectMgr,     // global instance
                                  env,                // pointer to Environment structure
                                  serverName );       // server Name
```

The parameter *serverName* is a string that specifies the name of the server. This is the name you define as Implementation Alias when you register your server in the Implementation Repository.

To find a server by ID, a client will call the **somdFindServer** method from the *DSOM Object Manager*. The following shows the syntax for the method in C.

```
myServer = _somdFindServer(SOMD_ObjectMgr,     // global instance
                           env,                // pointer to Environment structure
                           serverId );         // serverId
```

The parameter *serverId* is a string that specifies the Implementation ID of the server. This is the unique ID that is generated when you register your server in the Implementation Repository.

There are two ways to find a server by a class it supports. You can either use **somdFindServersByClass** to find all the servers that are capable of supporting the specified class. You then choose the server you want to use based on certain characteristics such as the location or the name. Or you can use **somdFindAnyServerByClass** to find any of the servers that supports the given class. The syntax for both methods in C are shown below:

```
sequence<SOMDServer> = _somdFindServersByClass(SOMD_ObjectMgr,     // global instance
                                               env,                // env structure
                                               objectClass);       // class name


myServer = _somdFindAnyServerByClass(SOMD_ObjectMgr,      // global instance
                                     env,                 // env structure
                                     objectClass);        // class name
```

The parameter *objectClass* is a string that specifies the name of the class that the server needs to be capable of creating. The classes that a server supports are specified during registration.

Once a server proxy is obtained using any of the above methods, the client can create a new object in the requested server using the **somdCreateObj** method.

```
myObject = _somdCreateObj(myServer,          // server proxy
                          env,               // pointer to Environment structure
                          objectClassName,   // name of the class
                          hints);            // create options(optional)
```

The parameter *myServer* is the pointer to the server that is capable of creating an instance of the specified class. The remaining parameters are the same as the parameters in **somdNewObject**.

The following shows how you will use **somdFindServerByName** to locate *myPersonServer* and then create a *Person* object on that server.

```
SOMDServer *myServer;
Person       *person;

myServer = SOMD_ObjectMgr->somdFindServerByName(ev, "myPersonServer");
if (myServer)
      person = (Person *) myServer->somdCreateObj(ev, "Person", "");
```

### 5.4.2.3    User Defined Metaclass

Any class that has a user-defined metaclass should not use the **somdNewObject** method to create a remote object. This is because the **somdNewObject** simply calls the default constructor. Instead, the **somdGetClassObj** method should be used to create the class object for the specified class.

In Section 3.8 on page 39, we used the *Animal* IDL to illustrate metaclass usage. We have modified it slightly so that it can be used in a distributed environment. The changes are presented in bold below:

```
#include <somobj.idl>
#include <somcls.idl>

interface Animal;
interface MetaAnimal : SOMClass
{
        Animal createAnimal(in string name);

        #ifdef __SOMIDL__
        implementation
        {
          releaseorder : createAnimal;
          dllname = "animal.dll";
        };
        #endif
};

interface Animal : SOMObject
{
        attribute string name;

        void sleep();

        #ifdef __SOMIDL__
        implementation
        {
          releaseorder : _get_name, _set_name,
                         sleep;
          name: noset;
          metaclass = MetaAnimal;
          dllname = "animal.dll";
        };
        #endif
};
```

The *noset* modifier is specified so that the *set_name* method can be implemented explicitly in the class. The *set_name* method allocates memory and makes a copy of the input name so that the value can be preserved after the *createAnimal* method is called. The implementation for the *createAnimal* method is the same as before.

A client program will do the following to create a remote *Animal* object with the name *Spot*.

```
// Find the Animal server
server = SOMD_ObjectMgr->somdFindAnyServerByClass(ev, "Animal");


// Get class object for Animal
metaAnimalClsObj = (MetaAnimal *) server->somdGetClassObj(ev, "Animal");


// Create remote animal object with the name "Spot"
animal = metaAnimalClsObj->createAnimal(ev, "Spot");
```

### 5.4.2.4    Destroying Remote Objects

A remote object that is created using **somdNewObject** or **somdCreateObj** can be destroyed using the method **somdDestroyObject**. The **somdDestroyObject** method deletes the remote object as well as its local proxy. The following shows how to use **somdDestroyObject** to destroy the *Person* object and its proxy.

```
// Create remote person object
person = (Person *) myServer->somdCreateObj(ev, "Person", "");
...
// Destroy remote person object and its proxy
SOMD_ObjectMgr->somdDestroyObject(ev, person);
```

If the client only wants to delete the local proxy, but not the remote object, the **somdReleaseObject** method should be used instead. The following shows how to use the **somdReleaseObject** method to delete the local *Person* proxy.

```
// Destroy the local person proxy
SOMD_ObjectMgr->somdReleaseObject(ev, person);
```

### 5.4.3    Finding Existing Objects

In a distributed environment, typically you will want to share objects among different processes. This means that a client might not necessarily want to use **somdNewObject** or **somdCreateObj** to create a new object all the time. Instead, a client might want to obtain the object reference to an existing object. To enable clients to share objects, DSOM supports the notion of *externalizing proxies*. The DSOM Object Manager provides methods to convert a proxy to a string ID, and vice-versa. The string ID can be saved in some persistent store. As long as the server that maintains the object exists, the string ID can be converted back to the proxy that points to the corresponding object. An example of this is given in the Distributed Calendar application in Section 5.10 on page 108.

To convert a proxy to a string ID, use the **somdGetIdFromObject** method:

```
objectId = _somdGetIdFromObject(SOMD_ObjectMgr,    // global instance
                                env,                // pointer to Environment structure
                                objectPtr);         // pointer to object
```

The parameter *objectPtr* is a proxy for which a string ID is returned. To convert the string ID back to a proxy, use the **somdGetObjectFromId** method:

```
objectPtr = _somdGetObjectFromId(SOMD_ObjectMgr,    // global instance
                                 env,                // pointer to Environment structure
                                 objectId);          // string Id representing object
```

## 5.5    CONFIGURATION

There are a few environment variables that need to be set before you can register or run your DSOM application. Table 5.1 lists all the environment variables related to OS/2 and indicates the ones that must be set.

The following shows an example of setting the variables on OS/2.

```
set USER=mary
set HOSTNAME=stealth
set SOMIR=d:\mydir\project.ir
set SOMDDIR=d:\mydir\somddir
```

## 5.6    BUILDING AND REGISTERING THE CLASSES

Once you have implemented your classes, your server (optional) and your client program, you have to compile them and register your classes and your server before they can be used. You should compile your classes into dynamic link libraries following the steps described in "Creating a DLL for SOM Classes" on page 79. Your server program should be compiled and linked with *somtk.lib*. Your client program should be complied and linked with *somtk.lib* and any other necessary libraries.

You must register the class's interface and implementation in the *Interface Repository* before an object can be accessed remotely by DSOM. You must also register a description of a server's implementation in the *Implementation Repository* before the server program, and the class libraries that it manages, can be used.

**Table 5.1**  DSOM Environment Variables on OS/2

| Environment Variables | Optional | Description |
| --- | --- | --- |
| HOSTNAME | no | Identifies the name of each machine running DSOM. |
| USER | no | Identifies the name of a DSOM user running a client program. |
| SOMIR | no | Specifies a list of files which, together, make up the Interface Repository. |
| SOMDDIR | yes | Specifies the directory where the files that make up the Implementation Repository should be located. This variable must be set before you register your server's implementation. If this variable is not set, DSOM will use the default directory %SOMBASE%\etc\DSOM. |
| SOMDPORT | yes | Specifes a well-known port number. The same well-known port number must be used on all machines in a workgroup in order for an application to establish connections successfully. |
| SOMSOCKETS | yes | Specifies the name of a class that implements communication services. This value is ignored by Workstation DSOM. |
| SOMDTIMEOUT | yes | Specifies how long a receiver should wait for a message or how long a sender should wait for an acknowledgement. The default value is 600 seconds. |
| SOMDDEBUG | yes | Enable DSOM run-time error reporting if set to 1. If set to 0, error reporting is disabled. |
| SOMDTRACELEVEL | yes | Enable DSOM run-time trace if set to 1. If set to 0, tracing is disabled. |
| SOMDMESSAGELOG | yes | Set to the name of the file where DSOM run-time error reporting or tracing messages are recorded. If not set, messages will be sent to the standard output device. |

### 5.6.1    Registering your Classes in the Interface Repository

DSOM uses the information stored in the Interface Repository extensively. The DSOM servers consult the Interface Repository to find the name of the DLL for a dynamically loaded class. Recall that you set the DLL name for a class in the *dllname* modifier in the implementation section of the class IDL. DSOM also uses the Interface Repository when transforming local method calls on proxies into messages that are sent to the remote objects.

The Interface Repository is a file that is located by the environment variable SOMIR. To populate the Interface Repository, you use the Interface Repository emitter, which can be invoked when you run the **sc** command with the **-u** option. If SOMIR is not set, the Interface Repository emitter creates a file named "som.ir" in the current directory. The following compiles the IDL file *person.idl* and creates an IR called "person.ir":

```
set SOMIR=c:\mydir\person.ir
sc -sir -u person.idl
```

Each class in the DLL must be compiled into the Interface Repository before running your DSOM application. DSOM uses the Interface Repository to find information on method parameters and return type. If a class has not been compiled into the Interface Repository, DSOM will generate a run-time error when an attempt is made to invoke a method from that class. The Interface Repository is described in more detail in Chapter 8.

The *SOMobjects Developer Toolkit* includes the utility **irdump** that can be used to find out if a class exists in the Interface Repository. For example, the following displays the definition of *SOMObject*:

```
irdump SOMObject
```

### 5.6.2    Registering your Server in the Implementation Repository

DSOM uses the Implementation Repository to find out information about a server's implementation. The Implementation Repository contains information such as the name of the server, the name of the executable for the server program, the name of the machine on which the server program is stored, and the classes that are associated with this server. DSOM uses this information to locate a server, and, if necessary, to activate the server so that clients can invoke methods on it.

The Implementation Repository consists of four files:

```
somdimpl.dat

somdimpl.toc

somdcls.dat

somdcls.toc
```

The location of the Implementation Repository is specified by the environment variable SOMDDIR. If SOMDDIR is not set, DSOM will attempt to use the default directory *%SOMBASE%\etc\dsom* on OS/2.

There are two ways that you can populate the Implementation Repository. The first is a static mechanism using the **regimpl** registration utility. The second is a dynamic mechanism where you can access and update the Implementation Repository using a programmable interface at run-time. These are described below.

### 5.6.3    Using the regimpl Registration Utility

The **regimpl** utility can be run either interactively or as a command. To run in interactive mode, type **regimpl** at the system command prompt. This brings up the DSOM Implementation Registration Utility menu, where you will be prompted for information. The command interface is perhaps more useful since you can invoke it from a makefile.

The following lists all the information that you can specify using the **regimpl** utility. The command flag that corresponds to each function is given in parentheses.

- Implementation alias (-i)
  This is the name you defined for your server.
- Server program name (-p)
  This is the name of the program that will execute as the server. The default program name is **somdsvr**, which is the DSOM generic server. If you have implemented your own application specific server, enter the full pathname for the program. If the program is located in PATH, then only the program name needs to be specified.
- Server class name (-v)
  This is the name of the class that will manage the objects in the server. The default is **SOMDServer**.
- Multi-threading (-m)
  This option specifies whether or not the server expects each method to be run in a separate thread. The default is no.
- Class name (-c)
  Use this option to specify the list of classes that are associated with this server.
- Host machine name (-h)
  This is the name of the machine on which the server program code is stored. The same name should be set in the HOSTNAME environment variable.
- Reference data file name (-f)
  This is an optional parameter that contains the full pathname of the file that is used to store *ReferenceData*[*] associated with object references created by this server.
- Backup reference data file name (-b)
- This is an optional parameter that contains the full pathname of the backup file that is used to mirror the primary *ReferenceData* file. This file can be used to restore the primary copy if it becomes corrupted.

Each of these options can add to, update, or delete from the Implementation Repository. For example, the following commands add the server, *myServer*, to the Implementation Repository. The name of the server program is *servprog.exe,* and the classes that are assoicated with *myServer* are *Class1, Class2,* and *Class3.*

```
regimpl -A -i myServer -p servprog.exe
regimpl -a -i myServer -c Class1 -c Class2 -c Class3
```

---

[*]Reference data is application-specific data if it is associated with an object reference. It can contain information such as the object location or state that is specific to the application. The SOMOA class provides the *create* and *create_constant* methods to create and associate reference data with the object reference.

You can list the information in the Implementation Repository. For example, the command,

    regimpl -L -i myServer

displays the list shown in Figure 5.3.

The Implementation ID is a unique ID that is generated by DSOM. This is the ID that you use when you invoke the **somFindServer** method to locate a server by its Implementation ID.

You can also list the classes associated with a server. For example, the command,

    regimpl -l -i myServer

displays the classes shown in Figure 5.4.

### 5.6.4   Using the Programmable Interface

The Implementation Repository can also be accessed and updated dynamically, using the programmable interface provided by the *ImplRepository* class. The following summarizes the methods provided by the *ImplRepository* class:

```
================================================================
Implementation id..............: 2cc7eff7-067c6140-7f-00-0100007f0000
Implementation alias..........: myServer
Program name...................: servprog.exe
Multithreaded....................: No
Server class......................: SOMDServer
Object reference file...........:
Object reference backup....:
Host name........................: localhost
```

**Figure 5.3** The Implementation Repository for myServer

```
Implementation alias                    Classes in this implementation

================================================================
myServer                                Class1
                                        Class2
                                        Class3
```

**Figure 5.4** The classes associated with myServer

- **add_impldef**—adds an implementation definition to the Implementation Repository.
- **add_class_to_impldef**—associates a class with a server.
- **remove_class_from_impldef**—removes the association of a class with a server.
- **delete_impldef**—deletes an implementation definition from the Implementation Repository.
- **update_impldef**—updates an implementation definition in the Implementation Repository.
- **find_impldef**—returns a server implementation definition given its ID.
- **find_impldef_by_alias**—returns a server implementation definition given its alias.
- **find_impldef_by_class**—returns a sequence of implementation definitions for servers that are associated with the specified class.
- **find_classes_by_impldef**—returns a sequence of class names associated with a server.

The code example of Figure 5.5 illustrates how you can retrieve a server implementation given the server's alias. The variable **SOMD_ImplRepObject** is initialized by **SOMD_Init** to point to the *ImplRepository* object. The *ImplementationDef* object contains attributes for setting and accessing the server's implementation definition.

## 5.7    EXECUTION

Once you have properly set up your environment variables and performed the necessary registration, you can run your DSOM application. To run a DSOM application, the DSOM daemon, **somdd**, must be started on each server machine. Client-only machines do not require an active DSOM daemon. The daemon can be started from a command line or from a start-up script. For example, **start somdd** can be used to start the daemon on OS/2.

The DSOM daemon is responsible for establishing a connection between a client process and a server. When a request is made to a server, if the server is not already running, the DSOM daemon will automatically start the server.

Once the DSOM daemon is running, the DSOM application can be started.

## 5.8    A CHECKLIST FOR DSOM CONFIGURATION

Configuring your environment for DSOM can be difficult and error-prone. The following checklist provides tips for configuring your DSOM and network environment. Refer to the product's Installation Guide for additional details.

1. Workstation DSOM can be run on a single OS/2 or AIX without any networking hardware, if it is not used with the Event Manager Framework. In this case, Workstation DSOM uses shared memory for communications.

```c
#include <stdlib.h>
#include <string.h>
#include <somd.xh>
#include <implrep.xh>
#include <stdio.h>

main(int argc, char **argv)
{
    Environment *ev;
    ImplementationDef *implDef;
    sequence(string) classes;
    short i;

    ev = SOM_CreateLocalEnvironment();
    SOMD_Init(ev);

    // Find the ImplementationDef object for the specified server alias
    implDef = SOMD_ImplRepObject->find_impldef_by_alias(ev, argv[1]);

    // Find the sequence of classes associated with this server Id
    classes = SOMD_ImplRepObject->find_classes_by_impldef(ev, implDef->_get_impl_id(ev));

    printf("Server : %s\n", argv[1]);
    printf("Program Name: %s\n", implDef->_get_impl_program(ev));
    printf("Server Class: %s\n", implDef->_get_impl_server_class(ev));
    printf("Host Name: %s\n", implDef->_get_impl_hostname(ev));

    for (i=0; i < sequenceLength(classes); i++)
    {
        printf("%s\n", sequenceElement(classes,i) );
    }

    SOMD_Uninit(ev);
    SOM_UninitEnvironment(ev);
}
```

**Figure 5.5** A program that accesses the Implementation Repository

2. Workstation DSOM, if used with the Event Manager Framework, requires TCP/IP to be installed.
3. Workgroup DSOM requires networking software for its operations. Table 5.2 lists the network products that are supported. Make sure at least one of them is installed and started before you use Workgroup DSOM.

**Table 5.2** Network software requirements for Workgroup DSOM

| OS/2 | AIX |
|---|---|
| TCP/IP Version 1.2.1 with CSD UN34109. This product includes Network File System (NFS). | TCP/IP and Network File System (NFS), Version 3.2, as shipped with the AIX Base Operationg System Network Facilities. |
| NetWare Requester for OS/2 v2.01. This product includes Novell IPX/SPX protocols. | Novell IPX/SPX transport, as shipped with Netware for AIX/6000 from IBM v3.11. |
| Network Transport Services/2 (NTS/2), v1.0. This product includes the NetBIOS protocol. | N/A |

4. Workgroup DSOM requires each machine to have a unique network address (Internet address), and a unique hostname. The association between hostnames and Internet address is maintained in a "hosts" file. The "hosts" file must be created on each machine, and must contain an entry for both the client and the server machines.

   If you are running NetWare, you also need an "ipxaddrs" file for each machine on the network. The "ipxaddrs" file entry maps an Internet address to a native Novell IPX/SPX address.

   If you are running NetBIOS, verify that you do not have a "resolv" file.

1. When using the Novell, or the NetBIOS protocol, there is an additional step in configuring Workgroup DSOM. This is because there is a software layer that maps Internet addresses onto local Novell, or native NetBIOS network addresses. If you are using the Novell protocol, you must run "ipxconf" which is supplied with the NetWare support for SOMobjects. If you are using the NetBIOS protocol, you must run "nbconf" which is supplied with the NetBIOS support of SOMobjects.

2. The environment variable ETC must be set on AIX for NetWare and on OS/2 for all supported protocols. It should be set to the pathname for the directory that contains the "hosts" file and the "ipxaddrs" file if NetWare is used.

3. The environment variable SOMSOCKETS must be set when using one of the communication protocols. The values are **TCPIPSockets** for TCP/IP, **IPXSockets** for NetWare, and **NBSockets** for NetBIOS. Note that this variable is ignored when using Workstation DSOM in a single machine and Event Management Framework is not used.

4. The following DSOM environment variables must be set when using either Workstation or Workgroup DSOM. They do not have default values.

       HOSTNAME=<name>
       MALLOCTYPE=3.1 (AIX ONLY)
       SOMIR=<file(s)>
       USER=<name>

5. The following DSOM environment variables have default values that can be redefined by the user if desired.

```
SOMDDIR=<directory>
SOMDPORT=<integer>
```

For Workgroup DSOM, the client and the server machines must have SOMD-
PORT set to the same value in order for connections to be established.

6. IDL must be compiled into the Interface Repository for all application classes. For Workgroup DSOM, the client and server machines must both have the application IDL in their Interface Repositories.

7. A server implementation (server program and class libraries) must be registered with DSOM by running the implementation registration utility, **regimpl**. For Workgroup DSOM, the client and server machines must share the Implementation Repository via a shared file system or have identical copies. Specifically, the automatically generated Implementation ID for a given implementation must be the same on both machines. The Implementation ID is used by DSOM to do the binding between client and server. They must be identical. Note that if you simply run **regimpl** on both machines, the ID that is generated might not be identical. Therefore, it is recommended that you share the Implementation Repository using a shared file system.

8. When moving a server from one machine to another, you should run **regimpl** with the update option to *update* the information associated with the server implementation. Do not simply create a new server implementation. This is because it will invalidate any existing references to the previous Implementation ID.

9. All class libraries and networking libraries must be in directories specified in LIBPATH. For Workgroup DSOM, both the client and server machines need the DLL that contains the classes. Note that for machines that will only be used to run client programs, a "stub" DLL may be built. A client-side "stub" DLL can be created by emiting the .xh, .xih and .cpp files or the .h, .ih and .c files from the IDL for a class and compiling these files in the same way that regular DLLs are compiled. A "stub" DLL provides the support for creating local proxy for the remote object.

10. The DSOM daemon, **somdd**, must be started on each server machine. Note that if the environment variable SOMIR has the value "...;som.ir" on OS/2 or "...:./som.ir" on AIX, the client programs, server programs and **somdd** must be started in the same directory as the "som.ir" file. Therefore, it is recommended that SOMIR contains fully-qualified file names. For example "...;d:\myir\som.ir" on OS/2, or "...:/u/joe/myir/som.ir" on AIX.

## 5.9    DYNAMIC INVOCATION INTERFACE

CORBA defines the dynamic invocation interface (DII), which allows the dynamic creation and invocation of requests to objects. A client using the DII to send a request to an object obtains the same semantics as a client that is using the language bindings which are generated from the interface specification. The DII is useful for applications that need to invoke objects without knowing all the object interfaces at compile-time.

DSOM supports the CORBA DII. Currently, you can use DII to invoke remote objects only. The **somDispatch** method, which is non-CORBA, can be used to invoke methods dynamically on either local or remote objects. The **somDispatch** method is discussed in Section 3.12.3.

To invoke a method using the DII, a client has to perform two steps:

1. Construct the request by using the **create_request** method from the *SOMDObject* class. A request comprises an object reference, an operation, and a list of parameters. The parameters are supplied as elements of an **NVList** object. The **create_request** method returns a *Request* object.
2. Initiate the request by invoking the **invoke** or the **send** method on the *Request* object. The **invoke** method will wait for the operation to complete, whereas the **send** method will not wait for the operation to complete. If **send** is used, the client can later call the **get_response** method on the *Request* object to determine if the operation has completed.

## 5.10    A DISTRIBUTED CALENDAR

To illustrate some of the concepts we have discussed in this chapter, we will develop a simple calendar system allowing you to record activities for a day. The following list is a summary of the functions:

- Allows a user to enter or delete activities
- Provides a graphical user interface (GUI) for user's actions
- Supports multiple users that are located across a network
- Allows sharing of any user's calendar

Since the purpose of this example is to illustrate the DSOM Framework, and not so much of the calendar functions, we will limit our calendar capability to support only hours, omitting minutes. Also, our calendar will support only a week's events. Nevertheless, one should easily be able to extend this example to a more realistic implementation.

### 5.10.1    What the User Sees

In this example, the client program is called PLANNER. When you invoke PLANNER, you can supply an optional parameter that specifies which calendar you want to work with. If you do not specify the parameter, it will default to my (Chris) calendar. The screen for my calendar is displayed in Figure 5.6.

The title of the screen indicates whose calendar it is. For example, if you type:

```
> PLANNER Kevin
```

This will invoke PLANNER with Kevin's calendar, and the title will show "Kevin Weekly Calendar".

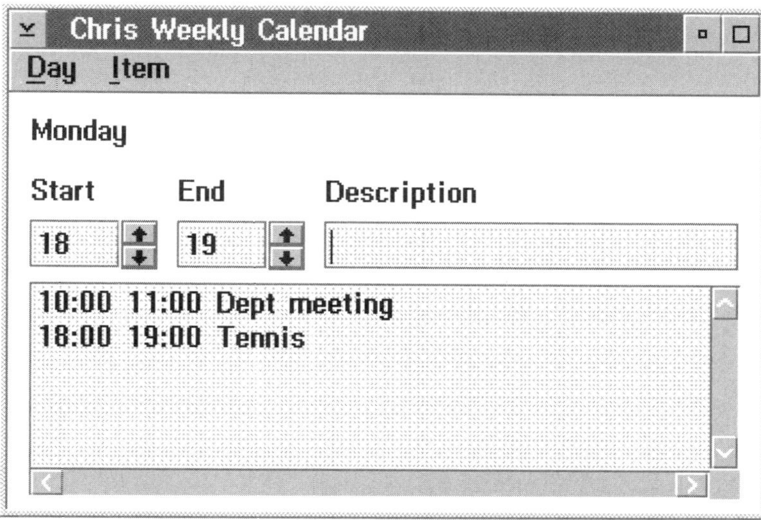


**Figure 5.6** Chris weekly calendar

Use the **Start** and **End** spin button control to select the start and end time for an activity, and type a description for the activity in the **Description** field. The **Item** menu allows you to Add or Delete an activity from your calendar. When you click on Add, the current activity will be added to the list. To delete an activity from the list, click on the activity to highlight it. Then select Delete from the **Item** menu and the activity will be deleted.

The **Day** menu lets you select what day of the week you want to work with. You can select either Sunday, Monday, Tuesday, Wednesday, Thursday, Friday, or Saturday. Initially, it is set to Monday. When you select a different day, the description text on the screen will be updated. If there are any activities for that day, they will be displayed. The **Day** menu also contains a Quit button that you can select to exit the PLANNER program.

### 5.10.2  Calendar Sharing

Multiple users can work with a particular calendar. For example, I can add activities to my calendar. Someone else can look at my calendar entries as well as make changes to them. Changes are local to each calendar. That is, if I add an activity to my calendar, the activity will only be added to my calendar and not to another person's calendar.

### 5.10.3  High-Level Design

To design our calendar application, we need to decide what our classes look like. Our classes need to capture information, like the start and end time for an activity, as well as the description of an activity. The classes also need to keep track of the activities for a particular day, and maintain activity lists for an entire week. Finally, the classes need to support multiple calendar users and allow sharing between them.

We also need to design the GUI front end. It is important to recognize that the GUI front end is the client of the classes that we used to model our calendar. The GUI client is not the calendar object. The GUI client will perform tasks such as creating the calendar object and exporting the corresponding proxy, so that the calendar object can be shared between multiple clients (users).

Our calendar is modeled using three classes: a work item class (*WorkItem*), a day class (*Day*), and a calendar directory class (*CalendarDir*). The *WorkItem* class is used to encapsulate the start time, the end time, and the description of an activity. The *Day* class is used to encapsulate the list of activities for a particular day. Individual activities can be added to, or deleted from, a *Day* object. The *CalendarDir* class is used to encapsulate a week so we can support up to seven days of activities.

The three classes are packaged into a DLL called *calendar.dll*. We will use the generic DSOM server program (*somdsvr*). To support different calendars for different users, we need to register multiple calendar servers. For example, we will have a server with alias "Chris" for my calendar, and another server with alias "Kevin" for Kevin's calendar.

Recall that the generic server program handles requests in a synchronous manner, using a FIFO queue. This ensures that when multiple updates are made to a calendar server, the requests will be queued and processed sequentially.

The GUI client is built using the IBM User Interface Class Library. Although it is not necessary to understand GUI in order to understand SOM, we believe future applications will make use of both the SOM Frameworks and the User Interface Frameworks. Therefore, it is included here for those who are interested in seeing how the two can be used together.

### 5.10.4   Implementation Details

This section will provide the details of the design and implementation of each of the components in our calendar application.

#### The WorkItem Class

The IDL for the *WorkItem* class is given in Figure 5.7. It introduces one new method and overrides two methods.

- The *mkEntry* method allocates storage for the strings *startTime, endTime,* and *task*, and then makes a copy of the input value. It is necessary to explicitly allocate memory for the strings so that the object will retain the values even after the caller falls out of scope.
- The **somInit** method is overridden to initialize the attributes to NULL.
- The **somUninit** method is overridden to free any storage that is allocated for the attributes when the object is destroyed.

```
#ifndef workitem_idl
#define workitem_idl

#include <somobj.idl>

interface WorkItem : SOMObject
{
    attribute string startTime;
    attribute string endTime;
    attribute string task;

    void mkEntry(in string sTime, in string eTime, in string taskDesc);

    #ifdef __SOMIDL__
    implementation
    {
      releaseorder : _get_startTime, _set_startTime,
                     _get_endTime, _set_endTime,
                     _get_task, _set_task,
                     mkEntry;

        somInit: override;
        somUninit: override;
        dllname = "calendar.dll";
    };
    #endif
};
#endif
```

**Figure 5.7** The WorkItem IDL

The C++ code that implements the methods for the *WorkItem* class is presented in Figure 5.8.

**The Day Class**

Figure 5.9 gives the IDL for the *Day* class. The *Day* class is used to capture the list of todo's for the day. It introduces two new methods and overrides two others.

- The *book* method adds a *WorkItem* object to the sequence *workList*. The sequence *workList* is a bounded sequence with a maximum of 50 *WorkItem* objects. We will restrict ourself to working a maximum of 50 tasks per day. Should you desire more, you can use an unbounded sequence and modify the implementation to manage storage.

```c
/*
 * This file was generated by the SOM Compiler and Emitter Framework.
 * Generated using:
 * SOM Emitter emitxtm: somc/smmain.c
 */


#define WorkItem_Class_Source
#include <workitem.xih>

SOM_Scope void SOMLINK mkEntry(WorkItem *somSelf, Environment *ev,
                                    string sTime, string eTime, string taskDesc)
{
    WorkItemData *somThis = WorkItemGetData(somSelf);
    WorkItemMethodDebug("WorkItem","mkEntry");

    if (somThis->startTime) SOMFree(somThis->startTime);
    somThis->startTime = (string)SOMMalloc(strlen(sTime)+1);
    strcpy (somThis->startTime, sTime);

    if (somThis->endTime) SOMFree(somThis->endTime);
    somThis->endTime = (string)SOMMalloc(strlen(eTime)+1);
    strcpy (somThis->endTime, eTime);

    if (somThis->task) SOMFree(somThis->task);
    somThis->task = (string)SOMMalloc(strlen(taskDesc)+1);
    strcpy (somThis->task, taskDesc);
}

SOM_Scope void SOMLINK somInit(WorkItem *somSelf)
{
    WorkItemData *somThis = WorkItemGetData(somSelf);
    WorkItemMethodDebug("WorkItem","somInit");

    WorkItem_parent_SOMObject_somInit(somSelf);

    somThis->startTime = NULL;
    somThis->endTime = NULL;
    somThis->task = NULL;
}
```

**Figure 5.8** The WorkItem class implementation (continues)

```
SOM_Scope void SOMLINK somUninit(WorkItem *somSelf)
{
    WorkItemData *somThis = WorkItemGetData(somSelf);
    WorkItemMethodDebug("WorkItem","somUninit");

    if (somThis->startTime) SOMFree(somThis->startTime);
    if (somThis->endTime) SOMFree(somThis->endTime);
    if (somThis->task) SOMFree(somThis->task);

    WorkItem_parent_SOMObject_somUninit(somSelf);
}
```

**Figure 5.8** continued

- The *removeItem* method removes a *WorkItem* object from the sequence *workList*. It searches the sequence for a *WorkItem* object that has the same *startTime*, *endTime,* and *task* values as the input parameters. If one is found, it will be removed from the sequence.
- The **somInit** method is overridden to initialize the sequence *workList*. It allocates storage for the sequence and sets the length and maximum field of the sequence.
- The **somUninit** method is overridden to free the storage that is allocated for the sequence *workList* when the object is destroyed.

The C++ code that implements the methods for the *Day* class is shown in Figure 5.10.

**The CalendarDir Class**

The IDL for the *CalendarDir* class is given in Figure 5.11. The *CalendarDir* class maintains a directory for a week of activities. It introduces two new methods and overrides two methods.

- The *addDay* method adds a *Day* object to the sequence *weekList*. The sequence *weekList* is a bounded sequence with a total of seven elements, one for each day of the week.
- The *getDay* method returns a *Day* object for the requested day.
- The **somInit** method is overridden to initialize the sequence *weekList*. It allocates storage for the sequence, and sets the length and maximum field of the sequence.
- The **somUninit** method is overridden to free the storage that is allocated for the sequence *weekList* when the object is destroyed.

The C++ code that implements the methods for the *CalendarDir* class is given in Figure 5.12.

```
#ifndef day_idl
#define day_idl

#include <somobj.idl>

interface WorkItem;
interface Day : SOMObject
{
    const unsigned long MAXITEM = 50;
    attribute long date;                                    // today's date
    attribute sequence<WorkItem,MAXITEM> workList;          // list of todo's

    short book(in WorkItem entry);
    short removeItem(in string start, in string end, in string desc);

    #ifdef __SOMIDL__
    implementation
    {
        releaseorder : _get_date, _set_date,
                       _get_workList, _set_workList,
                       book, removeItem;

        somInit: override;
        somUninit: override;
        dllname = "calendar.dll";
    };
    #endif
};
#endif
```

**Figure 5.9** The Day IDL


### The GUI Client

The PLANNER program is the client that uses the above classes in a distributed
fashion. The source files that make up the PLANNER program are *planwin.hpp*
and *planwin.cpp*. The listing for *planwin.hpp* is given in Figure 5.13.

The class *DayPlannerWindow* is derived from the *IFrameWindow, ICommandHandler,* and *ISelectHandler* classes from the IBM User Interface Class
Library. The *DayPlannerWindow* class handles the creation of the main window
and the processing of user events. It also handles the creation and management
of calendar objects. A summary of what each member function does is given
below:

```c
/*
 * This file was generated by the SOM Compiler and Emitter Framework.
 * Generated using:
 * SOM Emitter emitxtm: somc/smmain.c
 */

#define Day_Class_Source
#include <day.xih>
#include <workitem.xh>
#include <string.h>

SOM_Scope short SOMLINK book(Day *somSelf, Environment *ev,
                                    WorkItem* entry)
{
    DayData *somThis = DayGetData(somSelf);
    short rc;
    DayMethodDebug("Day","book");

    if (sequenceLength(somThis->workList) < sequenceMaximum(somThis->workList))
    {
      sequenceElement(somThis->workList, sequenceLength(somThis->workList)) = entry;
      sequenceLength(somThis->workList)++;
      rc = 0;
    }
    else
    {
      rc = -1;
    }
    return rc;
}

SOM_Scope short SOMLINK removeItem(Day *somSelf, Environment *ev,
                                      string start, string end, string desc)
{
    DayData *somThis = DayGetData(somSelf);
    short i;
    WorkItem *item;
    DayMethodDebug("Day","removeItem");

    for (i=0; i < sequenceLength(somThis->workList); i++ )
```

**Figure 5.10** The Day class implementation (continues)

```c
        {
          item = sequenceElement(somThis->workList,i);

          if ( (strcmp(start, item->_get_startTime(ev)) == 0) &&
            (strcmp(end, item->_get_endTime(ev)) == 0) &&
            (strcmp(desc, item->_get_task(ev)) == 0) )
          {
            // Found item. Delete it from the list.
            sequenceLength(somThis->workList)--;
            for (i; i < sequenceLength(somThis->workList); i++)
            {
                sequenceElement(somThis->workList,i) = sequenceElement(somThis->workList, i+1);
            }
            return 0;
          }
        }
        return -1;              // item not found
}


SOM_Scope void SOMLINK somInit(Day *somSelf)
{

      DayData *somThis = DayGetData(somSelf);
      DayMethodDebug("Day","somInit");

      Day_parent_SOMObject_somInit(somSelf);

      sequenceMaximum(somThis->workList) = MAXITEM;
      sequenceLength(somThis->workList) = 0;
      somThis->workList._buffer = (WorkItem**) SOMMalloc(sizeof (WorkItem *) * MAXITEM);
}


SOM_Scope void SOMLINK somUninit(Day *somSelf)
{

      DayData *somThis = DayGetData(somSelf);
      DayMethodDebug("Day","somUninit");

      if (somThis->workList._buffer)
        SOMFree(somThis->workList._buffer);

      Day_parent_SOMObject_somUninit(somSelf);
}
```

**Figure 5.10** continued

```
#ifndef caldir_idl
#define caldir_idl

#include <somobj.idl>

interface Day;
interface CalendarDir : SOMObject
{
    const unsigned long MAXDAY = 7;
    attribute sequence<Day, MAXDAY> weekList;

    long addDay(in short daynum, in Day entry);
    Day getDay(in short daynum);

    #ifdef __SOMIDL__
    implementation
    {
        releaseorder : _get_weekList, _set_weekList,
                       addDay, getDay;

        somInit: override;
        somUninit: override;
        dllname = "calendar.dll";
    };
    #endif
};
#endif
```

**Figure 5.11** The CalendarDir IDL

- The *constructor* constructs the frame window. It initializes the title bar using the name of the calendar server and creates the menu bar. It calls the *setup-Client* function to set up the client window. It then calls the *setupData* function to set up the DSOM environment. Finally, it calculates the size of the main window, sets focus to the main window, and displays it.
- The *command* function processes commands from the menu bar. The case MI_ADD handles the Add request. It adds the values from the input fields to the list box and calls the *book* function to add the item to the current activity list. The case MI_DEL handles the Delete request. It deletes the selected item from the list box as well as from the current activity list.

```
/*
 * This file was generated by the SOM Compiler and Emitter Framework.
 * Generated using:
 * SOM Emitter emitxtm: somc/smmain.c
 */

#define CalendarDir_Class_Source
#include <caldir.xih>

SOM_Scope long SOMLINK addDay(CalendarDir *somSelf, Environment *ev,
                                        short daynum, Day* entry)
{
    CalendarDirData *somThis = CalendarDirGetData(somSelf);
    long rc;
    CalendarDirMethodDebug("CalendarDir","addDay");

    if (sequenceLength(somThis->weekList) < sequenceMaximum(somThis->weekList))
    {
        sequenceElement(somThis->weekList, sequenceLength(somThis->weekList)) = entry;
        sequenceLength(somThis->weekList)++;
        rc = 0L;
    }
    else
    {
        rc = -1L;
    }
    return rc;
}

SOM_Scope Day* SOMLINK getDay(CalendarDir *somSelf, Environment *ev,
                                        short daynum)
{
    CalendarDirData *somThis = CalendarDirGetData(somSelf);
    CalendarDirMethodDebug("CalendarDir","getDay");

    return ( sequenceElement(somThis->weekList, daynum) );
}

SOM_Scope void SOMLINK somInit(CalendarDir *somSelf)
{
```

**Figure 5.12** The CalendarDir class implementation (continues)

```
    CalendarDirData *somThis = CalendarDirGetData(somSelf);
    CalendarDirMethodDebug("CalendarDir","somInit");


    CalendarDir_parent_SOMObject_somInit(somSelf);


    sequenceMaximum(somThis->weekList) = MAXDAY;
    sequenceLength(somThis->weekList) = 0;
    somThis->weekList._buffer = (Day**) SOMMalloc(sizeof (Day *) * MAXDAY);
}


SOM_Scope void SOMLINK somUninit(CalendarDir *somSelf)
{
    CalendarDirData *somThis = CalendarDirGetData(somSelf);
    CalendarDirMethodDebug("CalendarDir","somUninit");


    if (somThis->weekList._buffer)
        SOMFree(somThis->weekList._buffer);


    CalendarDir_parent_SOMObject_somUninit(somSelf);
}
```

**Figure 5.12** continued


The cases `MI_SUN`, `MI_MON`, etc., handle the selection of the day of the week. For instance, if Sunday is selected, the static field on the screen is updated to reflect the current day, and the *showItems* function is called to display the list of activities for Sunday.

The case `MI_QUIT` closes the application.

- The *selected* function handles the selected command from the list box. It sets the list box cursor to the selected item.
- The *setupClient* function creates a multi-cell canvas control as the client window. It also creates the spin-button controls, the static text controls, the entry field control, and the list box control, placing them on the multi-cell canvas.
- The *setupData* function initializes the DSOM environment and locates the specified calendar server. It then calls the *findProxy* function to determine if there is already an existing object reference to *CalendarDir* object that is managed by this server. If an object reference already exists, it will be used. Otherwise, a new *CalendarDir* object is created, and its reference is converted into a string ID. The string ID is written to a file to allow the sharing of the *CalendarDir* object.

A simple one-to-one mapping convention is used to identify the object reference for a calendar server. For example, if "`PLANNER Kevin`" is invoked for the

```
#ifndef PLANWIN_HPP
#define PLANWIN_HPP

#include <iframe.hpp>
#include <icmdhdr.hpp>
#include <imcelcv.hpp>
#include <ilistbox.hpp>
#include <iselhdr.hpp>
#include <istring.hpp>
#include <istattxt.hpp>
#include <imenubar.hpp>
#include <ispinbt.hpp>
#include <ientryfd.hpp>

#include <somd.xh>
#include "week.h"
#include "workitem.xh"
#include "day.xh"
#include "caldir.xh"

class DayPlannerWindow : public IFrameWindow,
                         public ICommandHandler,
                         public ISelectHandler
{
    public:
      DayPlannerWindow (unsigned long windowId, char *name);
      ~DayPlannerWindow();

    protected:
      virtual Boolean command(ICommandEvent& cmdevt);
      virtual Boolean selected(IControlEvent& evt);

    private:
      setupClient();
      setupData();
      short findProxy();
      showItems(short day);
      book(char *start, char *end, char *desc);
```

**Figure 5.13**  The DayPlannerWindow header file (continues)

```
            IEntryField *descT;
            IStaticText *weekday, *start, *end, *desc;
            ISpinButton *startT, *endT;

            IMultiCellCanvas *mc;
            IMenuBar *menuBar;
            short menuFlag;
            short createFile;

            IListBox *listBox;
            IListBox::Cursor *cursor;

            // DSOM related variables
            SOMDServer *server;
            char *serverName;
            Environment *ev;
            CalendarDir *curDirEntry;
            Day *curDay;
   };
   #endif
```

**Figure 5.13** continued

first time, a new *CalendarDir* object will be created for the Kevin calendar server. The reference to this object is converted to a string ID and stored in the file "Kevin". Later, when "PLANNER Kevin" is invoked again (say, by another user), the *findProxy* function will retrieve the string ID from the file "Kevin" and convert it back to the object reference so the second user can access Kevin's calendar.

- The *findProxy* function checks to see if there is already a string ID for the *CalendarDir* object that is managed by this server. If there is an existing string ID, it will be restored back into the object reference.
- The *showItems* function displays the list of activities for a particular day.
- The *book* function creates a new *WorkItem* object and adds it to the activitiy list for the day.
- The *destructor* performs cleanup. If this client has created a file to contain the string ID for the *CalendarDir* object, we assume it is the last remaining client and we call the **somdDestroyObject** method to destroy all the local proxies and the remote objects. The file is also erased.

  If this client is not the one that created a file, we assume that there are existing clients out there that are still working with the calendar objects. Therefore, we will not destroy the remote objects. Instead we call the **somdReleaseObject** method to release the local proxies.

The listing for the source file *planwin.cpp* is given in Figure 5.14.

```cpp
#include <ifont.hpp>
#include <ititle.hpp>
#include <iostream.h>
#include <fstream.h>
#include <imsgbox.hpp>

#include "planwin.hpp"

void main(int argc, char *argv[], char *envp[])
{
  IString filename;
  if (argc == 2)
  {
     filename = argv[1];
  }
  else
  {
     filename = "Chris";           // default to my calendar
  }
  DayPlannerWindow mainWindow(WND_MAIN, filename);
  IApplication::current().run();
}


DayPlannerWindow :: DayPlannerWindow(unsigned long windowId,
                                          char *name)
  : IFrameWindow (IFrameWindow::defaultStyle(), windowId)
  , serverName(name)
  , createFile(0)
{
  IString title(" Weekly Calendar");

  ICommandHandler::handleEventsFor(this);

  title = serverName + title;
  ITitle(this, title);

  menuBar = new IMenuBar(WND_MAIN,this);
  menuBar->setAutoDeleteObject();           // auto delete when window is closed
  menuBar->checkItem(MI_BASE);
```

**Figure 5.14** The DayPlannerWindow implementation (continues)

```
      menuFlag = MI_BASE;

      setupClient();
      setupData();

      if ( IWindow::desktopWindow()->size() > ISize(1000,700) )
      {
         sizeTo(ISize(460,330));
      }
      else                            // VGA
      {
         sizeTo(ISize(360,240));
      }

      setFocus();
      show();
}

DayPlannerWindow :: setupClient()
{
   mc = new IMultiCellCanvas(WND_CANVAS, this, this);
   mc->setAutoDeleteObject();
   setClient(mc);

   weekday = new IStaticText(WND_TEXT, mc, mc);
   weekday->setAutoDeleteObject();
   weekday->setText("Monday");

   start = new IStaticText(WND_TEXT, mc, mc);
   start->setAutoDeleteObject();
   start->setText("Start ");

   startT = new ISpinButton(WND_START,mc,mc);
   startT->setAutoDeleteObject();
   startT->setInputType(ISpinButton::numeric);
   startT->setRange(IRange(1,24));
   startT->setCurrent(8);
   startT->setLimit(2);
   startT->readOnly;
```

**Figure 5.14**  (continues)

```
end = new IStaticText(WND_TEXT, mc, mc);
end->setAutoDeleteObject();
end->setText("End ");

endT = new ISpinButton(WND_END,mc,mc);
endT->setAutoDeleteObject();
endT->setInputType(ISpinButton::numeric);
endT->setRange(IRange(1,24));
endT->setCurrent(6);
endT->setLimit(2);
endT->readOnly;

desc = new IStaticText(WND_TEXT, mc, mc);
desc->setAutoDeleteObject();
desc->setText("Description");
descT = new IEntryField(WND_DESC, mc, mc);

listBox = new IListBox(WND_LISTBOX,mc,mc,IRectangle(),
                       IListBox::defaultStyle() |
                       IControl::tabStop);
listBox->setAutoDeleteObject();
cursor = new IListBox::Cursor(*listBox);
ISelectHandler::handleEventsFor(listBox);

mc->addToCell(weekday,2,2);
mc->addToCell(start, 2,4);
mc->addToCell(startT, 2,5);
mc->addToCell(end, 4,4);
mc->addToCell(endT, 4,5);
mc->addToCell(desc, 6,4);
mc->addToCell(descT, 6,5);
mc->addToCell(listBox,2,7,5,1);

// Add some space between rows and columns to make it look pretty
mc->setRowHeight(3,2,true);
mc->setRowHeight(6,2,true);
mc->setRowHeight(8,2,true);
mc->setColumnWidth(3,2,true);
mc->setColumnWidth(5,2,true);
```

**Figure 5.14**  (continues)

```
        mc->setColumnWidth(7,2,true);
}


DayPlannerWindow :: setupData()
{
   short i, found;
   Day *day;

   string objectId;

   ev = SOM_CreateLocalEnvironment();
   SOMD_Init(ev);

   server = SOMD_ObjectMgr->somdFindServerByName(ev,serverName);
   found = findProxy();

   if (!found)
   {
       //****************************************************************************
       // Create a new CalendarDir object and adds 7 Days to the list
       //****************************************************************************
       curDirEntry = (CalendarDir *) server->somdCreateObj(ev,
                                                        "CalendarDir",
                                                        NULL);


       //****************************************************************************
       // Convert proxy to a string and save to a file with the same
       // name as the current server Name.
       //****************************************************************************
       objectId = SOMD_ObjectMgr->somdGetIdFromObject(ev,curDirEntry);

       ofstream outfile(serverName);
       outfile << objectId;
       outfile.close();

       createFile = 1;                 // remember this client created the file

       for (i=0; i<7; i++ )
       {
```

**Figure 5.14**  (continues)

```cpp
                day = (Day *) server->somdCreateObj(ev, "Day", NULL);
                day->_set_date(ev,i);
                curDirEntry->addDay(ev, i, day);
        }
    }


    // Set current day to Monday and show any existing activities
    curDay = curDirEntry->getDay(ev,1);
    showItems(1);
}

short DayPlannerWindow :: findProxy()
{
    ifstream infile(serverName);
    string objectId;
    char buffer[256];
    short found = 0;

    if (infile)             // proxy exists
    {
        //*******************************************
        // restore proxy from its string form
        //*******************************************
        objectId = (string) buffer;
        infile >> objectId;
        curDirEntry = (CalendarDir *) SOMD_ObjectMgr->somdGetObjectFromId(ev,
                                                                objectId);

        return 1;
    }
    return 0;
}

DayPlannerWindow :: ~DayPlannerWindow()
{
    short i,j;
    _IDL_SEQUENCE_WorkItem alist;

    if (createFile) // this client writes proxy to file
    {
```

**Figure 5.14**  (continues)

```
    //**********************************
    // perform clean up: delete the file
    //**********************************
    IString buffer("erase ");
    buffer = buffer + serverName;
    system(buffer);


    //**************************************
    // Destroy each Day object
    //**************************************
    for (i=0; i<7; i++ )
    {
            curDay = curDirEntry->getDay(ev,i);
            alist = curDay->_get_workList(ev);
            if (sequenceLength(alist) > 0 && sequenceLength(alist) < 50)
            {
                    //**********************************************************
                    // Destroy each WorkItem from the Day object
                    //**********************************************************
                    for (j=0; j < sequenceLength(alist) ; j++)
                    {
                            SOMD_ObjectMgr->somdDestroyObject(ev,
                                                        sequenceElement(alist,j));
                    }
            }
            SOMD_ObjectMgr->somdDestroyObject(ev,curDay);
    }

    // Destroy CalendarDir object
    SOMD_ObjectMgr->somdDestroyObject(ev, curDirEntry);
}
else
{
    //***************************************************
    // Release the proxy for each Day object
    //***************************************************
    for (i=0; i<7; i++ )
    {
            curDay = curDirEntry->getDay(ev,i);
```

**Figure 5.14**  (continues)

```
                        alist = curDay->_get_workList(ev);
                        if (sequenceLength(alist) > 0 && sequenceLength(alist) < 50)
                        {
                                //*****************************************************************
                                // Release proxy for each WorkItem from Day object
                                //*****************************************************************
                                for (j=0; j < sequenceLength(alist) ; j++)
                                {
                                SOMD_ObjectMgr->somdReleaseObject(ev,
                                                                        sequenceElement(alist,j));
                                }
                        }
                        SOMD_ObjectMgr->somdReleaseObject(ev,curDay);
                }

            // Release proxy for CalendarDir object
            SOMD_ObjectMgr->somdReleaseObject(ev,curDirEntry);
        }

    // release server proxy
    SOMD_ObjectMgr->somdReleaseObject(ev, server);

    SOMD_Uninit(ev);
    SOM_DestroyLocalEnvironment(ev);
}

Boolean DayPlannerWindow :: command(ICommandEvent & cmdEvent)
{
  IMessageBox msgbox(this);

  switch (cmdEvent.commandId())
  {
     case MI_ADD:
                if ( !(descT->text().size()) )
                {
                    msgbox.show("Enter a description", IMessageBox::okButton);
                }
                else
                {
```

**Figure 5.14**  (continues)

```
                            IString str;
                            IString pad("0");
                            IString trial(":00 ");
                            IString blank(" ");
                            IString sstr(startT->value());
                            IString estr(endT->value());

                            if ( startT->value() < 10 )
                            {
                                    sstr = pad + sstr;
                            }
                            if ( endT->value() < 10 )
                            {
                                    estr = pad + estr;
                            }

                            sstr = sstr + trial;
                            estr = estr + trial;

                            str = sstr + estr + descT->text();
                            listBox->addAscending(str);

                            book( sstr, estr, descT->text() );
                }
                return true;
                break;

                case MI_DEL:
                            if ( cursor->isValid() )
                            {
                                IString item, startTime, endTime, task;

                                item = listBox->elementAt(*cursor);
                                startTime = item.subString(1,6);
                                endTime = item.subString(7,6);
                                task = item.subString(13);
                                curDay->removeItem(ev, startTime, endTime, task);
                                listBox->removeAt(*cursor);
                            }
```

**Figure 5.14**  (continues)

```
                              return true;
                              break;

                case MI_SUN:
                              weekday->setText("Sunday");
                              showItems(0);
                              return true;

                case MI_MON:
                              weekday->setText("Monday");
                              showItems(1);
                              return true;

                case MI_TUE:
                              weekday->setText("Tuesday");
                              showItems(2);
                              return true;

                case MI_WED:
                              weekday->setText("Wednesday");
                              showItems(3);
                              return true;

                case MI_THU:
                              weekday->setText("Thursday");
                              showItems(4);
                              return true;

                case MI_FRI:
                              weekday->setText("Friday");
                              showItems(5);
                              return true;

                case MI_SAT:
                              weekday->setText("Saturday");
                              showItems(6);
                              return true;

                case MI_QUIT:
                          close();
                          return true;
                          break;
```

**Figure 5.14**  (continues)

```
      }
   return false;
}


Boolean DayPlannerWindow :: selected(IControlEvent & evt)
{
  cursor->setToFirst();
  return true;
}


DayPlannerWindow :: showItems(short day)
{
      _IDL_SEQUENCE_WorkItem alist;
      short i;
      IString str;
      long date;

      listBox->removeAll();                              // clear list

      menuBar->uncheckItem(menuFlag); // uncheck previous day
      menuBar->checkItem(MI_BASE+day); // check selected day
      menuFlag = MI_BASE + day;

      curDay = curDirEntry->getDay(ev,day);
      alist = curDay->_get_workList(ev);

      if (sequenceLength(alist) > 0 && sequenceLength(alist) < 50)
      {
         for (i=0; i < sequenceLength(alist) ; i++)
         {
               str = "";

               str = str +
                   sequenceElement(alist,i)->_get_startTime(ev) +
                   sequenceElement(alist,i)->_get_endTime(ev) +
                   sequenceElement(alist,i)->_get_task(ev);

               listBox->addAscending(str);
         }
      }
}
```

**Figure 5.14** (continues)

```
DayPlannerWindow :: book(char *start, char * end, char *task)
{
  WorkItem *item;


  item = (WorkItem *) server->somdCreateObj(ev,
                                                "WorkItem",
                                                NULL);
  item->mkEntry(ev, start, end, task);
  curDay->book(ev, item);

}
```

**Figure 5.14** continued

Note that in the member function, *showItems* and the *destructor*, there is an "if" statement to make sure that the length of the sequence is valid before proceeding. Normally, this is not necessary. However, at the time of writing this book, DSOM does not marshall empty sequences properly. As a result, the length of the sequence will show some huge number when the sequence is empty. Our example provides a quick patch for the problem. Another way is to add an element to the sequence right after the object is created. This ensures that the sequence will never be empty when marshalling occurs. This defect has been reported and should be fixed in future Corrective Service Distribution.

**The Makefile**

The source files that contain the classes *WorkItem, Day,* and *CalendarDir* are *workitem.cpp, day.cpp,* and *caldir.cpp.* The source files *initfunc.cpp* and *calendar.def* contain the initialization function and the module definition file. They are not listed here, but they are included on the diskette. These five files are needed to build the *calendar* DLL.

The source files *planwin.hpp, planwin.cpp, week.rc,* and *week.h* are needed to build the GUI client. The first two files are listed above. The file *week.rc* contains the resources for the application, and the file *week.h* contains constant definitions. They are included on the diskette.

The makefile for building the calendar application is given in Figure 5.15. It includes dependencies to build the Interface Repository and the Implementation Repository. The three classes are compiled into the Interface Repository file that is designated by the SOMIR environment variable. Two calendar servers, "Chris" and "Kevin", are registered with the Implementation Repository that is designated by the SOMDDIR environment variable.

```
.SUFFIXES:
.SUFFIXES: .idl .xih .xh .cpp .obj .def
#
# Need /Ge- to build DLL
#
OBJS = workitem.obj day.obj caldir.obj initfunc.obj
UILIB = dde4muii.lib dde4cci.lib dde4mbsi.lib os2386.lib

all: calendar.dll planner.exe som.ir somdimpl

.cpp.obj:
        icc /c+ /Ge- -I. $<
.idl.xh:
        sc -sxh $*.idl
.idl.xih:
        sc -sxih $*.idl
.idl.cpp:
        sc -sxc $*.idl

initfunc.obj: initfunc.cpp

clnimpl:
        -regimpl -D -i Chris
        -regimpl -D -i Kevin

workitem.obj: workitem.xih workitem.xh workitem.cpp
workitem.xih: workitem.idl
workitem.xh: workitem.idl
workitem.cpp: workitem.xih

day.obj: day.xih day.xh day.cpp
day.xih: day.idl
day.xh: day.idl
day.cpp: day.xih

caldir.obj: caldir.xih caldir.xh caldir.cpp
caldir.xih: caldir.idl
caldir.xh: caldir.idl
caldir.cpp: caldir.xih

initfunc.obj: initfunc.cpp
```

**Figure 5.15** The distributed PLANNER makefile (continues)

```
#
# Build the DLL
#
calendar.dll: $(OBJS) calendar.def
            icc @<<
            /Fe"calendar.dll" $(OBJS) calendar.def somtk.lib
<<
            implib calendar.lib calendar.def
#
# Build the executable
#
planwin.obj: planwin.cpp planwin.hpp week.h
            icc /c+ /Gd+ /Gm+ /Si+ -I. planwin.cpp

planner.exe: planwin.obj week.res
            icc /Fe"planner.exe" planwin.obj /B" /pm:pm /noi" \
            $(UILIB) somtk.lib calendar.lib planner.def
            rc week.res planner.exe

week.res: week.rc week.h
            rc -r week.rc
#
# Put the IDL descriptions into the Interface Repository
#
som.ir: workitem.idl day.idl caldir.idl
            sc -sir -u workitem.idl
            sc -sir -u day.idl
            sc -sir -u caldir.idl
#
# Build the DSOM Implementation Repository.
# Register two servers: Chris and Kevin
#
somdimpl: workitem.idl day.idl caldir.idl
            -regimpl -A -i Chris
            -regimpl -a -i Chris -c WorkItem -c Day -c CalendarDir
            -regimpl -L -i Chris
#
            -regimpl -A -i Kevin
            -regimpl -a -i Kevin -c WorkItem -c Day -c CalendarDir
            -regimpl -L -i Kevin
            @echo x > somdimpl
```

**Figure 5.15** continued

### Building the Application

To build the application, simply invoke NMAKE using the makefile shown above. Before you invoke NMAKE, make sure the following environment variables are set up properly.

- SOMIR
- SOMDDIR
- HOSTNAME

For example, you can use the following settings.

```
set SOMIR=%SOMBASE%\etc\som.ir;som.ir
set SOMDDIR=%SOMBASE%\etc\dsom
set HOSTNAME=localhost
```

The file *dsomenv.cmd* contains the commands you need to set up your environment for this example.

### Running the Application

We are ready to run our distributed calendar application. In the following, we assume we are running our application on a single OS/2 with the *SOMobjects Workstation Enabler*, or the *SOMobjects Developer Toolkit* installed. Note that it is possible to distribute the calendar objects to a AIX/6000 system by building a shared library for the AIX/6000, and using Workgroup DSOM to access the calendar objects.

Make sure the environment variables listed above are still set to the correct values in the session you are going to start the DSOM daemon. In addition, make sure the environment variable USERID is also set. For example:

```
set USERID=chris
```

Start the DSOM daemon by typing:

```
> start /f somdd
```

This starts the DSOM daemon in a separate window. Figure 5.16 shows the screen when the DSOM daemon is ready.

In the same window you started the DSOM daemon, type:

```
> planner
```

This starts the PLANNER program using the default ("Chris") server. Figure 5.17 shows the screen after PLANNER is started. Notice that the icon labelled *DSOM server somdsvr.exe* appears on the desktop when PLANNER is started. This is "Chris" server process.

**Figure 5.16** DSOM daemon

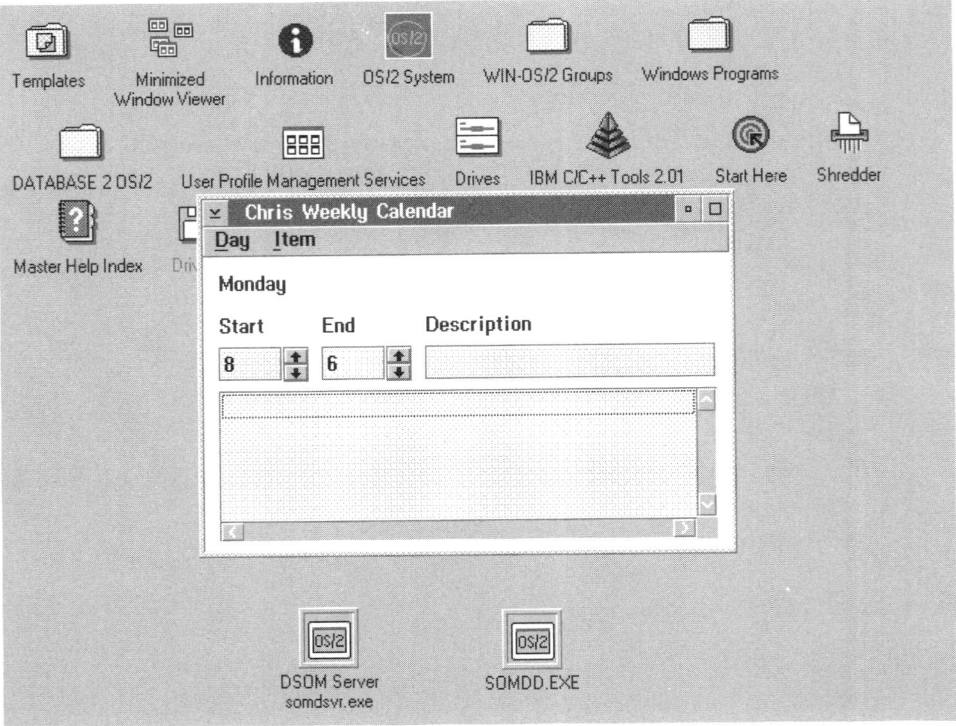


**Figure 5.17** Chris Client and Server Object on First Invocation

The file "Chris" should be created in your current directory. Take a look at it. It should contain an entry similar to the following:

```
SOM|2|2d149bb6-01791457-7f-00-0100007f0000|CalendarDir|4|b0984300
```

This entry is the string representation for the object reference we created for the object *CalendarDir*. The object reference is externalized to allow sharing.

Add some activities to Chris's calendar. For example, a department meeting is booked for Monday, from 10:00 to 11:00. A tennis game is booked for Tuesday, from 18:00 to 19:00.

In a separate window, run *dsomenv.cmd* to set up the environment variables. Then type "planner" to start a second PLANNER program using the "Chris" server. Notice how all of the activities that were added in the first PLANNER program appear in the second PLANNER program. This is because the two programs share the same calendar objects through the externalization of the proxy. If you add or delete activities from either calendar, they will be reflected on the other calendar when you refresh the list. Figure 5.18 shows the screen capture for the two "Chris Weekly Calendar" windows.

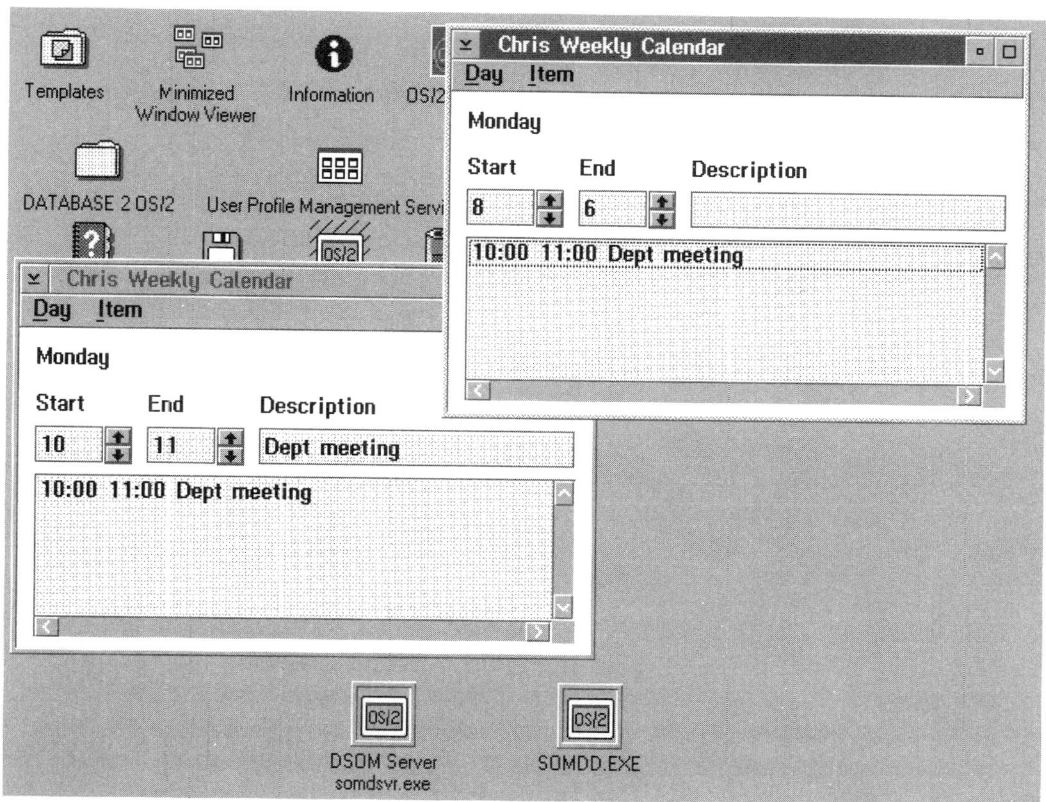


**Figure 5.18** Sharing Chris calendar

In a separate window, run *dsomenv.cmd* to set up the environment variables. Then type:

> planner Kevin

to start a PLANNER program using the Kevin calendar server. Figure 5.19 shows the screen after "PLANNER Kevin" is started. Notice that a second icon labelled *DSOM server somdsvr.exe* appears on the desktop when "PLANNER Kevin" is started. This is "Kevin" server process.

The activities that were added to the "Chris" calendar were not shown on the "Kevin" calendar because they do not share objects. The file "Kevin" should be created in the current directory to store the proxy to Kevin's *CalendarDir* object.

Now terminate the client programs by selecting Quit from the menu to exit. Notice that the two DSOM servers are still around. This is because the **somdDestroyObject** method only destroys the object that is managed by the server. It does not terminate the server. If you terminate the DSOM daemon, then the servers will be terminated.

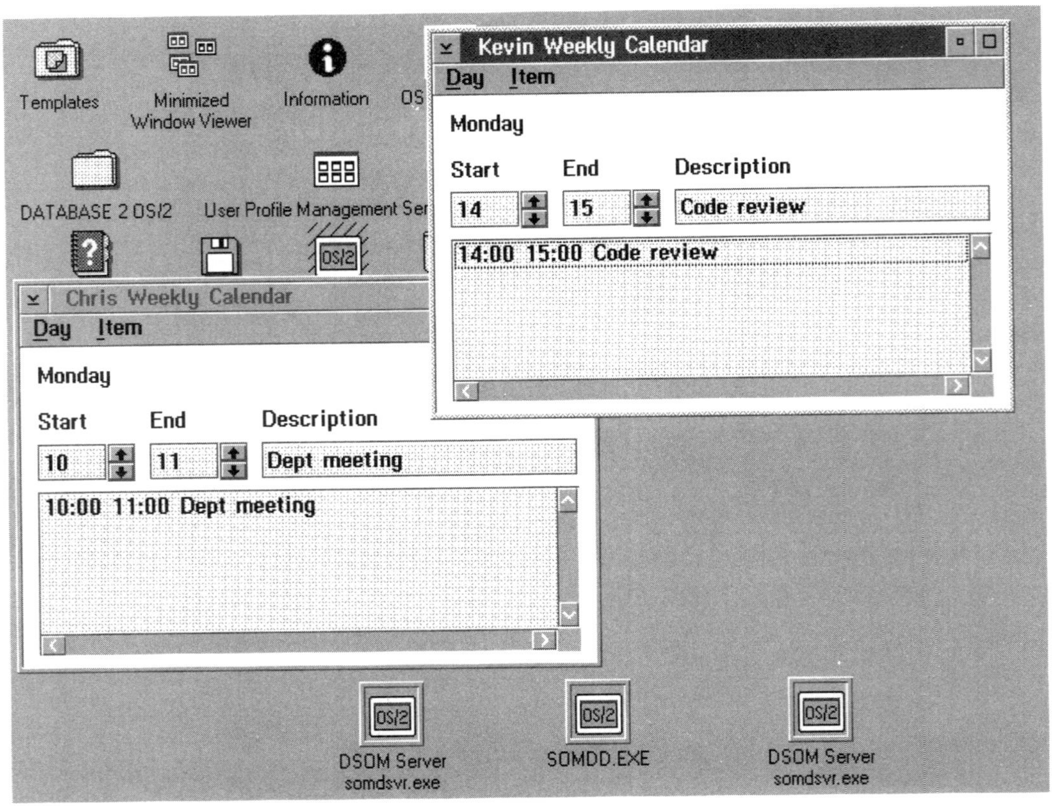


**Figure 5.19** Kevin's calendar

If you want the termination of a server to be controlled by a client, then you will need to implement your own server. You can create a new subclass of *SOMD-Server* and implement a *shutdown* method in this subclass. The *shutdown* method should perform the necessary cleanup and then terminate. The client can invoke the *shutdown* method using the server proxy it obtains from calling the **somdFindServerByName** method.

### Summary

The Calendar example illustrates some of the key concepts of developing and building a DSOM application. The task of building a distributed application has been greatly simplified with the availability of the Distributed SOM Framework. How many lines of code does a traditional program need to write to provide a similar form of interprocess or intermachine communications?

Notice that our calendars are not persistent. When the server process terminates, the states of the calendar objects are not preserved. In Chapter 6, we will add persistence to our calendar so that our calendar data can be preserved beyond the existence of the server process or the PLANNER program.

# 6

# Making Your Objects Persistent

The Persistence SOM (PSOM) Framework allows you to make all or part of a SOM object persistent. This means you can preserve the state of an object, even after the process that creates the object terminates. The Framework provides services that allow you to store an object to a file system or another form of persistent store. It also provides services that permit you restore objects from the persistent storage.

Most applications already use some form of persistence. For example, a spreadsheet or a word processor stores user data in a file. The implementation of a spreadsheet typically contains logic that converts the data in the cells into some format that can be written to a file for storage. When an existing spreadsheet is loaded, the reverse takes place. The logic converts the external data back to the cell format so the user can work with it.

The PSOM Framework simplifies these operations by providing a uniform interface to storage. A cell in a spreadsheet can be implemented as a persistent object, and its data can be stored and restored, using the services in the PSOM Framework. Any flattening and unflattening of data can be eliminated. Applications can also avoid writing low level I/O routines and therefore become more portable.

## 6.1   PSOM OVERVIEW

To use the PSOM Framework, both the object and the client program that accesses the object must be PSOM aware. What does this mean? From the object perspective, it must be derived from a special persistent class and the persistent data must be specified explicitly. This is different from the DSOM approach, where an object does not have to know in advance whether it is going to be distributed. The PSOM client is typically responsible for managing persistence by controlling when the persistent data is stored or restored.

The PSOM Framework can store and restore objects that are arbitrarily complex. This means that if an object contains pointers to other objects, the PSOM Framework can save and restore those referenced objects as well. In a hierarchy of objects, the client can control whether or not an object should be stored or restored with its children.

It should be noted that OMG is in the process of releasing a Persistence Service Specification. The goal of the Persistence Service Specification is to provide common interfaces to the mechanisms used for retaining and managing the persistent state of objects. It is expected that the next release of PSOM will comply with the OMG Persistence Service Specification. It is quite likely that the interfaces described in this chapter will change with the next release. However, the concepts behind them should remain the same. More on this can be found in Chapter 10.

The development of a PSOM application involves the following steps.

1. Define the interface for your persistent objects, and write code to implement your objects.
2. Create a client program that accesses and manages the objects.
3. Build your classes and register them with the Interface Repository.
4. Run the client program.

The following sections provide details on each of the above steps.

## 6.2    DEFINE AND IMPLEMENT A PERSISTENT OBJECT

To create a persistent object, we must first create a class that is derived from the *SOMPPersistentObject* class. The parent class for *SOMPPersistentObject* class is *SOMObject*. Therefore, your persistent object is still a SOM object, only it can potentially become persistent because it is dervied from the *SOMPPersistentObject* class.

All data that is to be stored persistently must be declared as an attribute of CORBA type. The *persistent* modifier must be set for each of these attributes in the implementation section of the IDL.

The following *Person* class is potentially persistent and contains two persistent and one non-persistent attributes.

```
#include <po.idl>
interface Person: SOMPPersistentObject
{
        attribute string name;
        attribute string birthdate;
        attribute short age;
```

```
#ifdef __SOMIDL__
implementation
{
  releaseorder : _get_name, _set_name,
                 _get_birthdate, _set_birthdate,
                 _get_age, _set_age;

  sompIsDirty: override;

  name: persistent;
  birthdate: persistent;
};
#endif
};
#endif
```

The *SOMPPersistentObject* class provides the **sompIsDirty** method, which is called by the PSOM Framework, to determine if an object has been changed. The PSOM Framework is optimized so it will only write out changed objects. Since the default implementation of **sompIsDirty** always returns TRUE, it is typically redefined by subclasses so that they can indicate whether an object has been changed. The implementation can invoke the **sompGetDirty** method to determine if the object has been changed. An example of overriding this method is given in the Persistent Calendar application in Section 6.6 on page 148.


## 6.3    CLIENT PROGRAM

Although not absolutely necessary, the storing and restoring of persistent objects is normally controlled by the client of the objects, so the client can decide when to store or restore the persistent state. To save and restore persistent objects, a client program must initialize the PSOM Framework, manage the assignment of persistent ID to the persistent object, and invoke the save or the restore methods.


### 6.3.1    PSOM Initialization

Every PSOM client must include the file *<somp.xh>* (or *<somp.h>* if using the C bindings). This file includes the constants, global variables, and run-time interfaces that are used by PSOM. The client also has to initialize the PSOM Framework by creating a *Persistent Storage Manager* object. The Persistent Storage Manager provides the interfaces for clients to save and restore persistent objects. The Persistent Storage Manager is created by instantiating the *SOMPPersistentStorageMgr* class using the *SOMPPersistentStorageMgrNew()* macro or the *new* operator.

There is only one instance of a Persistent Storage Manager object for a process. Therefore, it does not matter how many times you invoke *new* on the *SOMPPersistentStorageMgr* class. It is quite normal to invoke *new* on the *SOMPPersistentStorageMgr* class locally in each procedure instead of passing the pointer to this object around. You must not free the Persistent Storage Manager object. If you do, the PSOM Framework will forget about previously initialized and restored objects.

A typical implementation of PSOM initialization is presented below:

```
#include <somp.xh>
main()
{
        Environment                             *ev;
        SOMPPersistentStorageMgr                *psm;

        ev = SOM_CreateLocalEnvironment();      // create and initialize an Environment structure
        psm = new SOMPPersistentStorageMgr();   // initialize Persistent Storage Manager
        ...
        SOM_DestroyLocalEnvironment(ev);        // Free Environment structure
}
```

## 6.3.2    The Persistent ID

In order for a persistent object to be saved or restored, it must be assigned an ID. The ID you assign to a persistent object tells the Framework how and where to store the object. The persistent ID is an object with a string value. The string has the following format.

```
<IOGroupMgrClassName>:<IOGroupName>:<GroupOffset>
```

The first part of the string identifies what data store the object will be stored in. The second part of the string is a name that is understandable to the data store specified in the first part. The third part is an offset that identifies the object within a group of objects. An example of a persistent ID string is given below:

```
SOMPAscii:\\sample\\test.dat:0
```

The first part of the string "SOMPAscii" identifies that the object is to be stored in a file using ASCII format. The second part, "\\sample\\test.dat", is a file name that indicates the file in which the object will be stored. The third part of the string, "0", is a number that identifies the object within the file where it is stored.

The PSOM Framework provides two I/O Group Manager classes. You can either use the *SOMPAscii* I/O Group Manager to store data in a ASCII format, or you can use the *SOMPBinary* I/O Group Manager to store data in a binary format. You can choose which format by setting the first part of the persistent ID string accordingly. The following persistent ID indicates the object that is assigned to it will be stored using binary format.

```
SOMPBinary:\\sample\\test.dat:0
```

The PSOM Framework is available on both AIX and OS/2. The notation for specifying the file name is different on the two systems. The file name that is specified above uses the OS/2 notation. If the same string ID is to be created on AIX, the slashes need to be modified to the following.

```
SOMPAscii:/sample/test.dat:0
```

### 6.3.3    Assigning a Persistent ID to a Persistent Object

Typically, a client will create a persistent ID, initialize its string ID, and assign it to the object. The *SOMPPersistentId* class is responsible for creating the persistent ID and provides methods to initialize the string value in the persistent ID. The *SOMPPersistentObject* class provides methods to assign a persistent ID to a persistent object. Since all persistent objects must be derived from *SOMPPersistentObject*, it follows that every persistent object supports the methods for setting its persistent ID.

The *SOMPPersistentId* class provides the method **somutSetIdString** for setting the string value for a persistent ID. The following code segment shows how to create a persistent ID and assigns the string "SOMPAscii:\\sample\\test.dat:0" to it:

```
SOMPPersistentId *pid;

pid = new SOMPPersistentId();
pid->somutSetIdString(ev, "SOMPAscii:\\sample\\test.dat:0");
```

The *SOMPPersistentObject* class provides three methods for assigning a persistent ID to a persistent object. You can assign a persistent object to a specific ID, to a system-generated ID, or to an ID that is near some other specified object. The three methods are **sompInitGivenId**, **sompInitNextAvail**, and **sompInitNearObject**. The choice depends on how much control the client needs over the storage of the object. The client-assigned ID provides the most control while the system-generated ID might be more convenient in other cases.

### 6.3.4    The sompInitGivenId Method

The **sompInitGivenId** method assigns a persistent object to a specific persistent ID. The syntax for the method in C is given below:

```
_sompInitGivenId(persistentObject,     // pointer to persistent object
                 env,                   // pointer to Environment structure
                 pid);                  // pointer to persistent ID object
```

The parameter *persistentObject* is a pointer to the persistent object to which the specified persistent ID is to be assigned. The parameter *pid* is a pointer to a persistent ID object.

Below is how you would use the **sompInitGivenId** method to assign a persistent ID. The class *Document* is derived from the *SOMPPersistentObject* class.

```
Document            *doc;
SOMPPersistentId    *pid;

pid = new SOMPPersistentId();
pid->somutSetIdString(ev, "SOMPAscii:\\sample\\doc.dat:0");

doc = new Document();
doc->sompInitGivenId(ev,pid);
```

The object *doc* is assigned the persistent ID whose value is "SOMPAscii:\\sample\\doc.dat:0". This means that if a store operation is invoked on the *doc* object, it will be stored in the ASCII file "\sample\doc.dat".

### 6.3.4.1    The sompInitNextAvail Method

The **sompInitNextAvail** method assigns a system-generated ID to a persistent object. The ID must be generated using the *SOMPIdAssigner* class. The *SOMPIdAssignerClass* implements a method **sompGetSystemAssignedId**, which generates an ID, using a simple algorithim based on a path name and a file name. If the environment variable SOMP_PERSIST is set, it will be used as the path name. Otherwise, it will default to the current directory. The file name is the string "p" concatenated with a seven digit hex number. The number is read from a file called "somplast.id" which is updated everytime with the last generated ID. The offset portion of the persistent ID is always set to 0. You can change the default algorithm by subclassing from *SOMPIdAssigner* and override **sompGetSystemAssignedId**.

The syntax for the **sompInitNextAvail** method is given below:

```
_sompInitNextAvail(persistentObject,      // pointer to persistent object
                   env,                   // pointer to Environment structure
                   genPid);               // pointer to the next available PID object
```

The parameter *persistentObject* is a pointer to the persistent object to which the specified persistent ID is to be assigned. The parameter *genPid* is a pointer to an object of class *SOMPIdAssigner*, which represents the next available persistent ID.

Here is how you would use the **sompInitNextAvail** method to assign a persistent ID to the above *Document* class:

```
Document                *doc;
SOMPIdAssigner          *pid;


pid = new SOMPIdAssigner();


doc = new Document();
doc->sompInitNextAvail(ev,pid);
```

Assuming the environment variable SOMP_PERSIST is not set and the file "somplast.id" does not exist yet, the ID that is generated above would be:

```
SOMPAscii:.\\p0000000:0
```

And the file "somplast.id" is created in the current directory with the following entry:

```
0000001
```

### 6.3.4.2     The sompInitNearObject Method

The **sompInitNearObject** method gives a specified persistent object a persistent ID that is nearby the ID of another specified persistent object. This method is useful when you have composite objects you want to store near to the root object. You can initalize your parent object using either of the above methods and then use **sompInitNearObject** to initialize the children objects. The syntax for the method in C is given below:

```
_sompInitNearObject(persistentObject,    // pointer to persistent object
                    env,                 // pointer to Environment structure
                    nearObj);            // pointer to nearby persistent object
```

The parameter *persistentObject* is a pointer to the persistent object to which a persistent ID is to be assigned. The parameter, *nearObj*,is a pointer to another persistent object  with a persistent ID.

The following shows how to use **sompInitNearObject** to set the persistent ID for the *doc2* object.

```
Document                *doc1, *doc2;
SOMPPersistentId        *pid;


pid = new SOMPPersistentId();
pid->somutSetIdString(ev, "SOMPAscii:\\sample\\doc.dat:0");


doc1 = new Document();
doc2 = new Document();
```

```
doc1->sompInitGivenId(ev,pid);
doc2->sompInitNearObject(ev, doc1);        // set doc2 persistent ID to be near doc1
```

### 6.3.5    Saving a Persistent Object

Once you have assigned a persistent ID to each persistent object you want to store, you can invoke the store method from the Persistent Storage Manager to store the object. There are two store methods: **sompStoreObject** and **sompStoreObjectWithoutChildren**. The **sompStoreObject** method stores a persistent object and all of its persistent children. The syntax for the method in C is presented below:

```
_sompStoreObject(psm,              // pointer to Persistent Storage Manager
                 env,              // pointer to Environment Structure
                 persistentObject);  // pointer to the persistent object being stored
```

The **sompStoreObjectWithoutChildren** method stores a persistent object but does not store any of the persistent objects to which it points. It has the same signature as **sompStoreObject**.

### 6.3.6    Restoring a Persistent Object

To restore an object you stored using the above methods, you need to know the persistent ID for the object. The Persistent Storage Manager provides the **sompRestoreObject** and the **sompRestoreObjectWithoutChildren** methods for restoring objects. The **sompRestoreObject** method restores a persistent object and all of its persistent children. The syntax for the method in C follows:

```
persistentObject = _sompRestoreObject(psm,   // pointer to Persistent Storage Manager
                                      env,   // pointer to Environment Structure
                                      pid);  // pointer to PID object
```

The **sompRestoreObjectWithoutChildren** method restores a persistent object but does not restore any of the persistent objects to which it points. It has the same signature as **sompRestoreObject**.

## 6.4    BUILDING AND REGISTERING THE CLASSES

Building a PSOM application is very much like a regular SOM application. You compile your classes and your client program. Unlike DSOM, it is not mandatory that you build a DLL for your classes. If you want to build a DLL, follow the steps in "Creating a DLL for SOM Classes" on page 79.

You need to compile your PSOM classes into the Interface Repository. The PSOM Framework uses the Interface Repository to find out things such as whether a class is persistent and which attributes are persistent. The Interface Repository is described in more detail in Chapter 8, Working with the Interface Repository.

## 6.5    EXECUTION

Make sure the environment variable SOMIR points to the Interface Repository that contains the persistent classes. The PSOM application then can be started.

## 6.6    A DISTRIBUTED AND PERSISTENT CALENDAR

In this section, we will extend the calendar application that we built in the last chapter by adding persistence to it. This means that you can preserve your calendar data even after the termination of the PLANNER program. The user interface remains the same. When you exit the PLANNER program, the activities that you added to or deleted from your calendar will be saved. When you invoke the PLANNER program again for a calendar, the calendar items that you previously added for that calendar will be displayed.

### 6.6.1    High-Level Design

For the most part, the three classes (*WorkItem, Day,* and *CalendarDir*) that made up our *calendar* DLL remain the same. Modifications have to be made to make the objects persistent.

Our calendar objects were created in a server process that is separated from our client PLANNER process through the use of the DSOM runtime. Therefore, the management of the persistent calendar objects must be handled by the server process. Recall that the *SOMDServer* class is the base class that defines and implements methods for managing objects in a DSOM server process. We introduce a new server class, *PersistentServer*, by subclassing from *SOMDServer*. The *PersistentServer* class provides methods to manage persistent objects. A new DLL called *perserv.dll* is created to contain this class.

### 6.6.2    Implementation Details

This section will provide the details of the design and implementation of each of the components in our new version of the calendar application. The changes made to previous IDLs, or code, are shown in bold.

#### The WorkItem Class

The IDL for the *WorkItem* class is given in Figure 6.1. The class is now derived from *SOMPPersistentObject* so its objects can be persistent. The attributes *startTime, endTime,* and *task* are made persistent. The method **sompIsDirty** is redefined. It invokes the **sompGetDirty** method to determine if the object has been changed since it was last written out.

```
#ifndef workitem_idl
#define workitem_idl

#include <po.idl>

interface WorkItem : SOMPPersistentObject
{
    attribute string startTime;
    attribute string endTime;
    attribute string task;

    void mkEntry(in string sTime, in string eTime, in string taskDesc);

    #ifdef __SOMIDL__
    implementation
    {
      releaseorder : _get_startTime, _set_startTime,
                     _get_endTime, _set_endTime,
                     _get_task, _set_task,
                     mkEntry;

      somInit: override;
      somUninit: override;
      sompIsDirty: override;

      dllname = "calendar.dll";

      startTime: persistent;
      endTime: persistent;
      task: persistent;
    };
    #endif
};
#endif
```

**Figure 6.1** The WorkItem IDL

The C++ code which implements the methods for the *WorkItem* class is given In Figure 6.2. Note that the **somInit** and the **somUninit** methods have been modified to call the initalization and the un-initialization method from the *SOMPPersistentObject* class.

## The Day Class

The IDL for the *Day* class is given in Figure 6.3 (p. 153). The class is now derived from *SOMPPersistentObject* so its objects can be persistent. The attributes *date* and *workList* are made persistent. The method **sompIsDirty** is redefined to determine if the object has been changed since it was last written out.

The C++ code that implements the methods for the *Day* class is given in Figure 6.4 (p. 154). The *book* method invokes the **sompSetDirty** method to mark the current *Day* object as dirty. It also invokes the **sompInitNearObject** method on the *WorkItem* object that is being added to the *workList* and assigns it a persistent ID that is near to the persistent ID of the *Day* object. The *remove* method invokes the **sompSetDirty** method to mark the current *Day* object as dirty when an item is being removed from the *workList*. The **somInit** and the **somUninit** methods have been modified similar to the *WorkItem* class.

## The CalendarDir Class

The IDL for the *CalendarDir* class is given in Figure 6.5 (p. 156). Similar to the above classes, the *CalendarDir* class is derived from *SOMPPersistentObject* and the attribute *weekList* is made persistent. The method **sompIsDirty** is being redefined to determine if the object has been changed since it was last written out.

The C++ code that implements the methods for the *CalendarDir* class is given in Figure 6.6 (p. 157). The *addDay* method invokes the **sompSetDirty** method to mark the current *CalendarDir* object as dirty. It also invokes the **sompInitNearObject** method on the *Day* object that is being added to the *weekList* and assigns it a persistent ID that is near to the persistent ID of the *CalendarDir* object. The **somInit** and the **somUninit** methods have been modified similar to the *WorkItem* class and the *Day* class.

## The PersistentServer Class

The IDL for the *PersistentServer* class is presented in Figure 6.7 (p. 159). It introduces three new methods and overrides one method.

- The *getPerStorMgr* method creates the Persistence Storage Manager object for this process and returns the pointer to it. Clients that create remote persistent objects using this class can store them using the handle returned by this method.
- The *objectExists* method checks to see if the specified persistent object exists in the persistent store. If it does, it returns TRUE. Otherwise, it returns FALSE.
- The *restoreObjectFromId* method restores a persistent object and all its children from the object string ID.
- The **somdCreateObj** method is overridden to create a remote persistent object. It first creates the object by calling the parent implementation. It then

```
/*
 * This file was generated by the SOM Compiler and Emitter Framework.
 * Generated using:
 * SOM Emitter emitxtm: somc/smmain.c
 */

#define WorkItem_Class_Source
#include <workitem.xih>

SOM_Scope void SOMLINK mkEntry(WorkItem *somSelf, Environment *ev,
                               string sTime, string eTime, string taskDesc)
{
    WorkItemData *somThis = WorkItemGetData(somSelf);
    WorkItemMethodDebug("WorkItem","mkEntry");

    if (somThis->startTime) SOMFree(somThis->startTime);
    somThis->startTime = (string)SOMMalloc(strlen(sTime)+1);
    strcpy (somThis->startTime, sTime);

    if (somThis->endTime) SOMFree(somThis->endTime);
    somThis->endTime = (string)SOMMalloc(strlen(eTime)+1);
    strcpy (somThis->endTime, eTime);

    if (somThis->task) SOMFree(somThis->task);
    somThis->task = (string)SOMMalloc(strlen(taskDesc)+1);
    strcpy (somThis->task, taskDesc);
}

SOM_Scope void SOMLINK somInit(WorkItem *somSelf)
{
    WorkItemData *somThis = WorkItemGetData(somSelf);
    WorkItemMethodDebug("WorkItem","somInit");

    WorkItem_parent_SOMPPersistentObject_somInit(somSelf);

    somThis->startTime = NULL;
    somThis->endTime = NULL;
    somThis->task = NULL;
}
```

**Figure 6.2** The WorkItem class implementation (continues)

```
    SOM_Scope void SOMLINK somUninit(WorkItem *somSelf)
    {
        WorkItemData *somThis = WorkItemGetData(somSelf);
        WorkItemMethodDebug("WorkItem","somUninit");

        if (somThis->startTime) SOMFree(somThis->startTime);
        if (somThis->endTime) SOMFree(somThis->endTime);
        if (somThis->task) SOMFree(somThis->task);

        WorkItem_parent_SOMPPersistentObject_somUninit(somSelf);

    }

    SOM_Scope boolean SOMLINK sompIsDirty(WorkItem *somSelf, Environment *ev)
    {
        WorkItemData *somThis = WorkItemGetData(somSelf);
        WorkItemMethodDebug("WorkItem","sompIsDirty");

        return (somSelf->sompGetDirty(ev));
    }
```

**Figure 6.2** continued

checks to see if a string ID is supplied in the *hint* field. If a string ID is supplied, a persistent ID is created and initialized with the string ID. The persistent ID is then assigned to the persistent object.

The C++ code that implements the methods for the *PersistentServer* class is given in Figure 6.8 (p. 160). The initialization function **SOMInitModule** is included in the file for dynamic loading.

### The GUI Client

The PLANNER program is now modified to work with the Persistent Framework. The listing for *planwin.hpp* is given in Figure 6.9 (p. 163). The changes are highlighted in bold.

The following summarizes what the new member functions do and the changes to existing member functions.

• The *setupData* function is modified to initialize both the DSOM and the PSOM environment. An instance of the Persistence Storage Manager is created at the specified calendar server. There are two forms of object sharing in our new application. The first form is through an existing object reference, which is what we had before. The second form is through persistent data. We first call the *findProxy* function to determine if there is an existing object reference to the *CalendarDir* object that is managed by this server. If an object reference already exists, it will be used. Otherwise, we call the *findPersist* function to

```
#ifndef day_idl
#define day_idl

#include <po.idl>

interface WorkItem;
interface Day : SOMPPersistentObject
{
      const unsigned long MAXITEM = 50;
      attribute long date;
      attribute sequence<WorkItem,MAXITEM> workList;

      short book(in WorkItem entry);
      short removeItem(in string start, in string end, in string desc);

      #ifdef __SOMIDL__
      implementation
      {
        releaseorder : _get_date, _set_date,
                       _get_workList, _set_workList,
                       book, removeItem;

        somInit: override;
        somUninit: override;
        sompIsDirty: override;

        dllname = "calendar.dll";

        date: persistent;
        workList: persistent;
      };
      #endif
};
#endif
```

**Figure 6.3** The Day IDL

```
/*
 * This file was generated by the SOM Compiler and Emitter Framework.
 * Generated using:
 * SOM Emitter emitxtm: somc/smmain.c
 */

#define Day_Class_Source
#include <day.xih>
#include <workitem.xh>
#include <string.h>

SOM_Scope short SOMLINK book(Day *somSelf, Environment *ev,
                                  WorkItem* entry)
{
  DayData *somThis = DayGetData(somSelf);
  short rc;
  DayMethodDebug("Day","book");

  if (sequenceLength(somThis->workList) < sequenceMaximum(somThis->workList))
  {
     sequenceElement(somThis->workList, sequenceLength(somThis->workList)) = entry;
     sequenceLength(somThis->workList)++;
     somSelf->sompSetDirty(ev);
     entry->sompInitNearObject(ev, somSelf);
     rc = 0;
  }
  else
     rc = -1;

  return rc;
}

SOM_Scope short SOMLINK removeItem(Day *somSelf, Environment *ev,
                                  string start, string end, string desc)
{
     DayData *somThis = DayGetData(somSelf);
     short i;
     WorkItem *item;
     DayMethodDebug("Day","removeItem");

     for (i=0; i < sequenceLength(somThis->workList); i++ )
     {
         item = sequenceElement(somThis->workList,i);
```

**Figure 6.4** The Day class implementation (continues)

```
            if ( (strcmp(start, item->_get_startTime(ev)) == 0) &&
                 (strcmp(end, item->_get_endTime(ev)) == 0) &&
                 (strcmp(desc, item->_get_task(ev)) == 0) )
            {
                sequenceLength(somThis->workList)--;

                for (i; i < sequenceLength(somThis->workList); i++)
                {
                    sequenceElement(somThis->workList,i) = sequenceElement(somThis->workList, i+1);
                }

                somSelf->sompSetDirty(ev);
                return 0;
            }
        }
        return -1;                              // item not found
}

SOM_Scope void SOMLINK somInit(Day *somSelf)
{
    DayData *somThis = DayGetData(somSelf);
    DayMethodDebug("Day","somInit");

    Day_parent_SOMPPersistentObject_somInit(somSelf);

    sequenceMaximum(somThis->workList) = MAXITEM;
    sequenceLength(somThis->workList) = 0;
    somThis->workList._buffer = (WorkItem**) SOMMalloc(sizeof (WorkItem *) * MAXITEM);
}

SOM_Scope void SOMLINK somUninit(Day *somSelf)
{
    DayData *somThis = DayGetData(somSelf);
    DayMethodDebug("Day","somUninit");

    if (somThis->workList._buffer)
      SOMFree(somThis->workList._buffer);

    Day_parent_SOMPPersistentObject_somUninit(somSelf);
}

SOM_Scope boolean SOMLINK sompIsDirty(Day *somSelf, Environment *ev)
{
    DayData *somThis = DayGetData(somSelf);
    DayMethodDebug("Day","sompIsDirty");

    return (somSelf->sompGetDirty(ev));
}
```

**Figure 6.4** continued

```
#ifndef caldir_idl
#define caldir_idl

#include <po.idl>

interface Day;
interface CalendarDir : SOMPPersistentObject
{
      const unsigned long MAXDAY = 7;

      attribute sequence<Day, MAXDAY> weekList;

      long addDay(in short daynum, in Day entry);
      Day getDay(in short daynum);

      #ifdef __SOMIDL__
      implementation
      {
        releaseorder : _get_weekList, _set_weekList,
                    addDay, getDay;

        somInit: override;
        somUninit: override;
        somIsDirty: override;

        dllname = "calendar.dll";

        weekList: persistent;
      };
      #endif
};
#endif
```

**Figure 6.5** The CalendarDir IDL

```
/*
 * This file was generated by the SOM Compiler and Emitter Framework.
 * Generated using:
 * SOM Emitter emitxtm: somc/smmain.c
 */


#define CalendarDir_Class_Source
#include <caldir.xih>
#include "day.xh"
#include <stdio.h>


SOM_Scope long SOMLINK addDay(CalendarDir *somSelf, Environment *ev,
                                     short daynum, Day* entry)
{
   CalendarDirData *somThis = CalendarDirGetData(somSelf);
   long rc;
   CalendarDirMethodDebug("CalendarDir","addDay");

   if (sequenceLength(somThis->weekList) < sequenceMaximum(somThis->weekList))
   {
      sequenceElement(somThis->weekList, sequenceLength(somThis->weekList)) = entry;
      sequenceLength(somThis->weekList)++;
      somSelf->sompSetDirty(ev);
      entry->sompInitNearObject(ev, somSelf);
      rc = 0;
   }
   else
      rc = -1;

   return rc;
}


SOM_Scope Day* SOMLINK getDay(CalendarDir *somSelf, Environment *ev,
                                     short daynum)
{
```

**Figure 6.6** The CalendirDir class implementation (continues)

```
            return ( sequenceElement(somThis->weekList, daynum) );
}


SOM_Scope void SOMLINK somInit(CalendarDir *somSelf)
{
   CalendarDirData *somThis = CalendarDirGetData(somSelf);
   CalendarDirMethodDebug("CalendarDir","somInit");

   CalendarDir_parent_SOMPPersistentObject_somInit(somSelf);

   sequenceMaximum(somThis->weekList) = MAXDAY;
   sequenceLength(somThis->weekList) = 0;
   somThis->weekList._buffer = (Day**) SOMMalloc(sizeof (Day *) * MAXDAY);
}


SOM_Scope void SOMLINK somUninit(CalendarDir *somSelf)
{
   CalendarDirData *somThis = CalendarDirGetData(somSelf);
   CalendarDirMethodDebug("CalendarDir","somUninit");

   if (somThis->weekList._buffer)
      SOMFree(somThis->weekList._buffer);

   CalendarDir_parent_SOMPPersistentObject_somUninit(somSelf);
}


SOM_Scope boolean SOMLINK sompIsDirty(CalendarDir *somSelf,
                                      Environment *ev)
{
   CalendarDirData *somThis = CalendarDirGetData(somSelf);
   CalendarDirMethodDebug("CalendarDir","sompIsDirty");

   return (somSelf->sompGetDirty(ev));
}
```

**Figure 6.6** continued

```
#ifndef perserver_idl
#define perserver_idl


#include <somobj.idl>
#include <somdserv.idl>
#include <somdtype.idl>
#include <snglicls.idl>


interface PersistentServer : SOMDServer
{
     // Return the Persistent Storage Manager in this process
     SOMObject getPerStorMgr();


     // Check to see if the persistent object exists
     boolean objectExists(in string id);


     // Restore a persistent object from its string ID
     SOMObject restoreObjectFromId(in string id);


     #ifdef __SOMIDL__
     implementation
     {
       releaseorder: getPerStorMgr, objectExists,
                 restoreObjectFromId;


       somdCreateObj : override;
       dllname = "perserv.dll";
       metaclass = SOMMSingleInstance;
     };
     #endif
};
#endif
```

**Figure 6.7** The PersistentServer IDL

```
/*
 * This file was generated by the SOM Compiler and Emitter Framework.
 * Generated using:
 * SOM Emitter emitxtm: 2.7
 */

#define PersistentServer_Class_Source
#define SOMMSingleInstance_Class_Source
#include <perserv.xih>
#include <somp.xh>
#include <stdio.h>

#ifdef __IBMC__
      #pragma linkage(SOMInitModule,system)
#endif

SOMEXTERN void SOMLINK SOMInitModule(long majorVersion,
                                     long minorVersion,
                                     string className)
{
    SOM_IgnoreWarning(majorVersion);
    SOM_IgnoreWarning(minorVersion);
    SOM_IgnoreWarning(className);

    PersistentServerNewClass(PersistentServer_MajorVersion,
                    PersistentServer_MinorVersion);
}

SOM_Scope SOMObject* SOMLINK getPerStorMgr(PersistentServer *somSelf,
                                           Environment *ev)
{
    /* PersistentServerData *somThis = PersistentServerGetData(somSelf); */
    SOMPPersistentStorageMgr *psm;
    PersistentServerMethodDebug("PersistentServer","getPerStorMgr");

    psm = new SOMPPersistentStorageMgr();
    return psm;
}

SOM_Scope boolean SOMLINK objectExists(PersistentServer *somSelf,
                                       Environment *ev, string id)
```

**Figure 6.8** The PersistentServer class implementation (continues)

```
    {
        /* PersistentServerData *somThis = PersistentServerGetData(somSelf); */
        SOMPPersistentStorageMgr *psm;
        SOMPPersistentId *pid;
        boolean rc;
        PersistentServerMethodDebug("PersistentServer","objectExists");

        psm = new SOMPPersistentStorageMgr();
        pid = new SOMPPersistentId();
        pid->somutSetIdString(ev, id);

        if ( psm->sompObjectExists(ev, pid) )
        {
            rc = TRUE;
        }
        else
        {
            rc = FALSE;
        }
        delete pid;
        return rc;
    }

SOM_Scope SOMObject* SOMLINK restoreObjectFromId(PersistentServer *somSelf,
                                                 Environment *ev, string id)
    {
        /* PersistentServerData *somThis = PersistentServerGetData(somSelf); */
        SOMPPersistentStorageMgr *psm;
        SOMObject *obj;
        PersistentServerMethodDebug("PersistentServer","restoreObjectFromId");

        psm = new SOMPPersistentStorageMgr();

        obj = psm->sompRestoreObjectFromIdString(ev,id);

        return obj;
    }

SOM_Scope SOMObject* SOMLINK somdCreateObj(PersistentServer *somSelf,
                                           Environment *ev, Identifier objclass,
                                           string hints)
```

**Figure 6.8** (continues)

```
{
        /* PersistentServerData *somThis = PersistentServerGetData(somSelf); */
        SOMPPersistentObject *obj;
        SOMPPersistentId *pid;

        PersistentServerMethodDebug("PersistentServer","somdCreateObj");

        obj = (SOMPPersistentObject *)
                PersistentServer_parent_SOMDServer_somdCreateObj(somSelf,
                                                        ev,
                                                        objclass,
                                                        NULL);

        if (hints != NULL)
        {
            //****************************************
            // Assign persistent ID to object
            //****************************************
            pid = new SOMPPersistentId();
            pid->somutSetIdString(ev, hints);
            obj->sompInitGivenId(ev, pid);
        }

        return obj;
}
```

**Figure 6.8** continued

determine if there is a persistent object for this calendar. If a persistent form
exists, it will be restored. If neither the object reference nor the persistent
object exists, a new *CalendarDir* object is created, and the *externalizeProxy*
function is called to externalize the object reference.
- The *findPersist* function is a new function. It checks to see if the persistent
  objects for this calendar already exist. If the persistent objects already exist,
  they will be restored, and the *externalizeProxy* function is called to externalize
  the object reference to the *CalendarDir* object.

  A naming convention is used to determine the persistent ID string for the
  *CalendarDir* object. If the calendar server is "pChris", then the persistent ID
  will be "SOMAscii:.\pChris.dat:0". This means that the persistent calendar
  objects will be stored in the file "pChris.dat" in the current directory.
- The *externalizeProxy* function is a new function. It converts the object reference to the *CalendarDir* object into a string ID. The string ID is written to a
  file in order to allow sharing of the *CalendarDir* object.

```
#ifndef PLANWIN_HPP
#define PLANWIN_HPP

#include <iframe.hpp>
#include <icmdhdr.hpp>
#include <imcelcv.hpp>
#include <ilistbox.hpp>
#include <iselhdr.hpp>
#include <istring.hpp>
#include <istattxt.hpp>
#include <imenubar.hpp>
#include <ispinbt.hpp>
#include <ientryfd.hpp>

#include <somd.xh>
#include <somp.xh>

#include "week.h"
#include "workitem.xh"
#include "day.xh"
#include "caldir.xh"
#include "perserv.xh"

class DayPlannerWindow : public IFrameWindow,
                         public ICommandHandler,
                         public ISelectHandler
{
  public:
      DayPlannerWindow (unsigned long windowId, char *name);
      ~DayPlannerWindow();

  protected:
      virtual Boolean command(ICommandEvent& cmdevt);
      virtual Boolean selected(IControlEvent& evt);
```

**Figure 6.9** The DayPlannerWindow header file (continues)

```
    private:
        setupClient();
        setupData();
        short findProxy();
        short findPersist();
        externalizeProxy();
        showItems(short day);
        book(char *start, char *end, char *desc);

        IEntryField *descT;
        IStaticText *weekday, *start, *end, *desc;
        ISpinButton *startT, *endT;

        IMultiCellCanvas *mc;
        IMenuBar *menuBar;
        short menuFlag;
        short createFile;

        IListBox *listBox;
        IListBox::Cursor *cursor;

        // DSOM related variables
        PersistentServer *server;
        char *serverName;
        Environment *ev;
        CalendarDir *curDirEntry;
        Day *curDay;

        // PSOM related variables
        SOMPPersistentStorageMgr *psm;      // persistent storage manager
        char *pidString;                    // persistent ID string
    };
    #endif
```

**Figure 6.9** continued

- The *destructor* is modified to save the persistent objects in addition to performing cleanup.

The partial listing for the source file *planwin.cpp* appears in Figure 6.10. Any code that has been changed or added is shown. Member functions that have not been changed are not listed. A complete listing is included on the diskette.

```cpp
#include <ifont.hpp>
#include <ititle.hpp>
#include <iostream.h>
#include <fstream.h>
#include <imsgbox.hpp>

#include <stdio.h>
#include "planwin.hpp"

void main(int argc, char *argv[], char *envp[])
{
    IString filename;
    if (argc == 2)
    {
        filename = argv[1];
    }
    else
    {
        filename = "pChris";              // default to my persistent calendar
    }
    DayPlannerWindow mainWindow(WND_MAIN, filename);
    IApplication::current().run();
}

DayPlannerWindow :: setupData()
{
    short i, found;
    Day *day;

    ev = SOM_CreateLocalEnvironment();
    SOMD_Init(ev);
```

**Figure 6.10** The DayPlannerWindow implementation (changed code only)

```
        server = (PersistentServer *)
                        SOMD_ObjectMgr->somdFindServerByName(ev,serverName);
        psm = (SOMPPersistentStorageMgr *) server->getPerStorMgr(ev);


        found = findProxy();

        if (!found)                              // no current client yet
        {
                found = findPersist();
        }

        if (!found)
        {
            //******************************************************************************
            // Create a new CalendarDir object and add 7 Days to the list.
            // Pass pidString as "hints". The pidString parm is set in findPersist.
            //******************************************************************************
            curDirEntry = (CalendarDir *) server->somdCreateObj(ev,
                                                                "CalendarDir",
                                                                pidString);

            externalizeProxy();


            for (i=0; i<7; i++ )
            {
                day = (Day *) server->somdCreateObj(ev, "Day", NULL);
                day->_set_date(ev,i);
                curDirEntry->addDay(ev, i, day);
            }
        }


        // Set current day to Monday and show any existing activities
        curDay = curDirEntry->getDay(ev,1);
        showItems(1);
    }


    DayPlannerWindow :: externalizeProxy()
    {
        string objectId;
```

**Figure 6.10** (continues)

```
      objectId = SOMD_ObjectMgr->somdGetIdFromObject(ev,curDirEntry);

      ofstream outfile(serverName);
      outfile << objectId;
      outfile.close();

      createFile = 1;                          // remember this client created the file
   }


   short DayPlannerWindow :: findPersist()
   {
      //***********************************************************************
      // Create string for persistent ID. We will store the
      // persistent objects in a file using the following convention:
      // SOMPAscii:.\\<serverName>.dat:0
      //***********************************************************************
      pidString = new char[strlen(serverName) + strlen("SOMPAscii:.\\.dat:0") + 1];
      sprintf(pidString, "SOMPAscii:.\\%s.dat:0", serverName);

      if ( server->objectExists(ev, pidString) )
      {
         curDirEntry = (CalendarDir *) server->restoreObjectFromId(ev, pidString);
         externalizeProxy();
         return 1;
      }
      else
      {
         return 0;
      }
   }


   DayPlannerWindow :: ~DayPlannerWindow()
   {
      short i, j;
      _IDL_SEQUENCE_WorkItem alist;


      //****************************************************
      // Store all objects
      //****************************************************
```

**Figure 6.10** (continues)

```
          psm->sompStoreObject(ev, curDirEntry);

    if (createFile)                                    // this client writes proxy to file
    {
        //*************************************
        // perform clean up: delete the file
        //*************************************
        IString buffer("erase ");
        buffer = buffer + serverName;
        system(buffer);


        //*************************************
        // Destroy each Day object
        //*************************************
        for (i=0; i<7; i++ )
        {
                curDay = curDirEntry->getDay(ev,i);
                alist = curDay->_get_workList(ev);
                if (sequenceLength(alist) > 0 && sequenceLength(alist) < 50)
                {
                    //***********************************************************
                    // Destroy each WorkItem from the Day object
                    //***********************************************************
                    for (j=0; j < sequenceLength(alist) ; j++)
                    {
                        SOMD_ObjectMgr->somdDestroyObject(ev,
                                                            sequenceElement(alist,j));
                    }
                }
                SOMD_ObjectMgr->somdDestroyObject(ev,curDay);
        }

        // Destroy CalendarDir object
        SOMD_ObjectMgr->somdDestroyObject(ev, curDirEntry);
    }
    else
    {
        //****************************************************
        // Release the proxy for each Day object
        //****************************************************
```

**Figure 6.10** (continues)

```
        for (i=0; i<7; i++ )
        {
            curDay = curDirEntry->getDay(ev,i);
            alist = curDay->_get_workList(ev);
            if (sequenceLength(alist) > 0 && sequenceLength(alist) < 50)
            {
                //*******************************************************************
                // Release proxy for each WorkItem from Day object
                //*******************************************************************
                for (j=0; j < sequenceLength(alist) ; j++)
                {
                    SOMD_ObjectMgr->somdReleaseObject(ev,
                                            sequenceElement(alist,j));
                }
            }
            SOMD_ObjectMgr->somdReleaseObject(ev,curDay);
        }

        // Release proxy for CalendarDir object
        SOMD_ObjectMgr->somdReleaseObject(ev,curDirEntry);
    }

    // release server proxy
    SOMD_ObjectMgr->somdReleaseObject(ev, server);

    SOMD_Uninit(ev);
    SOM_DestroyLocalEnvironment(ev);
}
```

**Figure 6.10** (continues)

Observe that we only use one store and one restore operation to write and read all the persistent calendar objects. This is possible because our persistent objects are structured as a hierarchy of objects as shown in Figure 6.11. Furthermore, notice that we assigned an explicit persistent ID to the root object. The remaining persistent IDs were assigned using the **sompInitNearObject** method where each object is assigned an ID that is near to the previously assigned ID. This technique is very useful for applications that work with a hierarchy of objects that is saved and restored as a whole.

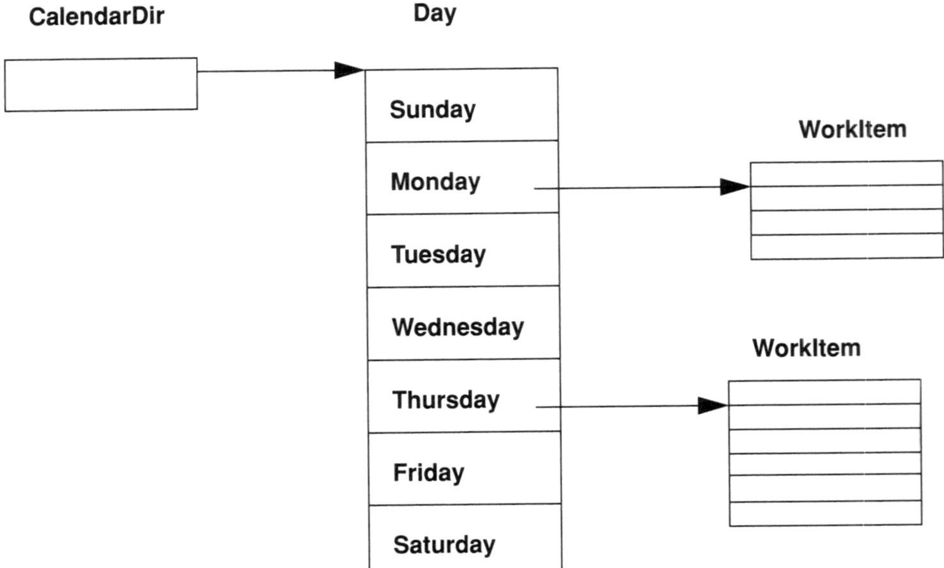


**Figure 6.11** Calendar Objects Hierarchy

### The Makefile

The makefile, listed in Figure 6.12, has been modified to build the distributed, persistent calendar. The source file that contains the class *PersistentServer* is *perserv.cpp*. The source file *perserv.def* contains the module definition file. It is not listed here but is included on the diskette. These two files are needed to build the *perserv* DLL.

The four classes are compiled into the Interface Repository file that is designated by the SOMIR environment variable. Two calendar servers, "pChris" and "pKevin", are registered with the Implementation Repository that is designated by the SOMDDIR environment variable. Note that the *PersistentServer* class is registered as the server class that will manage objects in the "pChris" and "pKevin" servers.

### Building the Application

The application is built by invoking NMAKE in a similar manner as before. The file *dsomenv.cmd* is provided to set up the environment variables for the application.

### Running the Application

Start the DSOM daemon as before.

> start /f somdd

Then start the PLANNER program using the default ("pChris") server.

> planner

Add some activities to pChris's calendar. Then select Quit to exit the application. The file "pChris.dat" should be created in your current directory. Take a look at it.

Start the PLANNER program again. The activities that were added before will be displayed.

You can try the sequences from the last chapter such as starting a second PLANNER program using the "pChris" server or start the PLANNER program using the "pKevin" server.

Observe the objects are only written out if they have been changed. Compare the time difference between exiting a calendar that has changed objects, versus one that does not have any changed objects.

**Summary**

Now that our calendar application is both distributed and persistent, what else is missing? You might have noticed that if you have multiple users sharing a calendar, then when one user makes a change to the calendar, the change is not automatically reflected in the other users' views. The other users need to either refresh their displays manually or restart the PLANNER program in order to see the changes. Can we extend this application so that a change is automatically propagated to all the views of the calendar? We will answer this question in the next chapter.

```
.SUFFIXES:
.SUFFIXES: .idl .xih .xh .cpp .obj .def
#
# Need /Ge- to build DLL
#
OBJS = workitem.obj day.obj caldir.obj initfunc.obj
POBJS = perserv.obj
UILIB = dde4muii.lib dde4cci.lib dde4mbsi.lib os2386.lib


all: calendar.dll perserv.dll planner.exe som.ir somdimpl


.cpp.obj:
        icc /c+ /Ge- -I. $<
.idl.xh:
        sc -sxh $*.idl
.idl.xih:
        sc -sxih $*.idl
.idl.cpp:
        sc -sxc $*.idl
```

**Figure 6.12** The distributed and persistent PLANNER Makefile (continues)

```
initfunc.obj: initfunc.cpp

clnimpl:
        -regimpl -D -i pChris
        -regimpl -D -i pKevin

workitem.obj: workitem.xih workitem.xh workitem.cpp
workitem.xih: workitem.idl
workitem.xh: workitem.idl
workitem.cpp: workitem.xih

day.obj: day.xih day.xh day.cpp
day.xih: day.idl
day.xh: day.idl
day.cpp: day.xih

caldir.obj: caldir.xih caldir.xh caldir.cpp
caldir.xih: caldir.idl
caldir.xh: caldir.idl
caldir.cpp: caldir.xih

initfunc.obj: initfunc.cpp

perserv.obj: perserv.xih perserv.xh perserv.cpp
perserv.xih: perserv.idl
perserv.xh: perserv.idl
perserv.cpp: perserv.xih

#
# Build the Calendar DLL
#
calendar.dll: $(OBJS) calendar.def
        icc @<<
        /Fe"calendar.dll" $(OBJS) calendar.def
        somtk.lib
<<
implib calendar.lib calendar.def

#
# Build the Persistent Server DLL
#
```

**Figure 6.12**  (continues)

```
perserv.dll: $(POBJS) perserv.def
        icc @<<
        /Fe"perserv.dll" $(POBJS) perserv.def
        somtk.lib
<<
implib perserv.lib perserv.def

#
# Build the executables
#
planwin.obj: planwin.cpp planwin.hpp week.h
        icc /c+ /Gd+ /Gm+ /Si+ -I. planwin.cpp
planner.exe: planwin.obj week.res
        icc /Fe"planner.exe" planwin.obj /B" /pm:pm /noi" \
        $(UILIB) somtk.lib calendar.lib perserv.lib planner.def
        rc week.res planner.exe

week.res: week.rc week.h
        rc -r week.rc
#
# Put the IDL descriptions into the Interface Repository
#
som.ir: workitem.idl day.idl caldir.idl perserv.idl
        sc -sir -u workitem.idl
        sc -sir -u day.idl
        sc -sir -u caldir.idl
        sc -sir -u perserv.idl
#
# Build the DSOM Implementation Repository.
# Register two servers: pChris and pKevin
#
somdimpl: workitem.idl day.idl caldir.idl perserv.idl
        -regimpl -A -i pChris -p $(SOMBASE)\bin\somdsvr.exe -v PersistentServer
        -regimpl -a -i pChris -c WorkItem -c Day -c CalendarDir
        -regimpl -L -i pChris
#
        -regimpl -A -i pKevin -p $(SOMBASE)\bin\somdsvr.exe -v PersistentServer
        -regimpl -a -i pKevin -c WorkItem -c Day -c CalendarDir
        -regimpl -L -i pKevin
        @echo x > somdimpl
```

**Figure 6.12**  (continues)

# 7

# Using Replicated Objects

The Replication SOM (RSOM) Framework allows you to replicate an object in several different processes distributed across a network. Each replica of the object can be updated, and the Framework handles the propagation of the update to all the other replicas. The updates are serialized by the Framework, and are propagated from the originating process to the other participants, without the use of secondary storage.

The RSOM Framework can be used to implement "groupware" type applications. For example, using the Replication Framework, a compound document consisting of text, diagrams, bitmaps, and graphics can be worked on collaboratively by multiple concurrent users located at different workstations on a network. Each user can see the changes made by others in the group. Traditionally, in a distributed environment, information sharing is achieved through the use of database servers. The Replication Framework provides a new way for sharing information that puts a user in direct contact with other users. Each user sees the changes made by others instantaneously.

Each replica is not aware of how many other replicas there are in the network, or where they are in the network. A participant can join or leave the group at any time, and the replicas in the network will not be aware of it. The Framework can tolerate process or node failure, and provides recovery.

## 7.1  RSOM OVERVIEW

To use the RSOM Framework, both the object, and the client program that accesses the object, must be RSOM aware. From the object perspective, it must be derived from a special replication class and provide methods to get and set the complete state of the object. The RSOM client is responsible for initializing the Replication Framework and to set up the main event processing loop for the application.

The development of an RSOM application involves the following steps.

1. Define the interface for your replicated objects, and write code to implement your objects.
2. Create a client program that accesses the objects.
3. Build your classes, and register them with the Interface Repository.
4. Start TCP/IP.
5. Run the client program.

The following sections provide details on each of the above steps.

## 7.2    DEFINE AND IMPLEMENT A REPLICATED OBJECT

To create a replicated object, we must first create a class derived from the *SOMRReplicbl* class. *SOMRReplicbl* is derived from *SOMRNameable* and *SOMRLinearizable*. Both *SOMRNameable* and *SOMRLinearizable* are subclassed from *SOMObject*.

Any class that is dervied either directly or indirectly from *SOMRReplicbl* can have groups of object instances that are replicas of each other. For an object to be replicable, a number of rules must be followed. These rules are discussed in the following sections.

### 7.2.1    Replica Name

A replicated object must have a name. All objects initialized for replication under the same name are replicas of one another. For example, assume the *Document* class is replicable. If process 1 creates an object of *Document* class and sets its name to "overview", and process 2 creates an object of *Document* class and sets its name to "overview", then these two objects are replicas of each other. Any update made to one replica will be propagated to the other, provided that the set of replication rules are followed.

The *SOMRNameable* class provides the **somrSetObjName** and the **somrGetObjName** methods to set and get the name of an object. The C syntax for the **somrSetObjName** method is given below:

```
_somrSetObjNamel(repObject,        // pointer to an object of SOMRNameable
                 env,              // pointer to Environment structure
                 name);            // pointer to the name of the object
```

The parameter *repObject* is a pointer to a replicated object to which the specified name is to be assigned. The parameter *name* is a null-terminated string that contains the name of the object.

## 7.2.2    Operation Vs. Value Logging

The Replication Framework defines two ways of propagating changes among replicas. They are:

1. Operation logging—each method that modifies a replica will execute at the site of the other replicas.
2. Value logging—the change in value of a replica is encoded after a method invocation, and the values of the other replicas are updated to reflect the changes.

The choice between the two depends on how long it takes to compute the new value of an object. For example, if you have a method that performs some very complex calculations, you should compute the result once, and use value logging to transfer the new value to the other replicas. On the other hand, if the method executes quickly, or transferring the results might take longer than having the replicas repeat the execution of the method, then operation logging should be used instead.

The *SOMRReplicbl* class provides the **somrRepInit** method to initialize an object for operation or value logging. The C syntax for the **somrRepInit** method follows:

```
_somrRepInit(repObject,      // pointer to an object of SOMRReplicbl
             env,            // pointer to Environment structure
             logType,        // type of logging
             mode);          // read or write mode
```

The parameter *repObject* is a pointer to a replicated object. The parameter *logType* indicates the type of logging used. It can be either 'o' for operation logging or 'v' for value logging. The parameter *mode* indicates whether or not the object can be written. If the mode is 'w', then the object can be written. If the mode is 'r', then the object can only be read by the Framework.

## 7.2.3    Replica Lock

A replicated object must obtain a replica lock before updating its data and must release the lock after the update. The *SOMRReplicbl* class provides different locking methods, depending on whether operation logging or value logging is used.

### 7.2.3.1    Operation Logging Lock

If *operation logging* is used, then a replicated class must invoke the **somrLockNlogOp** method to acquire a lock on the current replica, before the update is made. When the update is completed, the object must invoke the **somrReleaseNPropagateOperation** method to release the lock. In the case when the object wants to abort an update operation, it must invoke the **somrReleaseLockNAbortOp** method.

The C syntax for the **somrLockNlogOp** method follows:

```
_somrLockNlogOp(repObject,          // pointer to an object of SOMRReplicbl
                env,                // pointer to Environment structure
                className,          // name of class
                methodName,         // name of method
                ap);                // arguments
```

The parameter *repObject* is a pointer to a replicated object. The parameter *className* is the class name of the replicated object. The parameter *methodName* is the name of the method that performs the update. The parameter *ap* is a pointer to a va_list that specifies the arguments for the method.

The C syntax for **somrReleaseNPropagateOperation** and **somrReleaseLockNAbortOp** follow.

```
_somrReleaseNPropagateOperation(repObject,     // pointer to an object of SOMRReplicbl
                                env);          // pointer to Environment structure


_somrReleaseLockNAbortOp(repObject,            // pointer to an object of SOMRReplicbl
                         env);                 // pointer to Environment structure
```

### 7.2.3.2 Value Logging Lock

If *value logging* is used, then a replicated class must invoke the **somrLock** method to acquire a lock on the current replica before the update is made. When the update is completed, the object must invoke the **somrReleaseNPropagateUpdate** method to release the lock. In the case when the object wants to abort an update operation, it must invoke the **somrReleaseLockNAbortUpdate** method.

The C syntax for the **somrLock** method is presented below:

```
_somrLock(repObject,          // pointer to an object of SOMRReplicbl
          env);               // pointer to Environment structure
```

This method is similar to the **somrLockNlogOp** method except it does not log the method information.

The C syntax for **somrReleaseNPropagateUpdate** follows:

```
_somrReleaseNPropagateUpdate(repObject,     // pointer to an object of SOMRReplicbl
                             env,           // pointer to Environment structure
                             className,     // name of class
                             buf,           // buffer for update information
                             bufLen,        // size of buffer
                             objIntId);     // reserved for future use
```

The parameter *repObject* is a pointer to a replicated object. The parameter *className* is the class name of the replicated object. The parameter *buf* contains the information that is to be propagated. The parameter *bufLen* contains the size of the buffer. The parameter *objIntId* is reserved for future use and should be set to 0.

The C syntax for **somrReleaseLockNAbortUpdate** follows:

```
_somrReleaseLockNAbortUpdate(repObject,    // pointer to an object of SOMRReplicbl
                             env);         // pointer to Environment structure
```

## 7.2.4    Replica State

A replicated object must get and set the complete state of the object. The *SOMR-Linearizable* class provides two methods, **somrGetState** and **somrSetState**. These must be overridden by a replicated class. The **somrGetState** method encodes the internal state of the object into a byte string. The **somrSetState** method converts the byte string into its internal state. The Replication Framework calls these methods on the replicated object to synchronize new replicas with the existing ones. The **somrGetState** method is called on existing replicas and the **somrSetState** method is called on the new replicas.

The C syntax for the **somrGetState** method is presented below:

```
_somrGetState(repObject,    // pointer to an object of SOMRLinearizable
              env,          // pointer to Environment structure
              buf );        // buffer for outgoing byte string
```

The parameter *repObject* is a pointer to a replicated object. The parameter *buf* is the buffer that stores the internal state of the object. The caller must allocate the storage for the string, and the first four bytes must contain the length of the string.

The C syntax for the **somrSetState** method is shown below:

```
_somrSetState(repObject,    // pointer to an object of SOMRLinearizable
              env,          // pointer to Environment structure
              buf );        // buffer for incoming byte string
```

The parameter *repObject* is a pointer to a replicated object. The parameter *buf* is the buffer that contains the byte string for the internal state of the object. The first four bytes of the string contain the length of the string.

## 7.2.5    Replica Update

If value logging is used, the replicated object must override the method **somrApplyUpdates**. The **somrApplyUpdates** method receives and interprets messages propagated by other replicas. The C syntax for the **somrApplyUpdates** method follows:

```
_somrApplyUpdates(repObject,      // pointer to an object of SOMRReplicbl
                  env,            // pointer to Environment structure
                  buffer,         // buffer that contains update info
                  bufLen,         // size of buffer
                  objIntId );     // reserved for future use
```

The parameter *repObject* is a pointer to a replicated object. The parameter *buffer* contains the update information and is in the same format as the one passed by the **somrReleaseNPropagateUpdate** method. The parameter *bufLen* contains the size of the buffer. The parameter *objIntId* is reserved for future use, and should be set to 0.

### 7.2.6    Handle Directives

A replicated object must be able to receive and respond to data replication directives. A directive is a message sent from the Replication Framework to a replica, to indicate that some conditions have arisen asynchronously. The *SOMRReplicbl* class provides the method **somrDoDirective**, which should be overridden by a replicated subclass, to interpret the directives that are sent to the replica.

The C syntax for the **somrDoDirective** method is presented below:

```
_somrDoDirective(repObject,      // pointer to an object of SOMRReplicbl
                 env,            // pointer to Environment structure
                 directive );    // directive string
```

The parameter *repObject* is a pointer to a replicated object. The parameter *directive* is the string representing the directive. The current defined directives and their meanings are given in Table 7.1.

**Table 7.1**  RSOM directives

| Directives | Description |
| --- | --- |
| BECOME_STAND_ALONE | The replica lost its connection to other replicas, and RSOM has given up trying to reconnect to the other replicas. |
| CONNECTION_LOST | The replica has lost its connection to the other replicas, and RSOM is trying to reconnect. |
| CONNECTION_REESTABLISHED | The connection between the replica and other replicas has been reestablished. |
| LOST_RECOVERABILITY | RSOM cannot update the .scf[a] file to reflect the current state of the Framework, and recovery may be impacted. |

a. The .scf files are used by RSOM to establish communication among the replicas. It is an internal implementation detail that is exposed to the user. One should not make use of those files.

## 7.3    CLIENT PROGRAM

To use replicated objects, a client program must initialize the Replication Framework environment and set up the main loop for processing events. Because every operating system provides different mechanisms for processing events, the manner in which the event loop is set up will be different. SOM provides an Event Management Framework to organize events into groups, and to process them in a single event-processing loop.

### 7.3.1    RSOM Initialization

Every RSOM client must include the file *<somr.xh>* (or *<somr.h>* if using C bindings). This file includes the constants, global variables, and run-time interfaces that are used by RSOM. It must also include the file *<eman.xh>* (or *<eman.h>* if using C bindings). This file includes the run-time interfaces used by the Event Management Framework.

The client must also initialize the RSOM Framework by creating an instance of the *SOMR* class. The *SOMR* class creates and initializes several manager objects required by RSOM. The client must also initialize the Event Management Framework by creating an Event Manager object. The Event Manager object handles the registration and processing of input events.

A typical implementation of RSOM initialization follows:

```
#include <somr.xh>
#include <eman.xh>
main()
{
  Environment *ev;
  SOMR*repEnv;
  SOMEEMan*emgr;

  ev = SOM_CreateLocalEnvironment();  // create and initialize an Environment structure
  repEnv = new SOMR();                // create and initialize RSOM
  emgr = new SOMEEMan();              // create and initialize Event Management
  ...
}
```

### 7.3.2    Setup Event Processing Loop

The Event Manager class, *SOMEEMan*, provides the methods **someProcessEvent** and **someProcessEvents** for processing events. The **someProcessEvent** method processes one event and then returns. The **someProcessEvents** method loops forever waiting for events and dispatches them. Typically, a main program registers an interest in an event type and specifies a callback to be invoked, when the event occurs. The main program then calls **someProcessEvents** to wait on the registered events.

Note that in a single-threaded environment, such as AIX, once control is given to **someProcessEvents**, there is no way to respond to other input such as keyboard input. Therefore, one must register interest in "stdin" and provide a callback function to handle keyboard input before calling **someProcessEvents**. For multi-threaded environment such as OS/2, one can spawn a thread to execute **someProcessEvents** and another to handle keyboard input. This is demonstrated in our application.

## 7.4    BUILDING AND REGISTERING THE CLASSES

Building an RSOM application is very much like a regular SOM application. You compile your classes and your client program. It is not mandatory that you build a DLL for your classes. If you want to build a DLL, follow the steps in "Creating a DLL for SOM Classes" on page 79.

You need to compile your RSOM classes into the Interface Repository. The Interface Repository is described in more detail in Chapter 8, Working with the Interface Repository.

## 7.5    TCP/IP

The Replication Framework requires TCP/IP Version 1.2.1 with CSD UN34109 or later versions, to be installed and running. You can use the command file *\TCPIP\BIN\TCPSTART.CMD* to start TCP/IP execution. The Replication Framework uses sockets for inter-process communications. It also uses the Event Management Framework, which also uses sockets. The SOMobjects Developer Toolkit provides a *Sockets* class abstraction. *TCPIPSockets* is one of the dervied class of *Sockets* and uses the TCP/IP implementation.

## 7.6    EXECUTION

Make sure the environment variable SOMIR points to the Interface Repository that contains the replicated classes. The environment variable SOMSOCKETS must be set to the name of the socket implementation class. The default is TCPIPSockets. The RSOM application can then be started.

## 7.7    A REPLICATED CALENDAR

In this section, we will rewrite our calendar application using the RSOM Framework. We notice in our previous shared calendar that an update by one client is not automatically reflected in the other client's view. Say "Chris" calendar is accessed by two users and both are showing the work items for Monday. If the first user adds a calendar item to Monday, the second user will not see it until refreshing the Monday list. This is illustrated in Figure 7.1.

When user one adds a new work item (item3) to the shared calendar, user two will not see the new item. This is because even though the calendar data is shared by the two client processes, there is no mechanism in place to notify the other process when a change occurs in the shared data.

The Replication Framework can be used as a notification mechanism to solve the above problem. Using the Replication Framework, when an update occurs in a replica, the update is automatically propagated to the other replicas in the system. In other words, all the replicas of an object get notified by the Framework when a change occurs in any one of the replicas. On receiving the notification, a replica can refresh its view to show the current status.

In the following, we show the modifications that are needed to implement such a system. The user interface for the PLANNER program remains the same. However, you will notice when you make an update to the calendar, all the other views of that calendar will automatically be refreshed.

### 7.7.1    High-Level Design

Recall that the *Day* class is used to keep track of the list of work items for a particular day. We make the *Day* class replicable. When one client updates a *Day* object, say the Monday object, the update will be propagated to all the replicas of

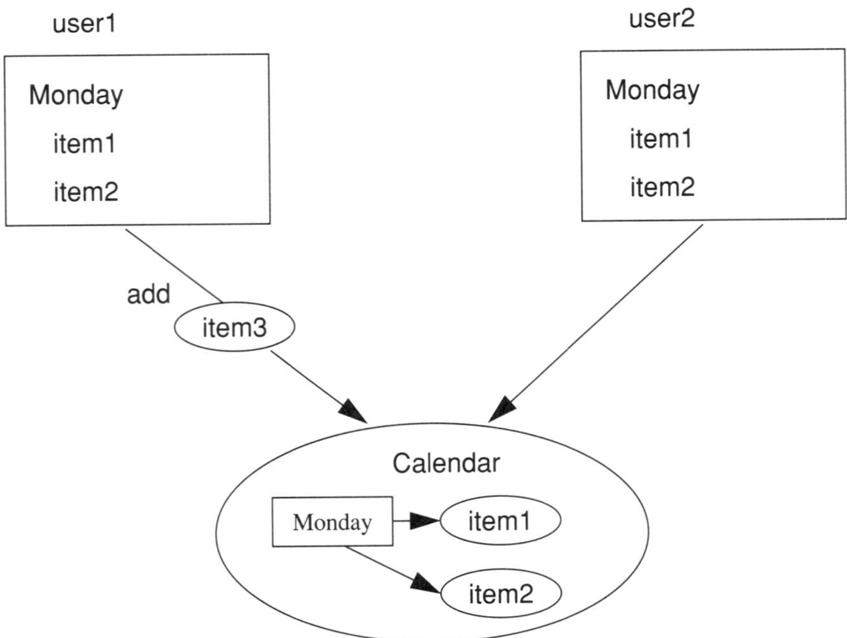


**Figure 7.1** Multiple users working with the same calendar

the Monday object in the system. The classes *WorkItem* and *CalendarDir* that make up our *calendar* DLL do not change. They are identical to the Distributed Calendar implementation in Section 5.10 on page 108.

In order for our client views of the calendar to show the updated list of work items for a particular day, a protocol must be in place so that whenever a *Day* object changes, a message is sent to each client views to inform them of the change. This is because the *Day* object, which contains only state information, has no idea of the possible views that are interested in its state.

We provide a simple registration protocol in our implementation. Any client that is interested in a change in a *Day* object will register such a desire with the *Day* class. The registration contains information as to what method to invoke when a change occurs. When a *WorkItem* is added to or removed from a *Day* object, it will invoke the registered method to notify the corresponding client.

A new SOM class *DayView* is added to provide the view encapsulation. The *DayView* class provides the bridge from the data object to the multiple views on the data object. Figure 7.2 shows the association between the view and the data.

When an update is made to a *Day* replica, the RSOM Framework will multicast the update to all the other replicas. Each replica can notify each view that has registered an interest in its state change. When the view receives the notification, it can update its display. This is summarized in Figure 7.3.

### 7.7.2  Implementation Details

This section provides the details on the design and implementation of each component in our replicated calendar.

### The WorkItem Class

The IDL for the *WorkItem* class is given in Figure 7.4. The *WorkItem* class encapsulates work items for a day.

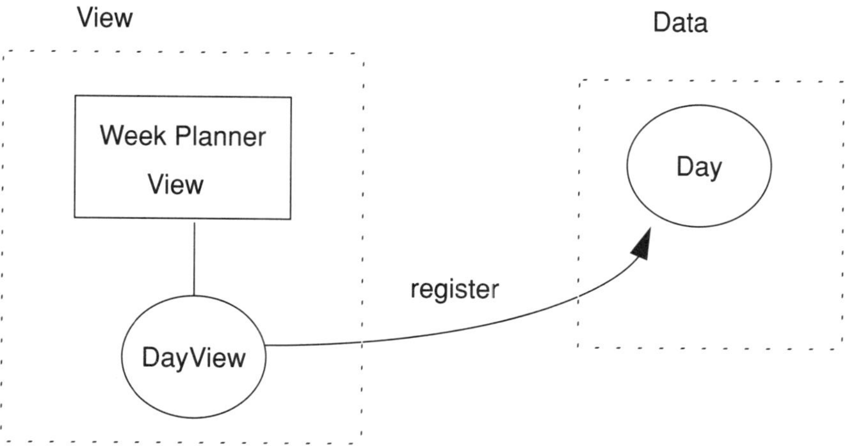


**Figure 7.2** Associating View with Data

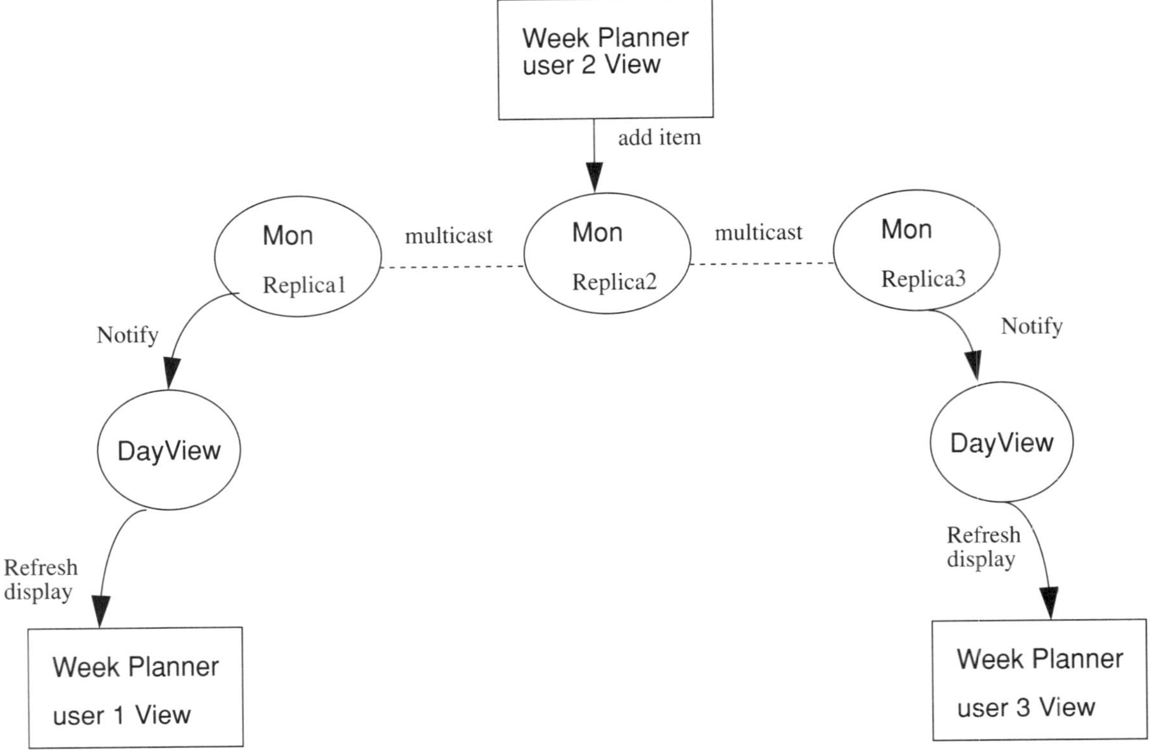



**Figure 7.3** RSOM multicast update on replica triggers refresh of display

The C++ implementation for the *WorkItem* class is the same as the one in the Distributed Calendar. Refer to Section 5.10.4 on page 110 for the details.

**The Day Class**

The IDL for the *Day* class is presented in Figure 7.5. This class is derived from *SOMRReplicbl* so that its objects are replicable.

- The *book2* method acquires a lock on the current replica. It creates a new *WorkItem* object, adds it to the sequence *workList,* and propagates the update to the other replicas. It then invokes the *notifyView* method to notify any view object that has registered an interest in the state change of the object.

  Observe that the *book2* method signature is different from the previous *book* method. The *book* method takes a *WorkItem* object as input parameter, while the *book2* method takes the *startTime, endTime,* and *task* values as input parameters and then constructs the *WorkItem* object. This is because we use operation logging to propagate changes. Operation logging executes this method at every existing replica. Had we passed a *WorkItem* object, the *WorkItem* object would not exist in the different address spaces. Therefore, we need to pass explicit values, and then create the *WorkItem* object in each address space.

```
#ifndef workitem_idl
#define workitem_idl

#include <somobj.idl>

interface WorkItem : SOMObject
{
   attribute string startTime;
   attribute string endTime;
   attribute string task;

   void mkEntry(in string sTime, in string eTime, in string taskDesc);

   #ifdef __SOMIDL__
   implementation
   {
       releaseorder : _get_startTime, _set_startTime,
                      _get_endTime, _set_endTime,
                      _get_task, _set_task,
                      mkEntry;

       somInit: override;
       somUninit: override;

       dllname = "calendar.dll";
   };
   #endif
};
#endif
```

**Figure 7.4** TheWorkItem IDL

- The *removeItem* method acquires a lock on the current replica and removes a *WorkItem* object from the sequence *workList* by searching the sequence for a *WorkItem* object that has the same *startTime, endTime,* and *task* values as the input parameters. If one is found, it will be removed from the sequence. The update is propagated to the other replicas and the *notifyView* method is called to notify any view object that has registered an interest in the state change of the object.
- The *initReplica* method sets the replica name and initializes the replica to use operation logging.
- The *registerView* method registers a view object that is interested in the state change of this replica. The registration information includes the name of the class and the name of the method to invoke when a change in replica state occurs.

```
#ifndef day_idl
#define day_idl

#include <replicbl.idl>

interface WorkItem;

interface Day : SOMRReplicbl
{
     const unsigned long MAXITEM = 50;
     attribute long date;
     attribute sequence<WorkItem,MAXITEM> workList;

     short book2(in string start, in string end, in string desc);
     short removeItem(in string start, in string end, in string desc);

     void initReplica(in string replicaName);

     void registerView(in SOMObject anyObj, in string methodName);
     void notifyView(in long eventId);
     SOMObject getViewObject();

     #ifdef __SOMIDL__
     implementation
     {
       releaseorder : _get_date, _set_date,
                     _get_workList, _set_workList,
                     book2, removeItem,
                     initReplica, registerView, notifyView,
                     getViewObject;

       string methodName;
       SOMObject objectPtr;

       somInit: override;
       somUninit: override;
       somrGetState: override;
       somrSetState: override;
       somrDoDirective: override;

       dllname = "calendar.dll";
     };
     #endif
};
#endif
```

**Figure 7.5** Day IDL

- The *notifyView* method uses dispatch-function resolution to invoke the registered method. The *notifyView* method is called whenever there is a change in the object state or whenever a directive is received.
- The *getViewObject* method returns the view object that is associated with this replica.
- The **somInit** method is overridden to initialize the sequence *workList*. It allocates storage for the sequence and sets the length and maximum field of the sequence.
- The **somUninit** method is overridden to free the storage that is allocated for the sequence *workList* when the object is destroyed.
- The **somrGetState** method is overridden to encode the internal state of the object into a byte string. The internal state of the object consists of all the *WorkItem* objects that are associated with this *Day* object. Therefore each *WorkItem* object has to be flattened and appended to the byte string. The flattened information contains the length and the value of each field in the *WorkItem* object.
- The **somrSetState** method is overridden to decode the byte string into the object internal state. Using the encoded length information, each field can be read in and a new *WorkItem* object can be re-created and added to the *workList* sequence.

  Note that the current release of RSOM does not support composite objects in the sense that there is no lock propagation. For example, a lock on the *Day* object does not lock the *WorkItem* objects in the *workList* sequence. Therefore, one must implement code similar to that presented here in order to save and restore the state of the *WorkItem* objects. This presents a difficulty when using RSOM. The support for composite objects will hopefully be added in future releases.
- The **somrDoDirective** method is overridden to handle the data replication directives. It calls *notifyView* to notify the interested view on the directive that this replica received.

The C++ code that implements the methods for the *Day* class is given in Figure 7.6. The **somrGetState** method encodes each *WorkItem* object into a byte string using the following sequence: startTime length, startTime value, endTime length, endTime value, task length, task value. It also stores the total number of *WorkItem* objects in the byte string. The **somrGetState** method is called by the Replication Framework on an existing replica whenever a new replica enters the system. The Framework then calls the **somrSetState** method on the new replia to synchronize the new replica data with the existing ones. Using the self-describing byte string, the **somrSetState** method reconstructs each *WorkItem* object and adds it to the new replica sequence.

### The CalendarDir Class

The IDL for the *CalendarDir* class is shown in Figure 7.7. It is used as a directory to keep track of the list of days of the week.

```
/*
 * This file was generated by the SOM Compiler.
 * Generated using:
 * SOM incremental update: 2.7
 */

#define Day_Class_Source
#include <day.xih>
#include <workitem.xh>
#include <stdio.h>
#include "eventid.h"                          // constants for our event Ids

SOM_Scope short SOMLINK book2(Day *somSelf, Environment *ev,
                                    string start, string end, string desc)

{
    DayData *somThis = DayGetData(somSelf);
    WorkItem *entry;
    short rc;
    DayMethodDebug("Day","book2");

    somSelf->somrLockNlogOp(ev, "Day", "book2", ev, start, end, desc);

    entry = new WorkItem;
    entry->mkEntry(ev, start, end, desc);

    if (sequenceLength(somThis->workList) < sequenceMaximum(somThis->workList))
    {
        sequenceElement(somThis->workList,
        sequenceLength(somThis->workList)) = entry;
        sequenceLength(somThis->workList)++;
        rc = 0L;
    }
    else
    {
        rc = -1L;
    }

    somSelf->somrReleaseNPropagateOperation(ev);

    //***************************************************************************
    // Notify the different views so that they can refresh their display
    //***************************************************************************
    somSelf->notifyView(ev, WM_REFRESH);
    return rc;
```

**Figure 7.6** The Day class implementation (continues)

```
        }

    SOM_Scope short SOMLINK removeItem(Day *somSelf, Environment *ev,
                                        string start, string end, string desc)
    {
        short rc, i;
        WorkItem *item;
        DayData *somThis = DayGetData(somSelf);
        DayMethodDebug("Day","removeItem");

        rc = -1;
        somSelf->somrLockNlogOp(ev, "Day", "removeItem", ev, start, end, desc);

        for (i=0; i < sequenceLength(somThis->workList); i++ )
        {
            item = sequenceElement(somThis->workList,i);

            if ( (strcmp(start, item->_get_startTime(ev)) == 0) &&
                 (strcmp(end, item->_get_endTime(ev)) == 0) &&
                 (strcmp(desc, item->_get_task(ev)) == 0) )
            {
                sequenceLength(somThis->workList)--;

                for (i; i < sequenceLength(somThis->workList); i++)
                {
                        sequenceElement(somThis->workList,i) =
                                        sequenceElement(somThis->workList, i+1);
                }
                rc = 0;
            }
        }

        somSelf->somrReleaseNPropagateOperation(ev);

        //*********************************************************************
        // Notify the different views so that they can refresh their display
        //*********************************************************************
        somSelf->notifyView(ev, WM_REFRESH);
        return rc;
    }

    SOM_Scope void SOMLINK initReplica(Day *somSelf, Environment *ev,
                                        string replicaName)
    {
```

**Figure 7.6** (continues)

```
        DayData *somThis = DayGetData(somSelf);
        DayMethodDebug("Day","initReplica");

        somSelf->somrSetObjName(ev, replicaName);
        somSelf->somrRepInit(ev, 'o', 'w');
}

SOM_Scope void SOMLINK registerView(Day *somSelf, Environment *ev,
                                      SOMObject* anyObj, string methodName)

{
        DayData *somThis = DayGetData(somSelf);
        DayMethodDebug("Day","registerView");

        somThis->objectPtr = anyObj;
        somThis->methodName = methodName;
}

SOM_Scope void SOMLINK notifyView(Day *somSelf, Environment *ev, long eventId)
{
        DayData *somThis = DayGetData(somSelf);
        DayMethodDebug("Day","notifyView");

        if (somThis->objectPtr)
        {
            (somThis->objectPtr)->somDispatch((somToken*)0,
                                    somIdFromString(somThis->methodName),
                                    somThis->objectPtr,
                                    ev,
                                    eventId);

        }
 }

SOM_Scope SOMObject* SOMLINK getViewObject(Day *somSelf, Environment *ev)
{
        DayData *somThis = DayGetData(somSelf);
        DayMethodDebug("Day","getViewObject");

        return (somThis->objectPtr);
}

SOM_Scope void SOMLINK somInit(Day *somSelf)
{
        DayData *somThis = DayGetData(somSelf);
        DayMethodDebug("Day","somInit");
```

**Figure 7.6** (continues)

```
        Day_parent_SOMRReplicbl_somInit(somSelf);

        sequenceMaximum(somThis->workList) = MAXITEM;
        sequenceLength(somThis->workList) = 0;
        somThis->workList._buffer = (WorkItem**) SOMMalloc(sizeof (WorkItem *) * MAXITEM);
    }

SOM_Scope void SOMLINK somUninit(Day *somSelf)
{
        DayData *somThis = DayGetData(somSelf);
        DayMethodDebug("Day","somUninit");

        if (somThis->workList._buffer)
            SOMFree(somThis->workList._buffer);

        Day_parent_SOMRReplicbl_somUninit(somSelf);
    }

SOM_Scope void SOMLINK somrGetState(Day *somSelf, Environment *ev,
                                    string* buf)
{
        long bufsize;
        long seqsize;
        short i, len;
        long infoLen;
        char *start;
        WorkItem *item;
        DayData *somThis = DayGetData(somSelf);
        DayMethodDebug("Day","somrGetState");

        bufsize = sizeof(long) + sizeof(unsigned long);

        for (i=0; i < sequenceLength(somThis->workList); i++ )
        {
            item = sequenceElement(somThis->workList,i);
            bufsize += strlen(item->_get_startTime(ev)) + 1 + sizeof(long) +
                       strlen(item->_get_endTime(ev)) + 1 + sizeof(long) +
                       strlen(item->_get_task(ev)) + 1 + sizeof(long);
        }

        *buf = (char *) SOMMalloc(bufsize);

        //*************************************************
        // Store total length
        //*************************************************
```

**Figure 7.6** (continues)

```
memcpy(*buf, &bufsize, sizeof(long));
len = sizeof(long);


//**************************************************
// Store sequence Length
//**************************************************
memcpy( (*buf+len),
            &sequenceLength(somThis->workList),
            sizeof(unsigned long));
len += sizeof(unsigned long);


//**************************************************
// Store sequence Elements
//**************************************************
for (i=0; i < sequenceLength(somThis->workList); i++ )
{
    item = sequenceElement(somThis->workList,i);

    //*****************************************************
    // Store length of startTime and startTime
    //*****************************************************
    infoLen = strlen(item->_get_startTime(ev)) + 1;

    memcpy((*buf+len), &infoLen, sizeof(long));
    len += sizeof(long);

    strcpy( (char*)(*buf+len), item->_get_startTime(ev));
    len += infoLen;

    //*****************************************************
    // Store length of endTime and endTime
    //*****************************************************
    infoLen = strlen(item->_get_endTime(ev)) + 1;

    memcpy((*buf+len), &infoLen, sizeof(long));
    len += sizeof(long);

    strcpy((char*)(*buf+len), item->_get_endTime(ev));
    len += infoLen;

    //*****************************************************
    // Store length of task and task
    //*****************************************************
    infoLen = strlen(item->_get_task(ev)) + 1;
```

**Figure 7.6** (continues)

```
                memcpy((*buf+len), &infoLen, sizeof(long));
                len += sizeof(long);

                strcpy((char*)(*buf+len), item->_get_task(ev));
                len += infoLen;
            }
    }

    SOM_Scope void SOMLINK somrSetState(Day *somSelf, Environment *ev,
                                                      string buf)
    {
        long totlen, seqlen;
        short len;
        long infoLen;
        WorkItem *entry;
        short i;
        char *start, *end, *task;
        DayData *somThis = DayGetData(somSelf);
        DayMethodDebug("Day","somrSetState");

        totlen = *(long *) buf;
        len = sizeof(long);

        seqlen = *( (unsigned long *)(buf + len) );
        len += sizeof(unsigned long);

        for (i=0; i < seqlen; i++)
        {
            //***********************************************
            // Get startTime
            //***********************************************
            infoLen = *( (long *)(buf+len) );
            len += sizeof(long);

            start = (char *)SOMMalloc(infoLen);
            memcpy(start, (buf + len), infoLen);
            len += infoLen;

            //***********************************************
            // Get endTime
            //***********************************************
            infoLen = *( (long *)(buf+len) );
            len += sizeof(long);
```

**Figure 7.6** (continues)

```
                    end = (char *)SOMMalloc(infoLen);
                    memcpy(end, (buf + len), infoLen);
                    len += infoLen;


                    //***********************************************
                    // Get task
                    //***********************************************
                    infoLen = *( (long *)(buf+len) );
                    len += sizeof(long);

                    task = (char *)SOMMalloc(infoLen);
                    memcpy(task, (buf + len), infoLen);
                    len += infoLen;


                    //***********************************************
                    // Create WorkItem
                    //***********************************************
                    entry = new WorkItem;
                    entry->mkEntry(ev, start, end, task);

                    sequenceElement(somThis->workList,i) = entry;
                    SOMFree(start);
                    SOMFree(end);
                    SOMFree(task);
                }

            sequenceLength(somThis->workList) = seqlen;
        }

    SOM_Scope void SOMLINK somrDoDirective(Day *somSelf, Environment *ev,
                                           string str)
    {
        DayData *somThis = DayGetData(somSelf);
        DayMethodDebug("Day","somrDoDirective");

        if (strcmp(str, "BECOME_STAND_ALONE") == 0)
        {
            somSelf->notifyView(ev, WM_STAND_ALONE);
        }
        else
        {
            if (strcmp(str, "CONNECTION_LOST") == 0)
            {
```

**Figure 7.6** (continues)

```
                        somSelf->notifyView(ev, WM_CONNECTION_LOST);
    }
    else
    {
        if (strcmp(str, "CONNECTION_REESTABLISHED") == 0)
        {
            somSelf->notifyView(ev, WM_CONNECTION_REESTABLISH);
        }
        else
        {
            if (strcmp(str, "LOST_RECOVERABLILTY") == 0)
            {
                somSelf->notifyView(ev, WM_LOST_RECOVER);
            }
        }
    }

    Day_parent_SOMRReplicbl_somrDoDirective(somSelf, ev, str);
}
```

**Figure 7.6** continued

The C++ implementation for the *CalendarDir* class is the same as the one in
the Distributed Calendar. Refer to Section 5.10.4 on page 110 for the details.

### The DayView Class

The IDL for the *DayView* class is given in Figure 7.8. The *DayView* class is used
to encapsulate the view for the *Day* class. Recall that our view of the calendar
objects is a GUI client, *DayPlannerWindow*, written using C++ classes. We would
like to store a pointer to the *DayPlannerWindow* object so that we can notify it
when there is a state change in the *Day* object. However, because IDL is language neutral, it does not allow the specification of C++ objects as parameter
types. To overcome the problem, we declare an attribute *owner* of type *void ** , so
we can store the pointer to the C++ object. We then cast it to the appropriate C++
class in the code.

The *DayView* class introduces one new method, *notifyDayPlanner*. This
method sends a message to the *DayPlannerWindow* object , so it can refresh its
display.

The C++ implementation for the *DayView* class is shown in Figure 7.9.

### The GUI Client

The PLANNER program is modified to work with the Replication Framework. The
listing for *planwin.hpp* appears in Figure 7.10.

```
#ifndef caldir_idl
#define caldir_idl

#include <somobj.idl>

interface Day;
interface CalendarDir : SOMObject
{
      const unsigned long MAXDAY = 7;

      attribute sequence<Day, MAXDAY> weekList;

      long addDay(in short daynum, in Day entry);
      Day getDay(in short daynum);

      #ifdef __SOMIDL__
      implementation
      {
        releaseorder : _get_weekList, _set_weekList,
                       addDay, getDay;

        somInit: override;
        somUninit: override;
        dllname = "calendar.dll";
      };
      #endif
};
#endif
```

**Figure 7.7**  The CalendarDir IDL

In addition to inheriting from the *IFrameWindow, ICommandHandler,* and *ISelectHandler* classes, the class *DayPlannerWindow* also inherits from the *PlannerHandler* class. The *PlannerHandler* class processes events that are specific to the *DayPlannerWindow.* A summary of each member function in *DayPlannerWindow* follows.

- The *plannerMessage* function provides the handling for a refresh event. When a WM_REFRESH event is received, it calls the *refreshListBox* function to refresh the list of work items for the current day. When a directive event is received, it pops up a message box to inform the user.
- The *setupClient* function creates a multi-cell canvas control as the client window. It also creates the spin-button controls, the static text controls, the entry field control, and the list box control, and places them on the multi-cell canvas.

```
#ifndef dayview_idl
#define dayview_idl

#include <somobj.idl>

interface DayView : SOMObject
{
    attribute void *owner;
    void notifyDayPlanner(in long eventId);

    #ifdef __SOMIDL__
    implementation
    {
      releaseorder: _get_owner, _set_owner,
                    notifyDayPlanner;
    };
     #endif
};
#endif
```

**Figure 7.8** The DayView IDL

```
/*
 * This file was generated by the SOM Compiler and Emitter Framework.
 * Generated using:
 * SOM Emitter emitxtm: 2.7
 */

#define DayView_Class_Source
#include <dayview.xih>
#include <iwindow.hpp>

SOM_Scope void SOMLINK notifyDayPlanner(DayView *somSelf, Environment *ev,
                                        long eventId)
{
    DayViewData *somThis = DayViewGetData(somSelf);
    IWindow *winOwner;
    DayViewMethodDebug("DayView","notifyDayPlanner");

    winOwner = (IWindow *) somThis->owner;
    winOwner->postEvent(eventId);
}
```

**Figure 7.9** The DayView class implementation

```
#ifndef PLANWIN_HPP
#define PLANWIN_HPP

#include <iframe.hpp>
#include <icmdhdr.hpp>
#include <imcelcv.hpp>
#include <ilistbox.hpp>
#include <iselhdr.hpp>
#include <istring.hpp>
#include <istattxt.hpp>
#include <imenubar.hpp>
#include <ispinbt.hpp>
#include <ientryfd.hpp>
#include <ithread.hpp>

#include <somr.xh>
#include <eman.xh>

#include "week.h"
#include "workitem.xh"
#include "day.xh"
#include "caldir.xh"

#include "planhdr.hpp"

class DayPlannerWindow : public IFrameWindow,
                         public ICommandHandler,
                         public ISelectHandler,
                         public PlannerHandler
{
    public:
        DayPlannerWindow (unsigned long windowId);
        ~DayPlannerWindow();
        void checkEvents();

    protected:
        Boolean command(ICommandEvent& cmdevt);
        Boolean selected(IControlEvent& evt);
        Boolean plannerMessage(IEvent& evt);

    private:
        setupClient();
```

**Figure 7.10** The DayPlannerWindow header (continues)

```
                setupData();
                showItems(short day);
                book(char *start, char *end, char *desc);
                remove(char *start, char *end, char *desc);
                refreshListBox();
                registerView(Day *day);

                IEntryField *descT;
                IStaticText *weekday, *start, *end, *desc;
                ISpinButton *startT, *endT;

                IMultiCellCanvas *mc;
                IMenuBar *menuBar;
                short menuFlag;

                IListBox *listBox;
                IListBox::Cursor *cursor;

                IThread thread;
                SOMEEMan *emgr;
                SOMR *repobj;
                Environment *ev;
                CalendarDir *curDirEntry;
                Day *curDay;
        };

class eventMgrThread : public IThreadFn
{
        public:
            eventMgrThread(DayPlannerWindow &obj)
            : planObj(obj)
            {;}

            void run() { planObj.checkEvents(); }

        private:
            DayPlannerWindow &planObj;
};

#endif
```

**Figure 7.10** continued

- The *setupData* function initializes the RSOM environment and the Event Manager. It creates a new *CalendarDir* object and seven *Day* objects. Each *Day* object is given a name. In addition, it calls *registerView* to register a view object with each *Day* object. It then starts a secondary thread for the SOM Event Manager.
- The *showItems* function displays the list of activities for a particular day.
- The *book* function creates a new *WorkItem* object and adds it to the activitiy list for the day.
- The *remove* function removes the selected *WorkItem* for the day.
- The *refreshListBox* function redisplays the work items for the current day.
- The *registerView* function creates a new *DayView* object and registers it with the specified *Day* object.

The listing for the source file *planwin.cpp* is given in Figure 7.11.

### The PlannerHandler Class

The *PlannerHandler* class provides a handler for the message that is specific to the *DayPlannerWindow*. It overrides the *dispatchHandlerEvent* member function and provides a virtual callback function to process the message. The listing for *planhdr.hpp* is shown in Figure 7.12. For more information on handlers and events, please refer to the Redbook for the IBM User Interface Class Library.

The listing for *planhdr.cpp* is shown in Figure 7.13 (p. 212). It filters the events so it will only call the *plannerMessage* function, when it is one of the expected events. The default implementation returns FALSE so that an event can be passed on to other handlers. The *plannerMessage* is overridden in the *DayPlannerWindow* to provide the specific event handling required.

### The Makefile

The source files for building the *calendar* DLL are *workitem.cpp*, *day.cpp*, *caldir.cpp*, *initfunc.cpp*, and *calendar.def*.

The source file *dayview.cpp* contains the *DayView* class. The source file *planhdr.cpp* contains the *PlannerHandler* class. The *planwin.hpp*, *planwin.cpp*, *dayview.hpp*, *dayview.cpp*, *planhdr.hpp*, *planhdr.cpp*, *week.rc*, and *week.h* source files are needed to build the GUI client.

The makefile for building the Replicated Calendar application is given in Figure 7.14 (p. 213). It includes dependencies to build the Interface Repository. The classes that make up the *calendar* DLL are compiled into the Interface Repository.

### Building the Application

To build the application, invoke NMAKE using the makefile shown in Figure 7.14.

### Running the Application

TCP/IP must be started before you can run the Replicated Calendar. The environment variable SOMIR must be set to point to the Interface Repository that

```
#define INCL_DOS
#define INCL_ERRORS
#define INCL_DOSPROCESS
#define INCL_DOSSEMAPHORES

#include <os2.h>
#include <stdio.h>
#include <stdlib.h>
#include <ctype.h>
#include <errno.h>

#include <eventmsk.h>

#include <ifont.hpp>
#include <ititle.hpp>
#include <iostream.h>
#include <fstream.h>
#include <imsgbox.hpp>

#include "planwin.hpp"

#include "dayview.xh"

HMTX keyboard_sem;

void main(int argc, char *argv[], char *envp[])
{
   DayPlannerWindow mainWindow(WND_MAIN);
   Application::current().run();
}

DayPlannerWindow :: DayPlannerWindow(unsigned long windowId)
   : IFrameWindow (IFrameWindow::defaultStyle(), windowId)
{
   IString title("Weekly Calendar");

   ICommandHandler::handleEventsFor(this);

   menuBar = new IMenuBar(WND_MAIN,this);
   menuBar->setAutoDeleteObject();                 // auto delete when window is closed
   menuBar->checkItem(MI_BASE);
   menuFlag = MI_BASE;
```

**Figure 7.11** The DayPlannerWindow implementation (continues)

```
        setupClient();
        setupData();

        if ( IWindow::desktopWindow()->size() > ISize(1000,700) )
        {
            sizeTo(ISize(460,330));
        }
        else // VGA
        {
            sizeTo(ISize(360,240));
        }

        setFocus();

        // Enable PlannerHandler to handle user-defined events
        PlannerHandler::handleEventsFor(this);
        show();
    }

    DayPlannerWindow :: setupClient()
    {
        mc = new IMultiCellCanvas(WND_CANVAS, this, this);
        mc->setAutoDeleteObject();
        setClient(mc);

        weekday = new IStaticText(WND_TEXT, mc, mc);
        weekday->setAutoDeleteObject();
        weekday->setText("Monday");

        start = new IStaticText(WND_TEXT, mc, mc);
        start->setAutoDeleteObject();
        start->setText("Start ");

        startT = new ISpinButton(WND_START,mc,mc);
        startT->setAutoDeleteObject();
        startT->setInputType(ISpinButton::numeric);
        startT->setRange(IRange(1,24));
        startT->setCurrent(8);
        startT->setLimit(2);
        startT->readOnly;

        end = new IStaticText(WND_TEXT, mc, mc);
```

**Figure 7.11**  (continues)

```
        end->setAutoDeleteObject();
        end->setText("End ");

        endT = new ISpinButton(WND_END,mc,mc);
        endT->setAutoDeleteObject();
        endT->setInputType(ISpinButton::numeric);
        endT->setRange(IRange(1,24));
        endT->setCurrent(6);
        endT->setLimit(2);
        endT->readOnly;

        desc = new IStaticText(WND_TEXT, mc, mc);
        desc->setAutoDeleteObject();
        desc->setText("Description");

        descT = new IEntryField(WND_DESC, mc, mc);
        descT->setAutoDeleteObject();

        listBox = new IListBox(WND_LISTBOX,mc,mc,
                              IRectangle(),
                              IListBox::defaultStyle() |
                              IControl::tabStop);
        listBox->setAutoDeleteObject();

        cursor = new IListBox::Cursor(*listBox);
        ISelectHandler::handleEventsFor(listBox);

        mc->addToCell(weekday,2,2);
        mc->addToCell(start, 2,4);
        mc->addToCell(startT, 2,5);
        mc->addToCell(end, 4,4);
        mc->addToCell(endT, 4,5);
        mc->addToCell(desc, 6,4);
        mc->addToCell(descT, 6,5);
        mc->addToCell(listBox,2,7,5,1);

        mc->setRowHeight(3,2,true);
        mc->setRowHeight(6,2,true);
        mc->setRowHeight(8,2,true);
        mc->setColumnWidth(3,2,true);
        mc->setColumnWidth(5,2,true);
        mc->setColumnWidth(7,2,true);
    }
```

**Figure 7.11**  (continues)

```
DayPlannerWindow :: setupData()
{
    short i, found;
    Day *day;
    char *dayName[] = {"Sun", "Mon", "Tue", "Wed", "Thu", "Fri", "Sat"};
    ULONG semattr;
    long rc;

    semattr = DC_SEM_SHARED;
    rc = DosCreateMutexSem((PSZ) NULL,
                           (PHMTX)&keyboard_sem, semattr, 0);
    if (rc != 0)
    {
        FILE *fp;
        fp = fopen("debug.dat", "a");
        fprintf(fp, "Error Allocating shared semaphore: rc = %d \n",rc);
        fclose(fp);
         exit(1);
    }

    ev = SOM_CreateLocalEnvironment();
    repobj = new SOMR();
    emgr = new SOMEEMan();

    curDirEntry = new CalendarDir();
    for (i=0; i < 7 ; i++ )
    {
        day = new Day();
        day->_set_date(ev,i);
        day->initReplica(ev, dayName[i]);          // set replica name
        curDirEntry->addDay(ev,i,day);
        registerView(day);                         // register view
    }

    //*************************************************************************
    // Set current day to Monday and show any existing activities
    //*************************************************************************
    curDay = curDirEntry->getDay(ev,1);
    showItems(1);

    //*************************************************************************
    // Start a new thread for SOM event manager
    //*************************************************************************
```

**Figure 7.11**  (continues)

```
        eventMgrThread *emgrFn = new eventMgrThread( *this );

    // Dispatch thread to run function
    thread.start( emgrFn );
}


//**************************************************************
// Register a DayView object with the Day object
//**************************************************************
DayPlannerWindow :: registerView(Day *day)
{
    DayView *dv;

    dv = new DayView;
    dv->_set_owner(ev, (void *)this);

    // register the notifyDayPlanner method
    day->registerView(ev, dv, "notifyDayPlanner");
}

DayPlannerWindow :: ~DayPlannerWindow()
{
    short i,j;
    _IDL_SEQUENCE_WorkItem alist;

    for (i=0; i < 7; i++ )
    {
        curDay = curDirEntry->getDay(ev,i);
        alist = curDay->_get_workList(ev);

        //********************************************************
        // Destroy each WorkItem from the Day object
        //********************************************************
        for (j=0; j < sequenceLength(alist) ; j++)
        {
                delete sequenceElement(alist,j);
        }
        //************************************************
        // Destroy DayView object
        //************************************************
        delete (curDay->getViewObject(ev));

        delete curDay;
    }
```

**Figure 7.11**  (continues)

```
        delete emgr;
        delete repobj;

        SOM_DestroyLocalEnvironment(ev);
}

Boolean DayPlannerWindow :: command(ICommandEvent & cmdEvent)
{
    IMessageBox msgbox(this);

    switch (cmdEvent.commandId())
    {
        case MI_ADD:
        if ( !(descT->text().size()) )
        {
            msgbox.show("Enter a description", IMessageBox::okButton);
        }
        else
        {
            IString str;
            IString pad("0");
            IString trial(":00 ");
            IString blank(" ");
            IString sstr(startT->value());
            IString estr(endT->value());

            if ( startT->value() < 10 )
            {
                sstr = pad + sstr;
            }
            if ( endT->value() < 10 )
            {
                estr = pad + estr;
            }

            sstr = sstr + trial;
            estr = estr + trial;

            str = sstr + estr + descT->text();
            listBox->addAscending(str);
            book( sstr, estr, descT->text() );
        }
```

**Figure 7.11**  (continues)

```
        return true;
        break;

    case MI_DEL:
        if ( cursor->isValid() )
        {
            IString item, startTime, endTime, task;

            item = listBox->elementAt(*cursor);
            startTime = item.subString(1,6);
            endTime = item.subString(7,6);
            task = item.subString(13);
            remove(startTime, endTime, task);
            listBox->removeAt(*cursor);
        }
        return true;
        break;

    case MI_SUN:
        weekday->setText("Sunday");
        showItems(0);
        return true;

    case MI_MON:
        weekday->setText("Monday");
        showItems(1);
        return true;

    case MI_TUE:
        weekday->setText("Tuesday");
        showItems(2);
        return true;

    case MI_WED:
        weekday->setText("Wednesday");
        showItems(3);
        return true;

    case MI_THU:
        weekday->setText("Thursday");
        showItems(4);
        return true;
```

**Figure 7.11**  (continues)

```cpp
        case MI_FRI:
           weekday->setText("Friday");
           showItems(5);
           return true;

        case MI_SAT:
           weekday->setText("Saturday");
           showItems(6);
           return true;

        case MI_QUIT:
           close();
           return true;
           break;
        }

        return false;
    }


//****************************************************
// Handler for user-defined messages
//****************************************************
Boolean DayPlannerWindow :: plannerMessage(IEvent& evt)
{
    IMessageBox msgbox(this);

    if (evt.eventId() == WM_REFRESH)
    {
       refreshListBox();
       return true;
    }
    if (evt.eventId() == WM_STAND_ALONE)
    {
       msgbox.show("Stand alone", IMessageBox::okButton);
       return true;
    }
    if (evt.eventId() == WM_CONNECTION_LOST)
    {
       msgbox.show("Connection lost", IMessageBox::okButton);
       return true;
    }
```

**Figure 7.11**   (continues)

```cpp
        if (evt.eventId() == WM_CONNECTION_REESTABLISH)
        {
            msgbox.show("Connection reestablished", IMessageBox::okButton);
            return true;
        }
        if (evt.eventId() == WM_LOST_RECOVER)
        {
            msgbox.show("Lost recoverability", IMessageBox::okButton);
            return true;
        }
         return false;
}


Boolean DayPlannerWindow :: selected(IControlEvent & evt)
{
    cursor->setToFirst();
    return true;
}


DayPlannerWindow :: showItems(short day)
{
    menuBar->uncheckItem(menuFlag);              // uncheck previous day
    menuBar->checkItem(MI_BASE+day);             // check selected day
    menuFlag = MI_BASE + day;

    curDay = curDirEntry->getDay(ev,day);
    refreshListBox();
}


DayPlannerWindow :: refreshListBox()
{
    _IDL_SEQUENCE_WorkItem alist;
    short i;
    IString str;

    alist = curDay->_get_workList(ev);

    listBox->removeAll();

    for (i=0; i < sequenceLength(alist); i++)
    {
        str = "";
```

**Figure 7.11**  (continues)

```
            str = str +
                    sequenceElement(alist,i)->_get_startTime(ev) +
                    sequenceElement(alist,i)->_get_endTime(ev) +
                    sequenceElement(alist,i)->_get_task(ev);
            listBox->addAscending(str);
        }
    }


    DayPlannerWindow :: book(char *start, char * end, char *task)
    {
        while (DosRequestMutexSem(keyboard_sem, SEM_INDEFINITE_WAIT) != 0);

        curDay->book2(ev, start, end, task);

        DosReleaseMutexSem(keyboard_sem);
    }


    DayPlannerWindow :: remove(char *start, char * end, char *task)
    {
        while (DosRequestMutexSem(keyboard_sem, SEM_INDEFINITE_WAIT) != 0);

        curDay->removeItem(ev, start, end, task);

        DosReleaseMutexSem(keyboard_sem);
    }


    //***********************************************************************
    // SOM Event Manager loop. It runs on its own thread
    //***********************************************************************
    void DayPlannerWindow :: checkEvents()
    {
        short rc;
        IMessageBox msgbox(this);

        while (1)
        {
            // Wait for 500 milliseconds
            DosSleep(500);

            // Wait on and take the mutual exclusion semaphore
            while (DosRequestMutexSem(keyboard_sem, SEM_INDEFINITE_WAIT) != 0);
```

**Figure 7.11**   (continues)

```
            // When control is obtained, process events
            emgr->someProcessEvent(ev, EMProcessTimerEvent | EMProcessSinkEvent);

            // Release the semaphore
            DosReleaseMutexSem(keyboard_sem);
        }
    }
```

**Figure 7.11**  continued

```
    #ifndef PLANHDR_HPP
    #define PLANHDR_HPP

    #include <ihandler.hpp>
    #include "eventid.h"                        // constants for event Ids

    class PlannerHandler : public IHandler
    {
      public:
          Boolean dispatchHandlerEvent( IEvent& evt);

      protected:
          virtual Boolean plannerMessage( IEvent& evt);
    };
    #endif
```

**Figure 7.12**  The PlannerHandler header file

contains the IDLs for the calendar classes. The environment variable SOMSOCK-
ETS must also be set. For example, you can use the following settings:

```
set SOMIR=%SOMBASE%\etc\som.ir;som.ir
set SOMSOCKETS=TCPIPSockets
```

The file *rsomenv.cmd* is provided to set up the enviromental variables.
Start the PLANNER program by typing:

```
> planner
```

Add some activities to the calendar. For example, a department meeting is
scheduled for Monday, from 10:00 to 11:00. A tennis game is booked for Tuesday,
from 17:00 to 18:00.

```
#include "planhdr.hpp"
#include <stdio.h>

Boolean PlannerHandler :: dispatchHandlerEvent(IEvent &evt)
{
    if (evt.eventId() == WM_REFRESH ||
      evt.eventId() == WM_STAND_ALONE ||
      evt.eventId() == WM_CONNECTION_LOST ||
      evt.eventId() == WM_CONNECTION_REESTABLISH ||
      evt.eventId() == WM_LOST_RECOVER)
    {
        //***********************************************************
        //events that are of interest to DayPlannerWindow
        //***********************************************************
        return plannerMessage(evt);
    }

    return false;
}

Boolean PlannerHandler :: plannerMessage(IEvent& evt)
{
    // Provides default return
    return false;
}
```

**Figure 7.13** The PlannerHandler implementation

In a separate window, run *rsomenv.cmd* to set up the environment variables. Then type "planner" to start a second PLANNER program. Notice how all the activities that were added in the first PLANNER program appear in the second PLANNER program. This is because the Replication Framework synchronizes the two replicas of the "Mon" object. If you add or delete an activity from either calendar, it will be automatically updated on the other calendar. You do not need to refresh the list explicitly. The multi-cast capability of RSOM, and the view notification mechanism that we implemented, gave us this function.

Try starting more PLANNER programs and terminating some and observe the following effects.

- When you start another PLANNER program, its data is synchronized with the rest.

```
.SUFFIXES:
.SUFFIXES: .idl .xih .xh .cpp .obj .def
#
# Need /Ge- to build DLL
#
OBJS = caldir.obj workitem.obj day.obj initfunc.obj
OBJS2 = dayview.obj planhdr.obj

UILIB = dde4muii.lib dde4cci.lib dde4mbsi.lib os2386.lib

all: calendar.dll planner.exe som.ir

.cpp.obj:
        cc /c+ /Ge- -I. $<
.idl.xh:
        sc -sxh $*.idl
.idl.xih:
        sc -sxih $*.idl
.idl.cpp:
        sc -sxc $*.idl

caldir.obj: caldir.xih caldir.xh caldir.cpp
caldir.xih: caldir.idl
caldir.xh: caldir.idl
caldir.cpp: caldir.xih

workitem.obj: workitem.xih workitem.xh workitem.cpp
workitem.xih: workitem.idl
workitem.xh: workitem.idl
workitem.cpp: workitem.xih

day.obj: day.xih day.xh day.cpp
day.xih: day.idl
day.xh: day.idl
day.cpp: day.xih

dayview.xih: dayview.idl
```

**Figure 7.14** The replicated PLANNER Makefile (continues)

```
dayview.xh: dayview.idl
dayview.cpp: dayview.xih

initfunc.obj: initfunc.cpp


#
# Build the DLL
#
calendar.dll: $(OBJS) calendar.def
        icc @<<
        /Fe"calendar.dll" $(OBJS) calendar.def
        somtk.lib
<<
        implib calendar.lib calendar.def
#
# Build the executables
#
planwin.obj: planwin.cpp planwin.hpp week.h
        cc /c+ /Gd+ /Gm+ /Si+ -I. planwin.cpp
planner.exe: $(OBJS2) planwin.obj week.res
        icc /Fe"planner.exe" $(OBJS2) planwin.obj /B" /pm:pm /noi" \
        $(UILIB) somtk.lib calendar.lib planner.def
        rc week.res planner.exe

planhdr.obj: planhdr.cpp planhdr.hpp
        icc /c+ /Gd+ /Gm+ /Si+ -I. planhdr.cpp
dayview.obj: dayview.cpp dayview.xh dayview.xih
        icc /c+ /Gd+ /Gm+ /Si+ -I. dayview.cpp

week.res: week.rc week.h
        rc -r week.rc
#
# Put the IDL descriptions into the Interface Repository
#
som.ir: caldir.idl workitem.idl day.idl
        sc -sir -u workitem.idl
        sc -sir -u day.idl
        sc -sir -u caldir.idl
```

**Figure 7.14** continued

- When you terminate a PLANNER program, existing PLANNER programs continue to function.
- When you terminate a PLANNER program, message boxes pop up with a "Connection Lost" message.

The "Connection Lost" message occurs when the *master* replica terminates or crashes. The RSOM Framework uses a *master/shadow* implementation model. One replica is designated as a *master,* and the other replicas are *shadows*. If a shadow crashes, it does not affect the group of replicas, and they continue to operate. However, if the master crashes, it takes some time before the shadows recognize this and elect a new master. The Framework sends the CONNECTION_LOST directive. You should not update the replica until a connection has been re-established. If a connection cannot be re-established by the Framework, you should reconnect the application.

A calendar can manifest itself in many different forms. A weekly planner like the one we have implemented is one form. Another form might be a daily reminder that only displays the calendar events for each day and beeps five minutes before each scheduled event. As an exercise, you might want to implement the following: Write a new GUI for a daily reminder and register its view with the replicated *Day* class so that whenever a new event is added to the weekly planner, the daily reminder will be notified as well.

**Summary**

This chapter explored an alternate implementation for sharing objects across different address spaces using the RSOM Framework. Although we have not made the replicated objects persistent, one could easily add this by inheriting from both *SOMRReplicbl* and *SOMPPersistentObject*.

The choice between DSOM and RSOM depends on a number of factors. While RSOM maintains a complete replica of an object in each process' address space, DSOM establishes a remote connection to the object which is maintained by a server process. For applications that involve multiple parties, and where the parties must feel like they are touching each other by receiving instantaneous feedback, RSOM might be a good candidate. For applications that require only the sharing of objects among multiple processes, with less emphasis on instantaneous feedback, DSOM might be sufficient.

Other factors that come into play include the availability and the limitations of each Framework. In the current release, RSOM does not support heterogeneous configuration. That is, one can only replicate objects within a single machine environment. The lack of support for composite objects in RSOM makes it difficult to support complex applications. Therefore, if any of these are required, DSOM could be your only choice.

# 8

# Working with the Interface Repository

The Interface Repository (IR) is a database that stores interface definitions. The SOMobjects Developer Toolkit includes an *Interface Repository emitter.* It can be invoked through the SOM compiler to create or update the Interface Repository. In addition, a set of classes are defined to provide access to the objects defined in the IR. This set of classes is known as the Interface Repository Framework. You can write programs to find information stored in the IDLs through the programming interfaces in the Interface Repository Framework.

## 8.1  WHO USES THE INTERFACE REPOSITORY

The Interface Repository is used by the Distributed, Persistence, and Replication Frameworks. All of them use the Interface Repository to find the class definitions and the method signatures. DSOM uses the information in the IR when creating local proxies and interpreting request messages. PSOM uses the IR to determine whether a class or its attributes are persistent. RSOM uses the IR to determine if a class is replicable.

The Interface Repository also assists in the dynamic loading of classes. The default implementation for methods like **somFindClass** and **somLocateClass-File** consult the IR for the value of the *dllname* modifier of the class.

## 8.2  MANAGING THE INTERFACE REPOSITORY

The Interface Repository is composed of a list of files that are located by the environment variable. When you install SOM, the install program adds the following statement to your "config.sys" file, assuming that SOM is installed on your C drive:

```
set SOMIR=C:\SOM\etc\som.ir;som.ir
```

The *%SOMBASE%\etc\som.ir* file contains objects that describe all the types, classes, and methods provided by the various Frameworks of the SOMobjects Developer Toolkit. Since all new classes will be derived from these predefined SOM classes, this file should always be included in your SOMIR path. The second file, som.ir, refers to the IR file in your current directory.

The Interface Repository emitter uses the environment variable SOMIR to locate the designated IR file. The SOMIR environment variable can consist of a list of files. The IR emitter will only update the last file that is on the list. If the file does not exist, the IR emitter creates it. If the SOMIR variable is not set, the IR emitter creates a file called "som.ir" in your current directory.

When running SOM programs that access the Interface Repository, the files that are listed by the SOMIR environment variable are processed from left to right. The SOM programs are not aware of the division of information across the separate files. The objects in the files appear as if they reside in a single interface repository file.

Therefore, by changing the environment variable SOMIR, you can control the interfaces that are visible to your programs. In a development environment, you might want to have separate IR files so you can separate the stable interfaces from those that are under development. For example, assuming the stable interfaces are in the file "c:\project\common.ir", developers John and Mary are working on separate classes. The SOMIR for John might be:

```
set SOMIR=%SOMBASE%\etc\som.ir;c:\project\common.ir;john.ir
```

And the SOMIR for Mary might be:

```
set SOMIR=%SOMBASE%\etc\som.ir;c:\project\common.ir;mary.ir
```

Since the Interface Repository emitter only updates the last file on the list, the changes made by John, when updating the IR, will not be reflected in Mary's IR. When either feels that the interfaces they are working on are stable enough, they can move the interfaces to the "common.ir" file so they can be included in other people's IRs.

In a production environment, it is also important to control your SOMIR settings. The path length and the size of each IR file have an impact on the performance for each IR access. The longer the path, or the bigger the file size, the slower the access. This is because the search for each class definition starts from the beginning of the path. The Interface Repository Framework does perform some internal caching to minimize the search. However, if you set the SOMIR variable to the minimum set of files that only contain the class definitions for your application, the performance of your application will be improved. In particular, if your application requires only a few of the base interfaces supplied with the SOM Toolkit in *%SOMBASE%\etc\som.ir*, then you can set SOMIR to point to a local som.ir and add in those extra base interfaces. This can have a big impact on performance.

## 8.3    BUILDING THE INTERFACE REPOSITORY

The Interface Repository is built by compiling IDL files with the Interface Repository emitter (**ir**) and the update (**-u**) option. For example, the following command compiles the file *car.idl* into the Interface Repository file that is designated by the SOMIR environment variable.

```
sc -u -sir car.idl
```

If the IR file does not exist, the Interface Repository emitter creates it. Otherwise, the Interface Repository emitter checks all the type information in the IDL source file being compiled for internal consistency and updates the contents of the IR file if necessary.

Note that it is also possible to invoke the Interface Repository emitter by simply using the **-u** option. In this case, the Interface Repository emitter, plus any other emitters that are indicated by the SMEMIT environment variable, will be run. By default, SMEMIT is set to run the emitters that emit C binding files (*.h* and *.ih*). For example, the following command compiles the file *car.idl* into the Interface Repository and generates the files *car.h* and *car.ih*.

```
sc -u car.idl
```

If the IDL source file contains private information that is defined using the __*PRIVATE*__ preprocessor macro, the SOM compiler will not compile the private information into the Interface Repository unless the **-p** option is also used. For example, the following command will place both the public and the private information in *car.idl* into the Interface Repository.

```
sc -up -sir car.idl
```

## 8.4    ACCESSING THE INTERFACE REPOSITORY

The Interface Repository Framework allows you to retrieve information from the Interface Repository. The information in the Interface Repository is maintained as a set of objects. The class names for these objects are listed below:

1. *Repository*: there is only one instance of this class for the entire Interface Repository. It contains modules, interfaces, constants, typedefs, and exceptions.

2. *ModuleDef*: an instance of this class exists for each **module** defined in an IDL file. It contains constants, typedefs, exceptions, interface definitions and other modules.
3. *InterfaceDef*: an instance of this class exists for each **interface** defined in an IDL file. It contains constants, types, exceptions, operations, and attributes.
4. *AttributeDef*: an instance of this class exists for each **attribute** defined in an IDL file.
5. *OperationDef*: an instance of this class exists for each **method** defined in an IDL file. It contains lists of parameters and exceptions raised by this method.
6. *ParameterDef*: an instance of this class exists for each **parameter** of each method defined in an IDL file.
7. *TypeDef*: an instance of this class exists for each **typedef**, **struct**, **enum**, or **union** defined in an IDL file.
8. *ConstantDef*: an instance of this class exists for each **constant** defined in an IDL file.
9. *ExceptionDef*: an instance of this class exists for each **exception** defined in an IDL file.

These objects are accessible from a program. They can be useful when an application needs to find information about an object it encounters at run-time. A common set of operations are defined for locating objects within the Interface Repository. These operations are defined using two generic interfaces, *Container* and *Contained*.

### 8.4.1    Understanding Container and Contained

The *Container* interface provides methods for locating objects that a particular container contains. *Repository, ModuleDef, InterfaceDef,* and *OperationDef* are all containers. They are derived from the *Container* interface and they can contain, or hold, other objects. For example, an *OperationDef* can contain *ParameterDefs*.

The *Contained* interface provides methods for accessing information in the specified contained object. *AttributeDef, ConstantDef, TypeDef, ParameterDef,* and *ExceptionDef* are all contained objects and are derived from the *Contained* interface. Each of them provides access to the corresponding definition in the Interface Repository. For example, an *AttributeDef* object returns information on an attribute definition in an IDL.

*ModuleDef, InterfaceDef,* and *OperationDef* are also contained objects. That is, they are derived from both the *Container* and *Contained* classes. This is because they are all contained by the *Repository* class.

### 8.4.2    The Container Class

The *Container* class provides three methods for navigating through a container to locate other objects.

1. **contents**—this method returns a list of objects contained by the specified *Container* object. It can be used to navigate the hierarchy of objects within the Interface Repository. For example, you can invoke this method on the *Repository* Container object. Then, for each object that is returned, if it is a *Container* object, invoke the **contents** method on it. This process can be repeated until you have iterated through each object in each container. The C syntax for **contents** follows:

```
sequence<Contained> _contents(container,      // pointer to Container object
                              env,             // pointer to Environment structure
                              limitType,       // what type of objects
                              excludeInherited);  // flag to include/exclude inherited obj
```

The parameter *container* is a pointer to a *Container* object whose contained objects are to be returned. The parameter *limitType* specifies what type of objects this method should return. It can be set to one of the following values: "AttributeDef", "ConstantDef", "ExceptionDef", "InterfaceDef", "ModuleDef", "ParameterDef", "OperationDef", "TypeDef", or "all". If it is set to "all", then objects of all interface types will be returned. Otherwise, only objects of the requested types are returned.

The parameter *excludeInherited* is a boolean. If it is set to TRUE, then any inherited objects will not be returned.

2. **describe_contents**—this method combines the operations of the **contents** method and the **describe** method described below.

3. **lookup_name**—this method locates an object by name within a specified *Container* object.

Objects that are containers inherit these navigation methods from the *Container* class. We will use the **contents** method to navigate through the *Repository* and the *InterfaceDef* objects in our Browser example in Section 8.6 on page 222.


### 8.4.3    The Contained Class

The *Contained* class provides the generic interface for all objects in the Interface Repository, since all objects in the Interface Repository, except the root *Repository* object, can be contained by some other objects. It provides the following methods:

1. **within**—this method returns a sequence of *Container* objects within the Interface Repository that contain the specified *Contained* object.

2. **describe**—this method returns a structure containing IDL information of the specified *Contained* object. The C syntax for **describe** follows:

```
Description _describe(contained,      // pointer to Container object
                      env);           // pointer to Environment structure
```

The structure of **Description** follows:

```
struct Description {
   Identifier  name;
    any        value;
};
```

The information that is returned in the **Description** structure depends on the type of the contained object. For example, if the contained object is an *AttributeDef*, the *name* field of the returned **Description** will contain the identifier "AttributeDescription" and the *value._value* field will contain a pointer to an **AttributeDescription** structure.

Every contained object has its own **Description** structure. For example, *ConstantDef* has a **ConstantDescription** structure, *InterfaceDef* has an **InterfaceDescription** structure. The structure of a **ConstantDescription** follows:

```
struct ConstantDescription {
   Identifier      name;          // non-unique name that identifies object within its containment
   RepositoryId    id;            // unique Id that identifies object in IR
   RepositoryId    defined_in;    // unique Id that identifies container for this ConstantDef object
   TypeCode        type;          // the type of this constant
   any             value;         // the value of this constant
};
```

### 8.4.4    The Repository Class

The *Repository* class provides global access to the Interface Repository. You can obtain an instance of the *Repository* class by using the *RepositoryNew()* macro in C, or by using the *new* operator in C++. Once you have a pointer to the *Repository* object, you can use methods like **contents** or **lookup_name** that it inherits from the *Container* class to look up any objects in the Interface Repository. The *Repository* class also introduces its own **lookup_id** and **lookup_modifier** methods for returning an object with a specified Repository ID.

All objects in the Interface Repository have both a *name* and a *Repository ID*. A name is not necessarily unique within an Interface Repository. However, it is unique within the context of the object that contains it. A Repository ID is guaranteed to be unique within an Interface Repository.

## 8.5    TypeCode

Much of the information contained in the Interface Repository is represented in the form of **TypeCode**s. A **TypeCode** is an architected way of describing everything known about a particular data type in the IDL, regardless of whether it is a built-in type, or a user-defined type.

Every **TypeCode** contains a *kind* field, which describes what it is, and a *parameter list*, which carries descriptive information for that particular kind of **TypeCode**. For example, the IDL type *long* has **TypeCode** *tk_long* and no parameters. The IDL type *sequence<char,10>* has **TypeCode** *tk_sequence* and two parameters, *10* and *char*. Table 8.1 lists the combinations of *kind* and *parameter list* as well as the type of the parameters and their functions.

As you can see, **TypeCode**s can be nested, so they can describe any kind of data. In the cases of *struct*, *union* and *enum*, they can have repeated members as indicated by the number "N" in the Parameters column.

A number of functions are provided to obtain information about a **TypeCode**. Some of them are listed below.

- **TypeCode_kind**—this function returns the kind of the specified **TypeCode**.
- **TypeCode_param_count**—this function returns the number of parameters in a given **TypeCode**.
- **TypeCode_parameter**—this function returns a specified parameter from a given **TypeCode**.


## 8.6    A SIMPLE IR BROWSER

The BROWSER program source code is presented in this section. Browser traverses the Interface Repository and prints out information on every interface definition. The main line creates an instance of the *Repository* class and invokes the **contents** method with the "all" option to retrieve all the objects in the Interface Repository. If an object is an *InterfaceDef*, then the *displayInterfaceDef* function is called to display the information on the interface definition. Note that another way is to invoke the **contents** method with the "InterfaceDef" option, but we want to show you how you can find out the type of the returned object by invoking the **describe** method.

Recall that an *InterfaceDef* can contain *ConstantDefs*, *TypeDefs*, *ExceptionDefs*, *AttributeDefs,* and *OperationDefs*. The *displayInterfaceDef* function prints out information on the constants, types, attributes, and methods contained in an interface definition. Although exceptions are not included, they can be added easily as an exercise.

The *browse.cpp* file is listed in Figure 8.1.


### 8.6.1    Constant Definition

The *displayConstantDef* function in the BROWSER program prints out the name, type, and value of a constant, as well as where it is defined. The following code excerpt illustrates how the type and the value of a constant is extracted from the *value* field in the **ConstantDescription** structure.

```
switch (TypeCode_kind(cd->value._type, ev))
{
    case tk_string:
```

**Table 8.1**  TypeCode functions and parameters

| TypeCode kind | Parameters | Type | Function |
|---|---|---|---|
| tk_null | 0 | - | - |
| tk_void | 0 | - | - |
| tk_short | 0 | - | - |
| tk_long | 0 | - | - |
| tk_ushort | 0 | - | - |
| tk_ulong | 0 | - | - |
| tk_float | 0 | - | - |
| tk_double | 0 | - | - |
| tk_boolean | 0 | - | - |
| tk_char | 0 | - | - |
| tk_octet | 0 | - | - |
| tk_any | 0 | - | - |
| tk_TypeCode | 0 | - | - |
| tk_Principal | 0 | - | - |
| tk_objref | 1 | string | The ID of the corresponding InterfaceDef in the Interface Repository |
| tk_struct | 2N + 1 | string | The name of the struct |
| | | | —— repeat for each member —— |
| | | string | The name of the struct member |
| | | TypeCode | The type of the struct member |
| tk_union | 3N + 2 | string | The name of union |
| | | TypeCode | The type of the discriminator |
| | | | —— repeat for each member —— |
| | | long | The name of the label |
| | | string | The name of the member |
| | | TypeCode | The type of the member |
| tk_enum | N + 1 | string | The name of the enum |
| | | | —— repeat for each enumerator —— |
| | | string | The name of the enumerator |
| tk_string | 1 | long | The maximum string length or 0. |
| tk_sequence | 2 | TypeCode | Element type in sequence |
| | | long | The maximum number of elements or 0. |
| tk_array | 2 | TypeCode | Element type in array |
| | | long | The maximum number of elements |
| tk_pointer | 1 | TypeCode | The type of the referenced datum |
| tk_self | 1 | string | The name of the referenced enclosing struct or union |
| tk_foreign | 3 | string | The name of the foreign type |
| | | string | The implementation context |
| | | long | The size of an instance |

```
#include <repostry.xh>
#include <containd.xh>
#include <stdio.h>
#include <intfacdf.xh>        // InterfaceDef include
#include <attribdf.xh>        // AttributeDef include
#include <constdef.xh>        // ConstantDef include
#include <typedef.xh>         // TypeDef include
#include <string.h>

Environment *ev;

// Function Prototypes
displayInterfaceDef(InterfaceDef *);
displayTypeDef(TypeDef *);
displayConstantDef(ConstantDef *);
displayTypeCode(TypeCode);
printType(TypeCode);


//*******************************************************************
// Simple Interface Repository Browser
//*******************************************************************
main(int argc, char *argv[], char *envp[])
{
   Repository *repo;
   _IDL_SEQUENCE_Contained allObj;
   short i ;

   ev = SOM_CreateLocalEnvironment();

   repo = new Repository();
   allObj = repo->contents(ev, "all", TRUE);

   for (i=0; i < sequenceLength(allObj); i++ )
   {
      Contained *contained;
      Description desc;

      contained = sequenceElement(allObj,i);
      desc = contained->describe(ev);

      if (strcmp(desc.name, "InterfaceDescription") == 0)
      {
```

**Figure 8.1** The BROWSER program (continues)

```
                              displayInterfaceDef( (InterfaceDef *) contained);
        }
    }
}

displayInterfaceDef(InterfaceDef *intdef)
{
    short i, j;
    FullInterfaceDescription fid;
    TypeCode tc;
    Description desc;
    InterfaceDescription *id;

    _IDL_SEQUENCE_Contained allObj;

    desc = intdef->describe(ev);
    id = (InterfaceDescription *) desc.value._value;
    printf("Interface Name: %s\n", id->name);

    //*************************************************************************
    // An Interface Defn can contain ConstantDef, TypeDef,
    // ExceptionDef, AttributeDef and OperationDef.
    // In the following, we display TypeDef and ConstantDef
    //*************************************************************************
    allObj = intdef->contents(ev, "all", TRUE);
    for (i=0; i < sequenceLength(allObj); i++ )
    {
        Contained *contained;
        Description desc;

        contained = sequenceElement(allObj,i);
        desc = contained->describe(ev);

        if (strcmp(desc.name, "ConstantDescription") == 0)
        {
            displayConstantDef( (ConstantDef *) contained);
        }
        if (strcmp(desc.name, "TypeDescription") == 0)
        {
            displayTypeDef( (TypeDef *) contained);
        }
    }
```

**Figure 8.1**  (continues)

```c
// Get a description of all the methods and attributes in the IR
fid = intdef->describe_interface(ev);


//***********************************************************
// Display all the attributes in this Interface Defn
//***********************************************************
_IDL_SEQUENCE_AttributeDescription attrd;
attrd = fid.attributes;

printf("List of attributes\n");
for (i=0; i< sequenceLength(attrd); i++)
{
    printf("<Attribute Name:> %s", sequenceElement(attrd,i).name);
    printf(" <Type:> ");
    printType(sequenceElement(attrd,i).type);

    if (sequenceElement(attrd,i).mode == AttributeDef_READONLY)
    {
        printf(" (readonly)");
    }
    printf("\n");
}


//***********************************************************
// Display all the methods in this Interface Defn
//***********************************************************
_IDL_SEQUENCE_OperationDescription opd;
opd = fid.operation;

printf("\nList of methods\n");
for (i=0; i < sequenceLength(opd); i++)
{
    printf("<Method Name:> %s <Return Type:> ",
    sequenceElement(opd,i).name);
    printType(sequenceElement(opd,i).result);
    printf("\n");

    //***************************************************
    // Display all parameters
    //***************************************************
    _IDL_SEQUENCE_ParameterDescription parmd;
```

**Figure 8.1**  (continues)

```
            parmd = sequenceElement(opd,i).parameter;
            for (j=0; j < sequenceLength(parmd); j++ )
            {
                    switch (sequenceElement(parmd,j).mode)
                    {
                       case ParameterDef_IN:
                                printf(" in ");
                                break;
                       case ParameterDef_OUT:
                                printf(" out ");
                                break;
                       default:
                                printf(" inout ");
                    }
                    printf("%s ", sequenceElement(parmd,j).name);
                    printType(sequenceElement(parmd,j).type);
                    printf("\n");
        }
 }
 printf("\n**********************************************\n");
}


displayTypeDef(TypeDef *typdef)
{
    Description desc;
    TypeDescription *td;

    desc = typdef->describe(ev);
    td = (TypeDescription *) desc.value._value;

    printf("Typedef %s defined in %s\n", td->name, td->defined_in);
    displayTypeCode(td->type);
    printf("\n");
}


displayConstantDef(ConstantDef *condef)
{
    Description desc;
    ConstantDescription *cd;

    desc = condef->describe(ev);
    cd = (ConstantDescription *) desc.value._value;
```

**Figure 8.1**  (continues)

```c
            printf("Constant %s defined in %s\n", cd->name, cd->defined_in);
            printf("<Type:> ");

            switch (TypeCode_kind(cd->value._type, ev))
            {
                case tk_string:
                        printf("string <Value:> %s\n", *((string *) cd->value._value));
                        break;
                case tk_long:
                        printf("long <Value:> %ld\n", *((long *) cd->value._value));
                        break;
                case tk_float:
                        printf("float <Value:> %f\n", *((float *) cd->value._value));
                        break;
                case tk_ushort:
                        printf("unsigned short <Value:> %d\n", *((unsigned short *) cd->value._value));
                        break;
                case tk_ulong:
                        printf("unsigned long <Value:> %d\n", *((unsigned long *) cd->value._value));
                        break;
            }
            printf("\n");
}

printType(TypeCode tc)
{
    switch (TypeCode_kind(tc, ev))
    {
        case tk_null:
                printf("null ");
                break;
        case tk_void:
                printf("void ");
                break;
        case tk_short:
                printf("short ");
                break;
        case tk_long:
                printf("long ");
                break;
```

**Figure 8.1**  (continues)

```
                    case tk_ushort:
                            printf("unsigned short ");
                            break;
                    case tk_ulong:
                            printf("unsigned long ");
                            break;
                    case tk_float:
                            printf("float ");
                            break;
                    case tk_double:
                            printf("double ");
                            break;
                    case tk_boolean:
                            printf("boolean ");
                            break;
                    case tk_char:
                            printf("char ");
                            break;
                    case tk_octet:
                            printf("octet ");
                            break;
                    case tk_any:
                            printf("any ");
                            break;
                    case tk_TypeCode:
                            printf("TypeCode ");
                            break;
                    case tk_Principal:
                            printf("Principal ");
                            break;
                    case tk_objref:
                            printf("Object Reference ");
                            break;
                    case tk_struct:
                            printf("struct ");
                            break;
                    case tk_union:
                            printf("union ");
                            break;
                    case tk_enum:
                            printf("enum ");
                            break;
```

**Figure 8.1**  (continues)

```
                case tk_string:
                        printf("string ");
                        break;
            case tk_sequence:
                        printf("sequence ");
                        break;
            case tk_array:
                        printf("array ");
                        break;
            case tk_pointer:
                        printf("pointer ");
                        break;
            case tk_self:
                        printf("Self ");
                        break;
            case tk_foreign:
                        printf("foreign ");
                        break;
        default:
                        printf("not valid data type\n");
                        break;
    }
}


//*********************************************************************
// Navigate TypeCode to display data types
//*********************************************************************
displayTypeCode(TypeCode tc)
{
    TypeCode membertc, seqtc;
    short i;
    any parm;
    long len;
    string memname;

    switch (TypeCode_kind(tc, ev))
    {
        case tk_short:
                    printf("short\n");
                    break;

        case tk_long:
```

**Figure 8.1**  (continues)

```
                    printf("long\n");
                    break;

            case tk_ushort:
                    printf("unsigned short\n");
                    break;

            case tk_ulong:
                    printf("unsigned long\n");
                    break;

            case tk_float:
                    printf("float\n");
                    break;

            case tk_double:
                    printf("double\n");
                    break;

            case tk_boolean:
                    printf("boolean\n");
                    break;

            case tk_char:
                    printf("char\n");
                    break;

            case tk_octet:
                    printf("octet\n");
                    break;

            case tk_any:
                    printf("any\n");
                    break;

            case tk_objref:
                    parm = TypeCode_parameter(tc, ev, 0);
                    printf("%s\n", *((string *)parm._value));
                    break;

            case tk_struct:
                    parm = TypeCode_parameter(tc, ev, 0);
```

**Figure 8.1**  (continues)

```c
        printf("<Structure:> %s\n", *((string *)parm._value));
        //*************************************************************
        // Get the name and type for each struct member
        //*************************************************************
        for (i=1; i < TypeCode_param_count(tc,ev); i+=2 )
        {
            parm = TypeCode_parameter(tc,ev,i);
            printf(" <Member Name:> %s", *((string *)parm._value));

            parm = TypeCode_parameter(tc,ev,i+1);
            printf(" <Member Type:> ");
            //*********************************************************************
            // Recursively call displayType to display the type of each member
            //*********************************************************************
            displayTypeCode( *( (TypeCode *)parm._value ) );
        }
        printf("\n");
        break;

case tk_union:
        parm = TypeCode_parameter(tc, ev, 0);
        printf("<Union:> %s\n", *((string *)parm._value));
        //*********************************************
        // Get the union switch type
        //*********************************************
        parm = TypeCode_parameter(tc, ev, 1);
        printf("<Discriminator Type:> ");
        printType( *((TypeCode *)parm._value) );

        for (i=2; i < TypeCode_param_count(tc,ev); i+=3)
        {
            // Get label value
            parm = TypeCode_parameter(tc,ev,i);
            printf("\n <Label:> %ld ", *((long *)parm._value) );

            // Get member name
            parm = TypeCode_parameter(tc,ev,i+1);
            memname = *((string *)parm._value);
```

**Figure 8.1**   (continues)

```
                // Get member type
                parm = TypeCode_parameter(tc,ev,i+2);
                printf("<Member Type:> ");
                printType( *((TypeCode *)parm._value) );
                printf(" <Member Name:> %s", memname);
            }
            printf("\n\n");
            break;

    case tk_enum:
            parm = TypeCode_parameter(tc, ev, 0);
            printf("<Enum:> %s\n", *((string *)parm._value));
            //**************************************************
            // Get the name for all enumerators
            //**************************************************
            for (i=1; i < TypeCode_param_count(tc,ev); i++ )
            {
                parm = TypeCode_parameter(tc,ev,i);
                printf(" <enumerator:> %s\n", *((string *)parm._value));
            }
            printf("\n");
            break;

    case tk_string:
            parm = TypeCode_parameter(tc, ev, 0);
            len = *((long *)parm._value);
            if (len != 0)
            {
                printf("string, maximum length: %ld\n", len);
            }
            else
            {
                printf("string\n");
            }
            break;

    case tk_sequence:
            printf("sequence\n");
            //**************************************************
```

**Figure 8.1**  (continues)

```c
                    // First parm contains the sequence type
                    //***************************************************
                    parm = TypeCode_parameter(tc, ev, 0);
                    printf("<Sequence Type:> ");
                    printType( *((TypeCode *)parm._value) );
                    //*************************************************************
                    // Second parm contains the sequence maximum len
                    //*************************************************************
                    parm = TypeCode_parameter(tc,ev,1);
                    len = *((long *)parm._value);
                    if (len != 0)
                    {
                        printf(" <Maximum Length:> %ld\n", len);
                    }
                    printf("\n");
                    break;

        case tk_array:
                    printf("array\n");
                    //********************************************
                    // First parm contains the array type
                    //********************************************
                    parm = TypeCode_parameter(tc, ev, 0);
                    printf("<Array Type:> ");
                    printType( *((TypeCode *)parm._value) );
                    //********************************************
                    // Second parm contains array size
                    //********************************************
                    parm = TypeCode_parameter(tc, ev, 1);
                    printf("<Size:> %ld\n", *((long *)parm._value));
                    break;

        default:
                    printf("not supported ...");
                    break;
    }
}
```

**Figure 8.1**  continued

```
                printf("string <Value:> %s\n", *((string *) cd->value._value));
                break;
        case tk_long:
                printf("long <Value:> %ld\n", *((long *) cd->value._value));
                break;

        ...
    }
```

The *value* field is of type **any**. Recall that the type **any** is made up of two fields, a **_type** field and a **_value** field. The **_type** field is a **TypeCode** that describes the data in the **_value** field. Therefore, we use the **TypeCode_kind** function to determine what the data type is, and extract the corresponding value by using the appropriate cast.

We did not code all of the possible valid types for a constant definition. We leave this as an easy exercise for the reader.

## 8.6.2   Type Definition

The *displayTypeDef* function in the BROWSER program prints out the name of the type and where it is defined and then calls *displayTypeCode* with the *type* field from the **TypeDescription** structure. The *type* field is a **TypeCode** that represents the type of the typedef.

The function *displayTypeCode* demonstrates how you can navigate a **Type-Code** to find out arbitrary complex type information. The following code is used to handle the type **struct**:

```
    case tk_struct:
            parm = TypeCode_parameter(tc, ev, 0);
            printf("<Structure:> %s\n", *((string *)parm._value));
            //****************************************************************
            // Get the name and type for each struct member
            //****************************************************************
            for (i=1; i < TypeCode_param_count(tc,ev); i+=2 )
            {
                parm = TypeCode_parameter(tc,ev,i);
                printf(" <Member Name:> %s", *((string *)parm._value));

                parm = TypeCode_parameter(tc,ev,i+1);
                printf(" <Member Type:> ");
                //**********************************************************************
                // Recursively call displayType to display the type of each member
                //**********************************************************************
                    displayTypeCode( *( (TypeCode *)parm._value ) );
            }
            printf("\n");
            break;
```

Recall that a **tk_struct** has 2N+1 parameters, where the first parameter is the name of the *struct*, and the next two parameters are repeated for the name and the type of a *struct member*. We use the function **TypeCode_param_count** to obtain the number of parameters, and **TypeCode_parameter** to obtain the parameters from the **TypeCode**. Since the type of the *struct member* is also a **TypeCode**, we call *displayTypeCode* recursively so that we can display the type of the *struct member*.

### 8.6.3    Attribute and Method Definition

The *InterfaceDef* class introduces a new method, **describe_interface**, that returns a description of all the methods and attributes of an interface definition. The *displayInterfaceDef* function in the BROWSER program invokes it.

```
fid = intdef->describe_interface(ev);
```

The returned structure is a **FullInterfaceDescription**.

```
struct FullInterfaceDescription {
    Identifier                                              name;
    RepositoryId                                            id;
    RepositoryId                                            defined_in;
    sequence<OperationDef::OperationDescription> operation;
    sequence<AttributeDef::AttributeDescription>    attributes;
};
```

The *displayInterfaceDef* function iterates through the *attribute* sequence to print out the name and type of each attribute. If an attribute is readonly, it will be indicated.

Similarly, the *operation* sequence is looped through to print out the name, return type, and parameters for each method.

### 8.6.4    Running the Program

Make sure the environment variable SOMIR is set. The BROWSE program will return all the interface definitions that are in the interface repository list. You might want to set SOMIR to a smaller subset of IRs if you do not want to see the information from the pre-defined SOM classes.

You can use the *test.idl* file shown in Figure 8.2 as a test case. It contains various type, attribute, and method definitions.

Figure 8.3 shows the output list for the *Test* interface. Observe the output for the struct *Dummy* . The types that are within *Dummy* are printed out because of the recursion.

```
#include <somobj.idl>
interface Test: SOMObject
{
    enum Fruit { apple, orange, strawberry };

    struct Dummy {
      short x, y;
      SOMObject obj;
      string name;
      Fruit afruit;
      sequence<Fruit, 50> flist;
      long counts[10];
    };

    union Foo switch (long)
    {
      case 1: long x;
      case 2: float y;
      default: char z;
    };

    const unsigned long MAXSIZE = 50;

    attribute Foo myfoo;
    attribute double mydouble;
    readonly attribute any anyvalue;
    attribute sequence<long,MAXSIZE> longList;

    void add(in string name);
    string query(in short index, inout octet aByte);
    long print(out boolean status);

    #ifdef __SOMIDL__
    implementation
    {
      releaseorder : _get_myfoo, _set_myfoo,
                     _get_mydouble, _set_mydouble,
                     _get_anyvalue, _set_anyvalue,
                     _get_longList, _set_longList,
                     add, query, print;
    };
    #endif
};
```

**Figure 8.2** An IDL to illustrate the BROWSER program

```
Interface Name: Test
Typedef Fruit defined in ::Test
<Enum:> Fruit
   <enumerator:> apple
   <enumerator:> orange
   <enumerator:> strawberry

Typedef Dummy defined in ::Test
<Structure:> Dummy
   <Member Name:> x                 <Member Type:> short
   <Member Name:> y                 <Member Type:> short
   <Member Name:> obj               <Member Type:> ::SOMObject
   <Member Name:> name              <Member Type:> string
   <Member Name:> afruit            <Member Type:> <Enum:> Fruit
   <enumerator:> apple
   <enumerator:> orange
   <enumerator:> strawberry

   <Member Name:> flist             <Member Type:> sequence
   <Sequence Type:> enum            <Maximum Length:> 50

   <Member Name:> counts            <Member Type:> array
   <Array Type:> long <Size:> 10

Typedef Foo defined in ::Test
   <Union:> Foo
   <Discriminator Type:> long
   <Label:> 1 <Member Type:> long <Member Name:> x
   <Label:> 2 <Member Type:> float <Member Name:> y
   <Label:> 0 <Member Type:> char <Member Name:> z

Constant MAXSIZE defined in ::Test
   <Type:> string <Value:> 50

List of attributes
<Attribute Name:> myfoo              <Type:> union
<Attribute Name:> mydouble           <Type:> double
<Attribute Name:> anyvalue           <Type:> any (readonly)
<Attribute Name:> longList           <Type:> sequence

List of methods
<Method Name:> add                   <Return Type:> void
   in name string
<Method Name:> query                 <Return Type:> string
   in index short
   inout aByte octet
<Method Name:> print                 <Return Type:> long
   out status boolean
```

**Figure 8.3**  Output from the BROWSER program

# 9

# Writing Your Own Emitter

One of the features of SOM is that it allows you to do object-oriented design and programming without restricting you to a particular programming language. In addition, SOM allows applications to access objects, regardless of the programming languages in which they were created. This means that a C++ program can use classes developed in Smalltalk and vice-versa. These characteristics are often referred to as language neutral. It is believed that this will significantly increase reuse and promote better inter-operability between programming languages.

To be language neutral, the interface for a class must be defined separately from its implementation. In SOM, the class interface is defined using SOM IDL. The IDL is then compiled by the SOM compiler to create an implementation file where the class implementation is added. To make it easier for programmers to implement SOM classes, and clients to use SOM classes, the SOM compiler can also invoke specific *emitters* to produce language specific *bindings*. Bindings are a set of macros and procedures that tailor the IDL interface to a particular programming language. For example, the C bindings allows C programs to invoke methods on SOM objects in the same way they make ordinary procedure calls. The C++ bindings allow C++ programs to invoke methods on SOM objects in the same way they invoke methods on C++ objects.

Currently, C and C++ bindings are available for the IBM and Borland compilers. Vendors of other language compilers may offer their own language bindings in the future. To help implementors write their own language bindings, SOM provides an Emitter Framework. The Emitter Framework is a collection of SOM classes that allows programmers to write their own emitters.

## 9.1    WHAT IS AN EMITTER?

We have seen a number of emitters already; for example, the Interface Repository emitter (*ir*), the C binding files and implementation template emitters (*h*, *ih*, *c*), the C++ binding files and implementation template emitters (*xh*, *xih*, *xc*), and the export file emitter (*def*). The term *emitter* can be thought of as *the back-end output component of the SOM compiler*:

- The input to an emitter is information about an IDL interface. This information is produced by the SOM compiler as it parses an IDL file.
- The output from an emitter is a file that contains information translated from an IDL interface file into a different format that is specific to the purpose of the emitter.

What this means is that programmers do not have to write their own IDL parsers if they want to understand or analyze an IDL file. Instead, they write an emitter using the classes in the Emitter Framework. The parsing is handled by the SOM compiler. The parsed information is passed to the emitter as an object. The emitter determines what information is needed for output, and writes it out accordingly.

## 9.2    DEVELOPING AN EMITTER

The development of an emitter involves the following steps.

1. Run the **newemit** program to generate a complete working emitter.
2. Customize the output template.
3. Customize the emitter implementation file.
4. Build the emitter.
5. Invoke the emitter via the SOM compiler.

The following sections provide details on each of the above steps.

### 9.2.1    The newemit Program

The **newemit** program is an emitter generator that generates a complete working emitter. You can then customize the emitter to your needs. The **newemit** program takes two parameters: the name of the emitter class and a *file stem*. The file stem represents the name of your emitter. The **newemit** program generates the following files in your current directory:

- *<filestem>*.idl—The IDL definition for your new emitter. Your emitter is always derived from the *SOMTEmitC* class. The *SOMTEmitC* class provides overall control for the emitting process. The IDL specifies that the **somtGenerateSections** method is overridden.

- *<filestem>*.c[*]—The C implementation file for your emitter class. This file contains a default implementation for the **somtGenerateSections** method.
- *<filestem>*.efw—A sample output template file.
- emit*<filestem>*.c—An emitter driver program. Notice that the driver program name is always *emit* followed by the specified file stem. Therefore, the length of your file stem should not be more than four characters long on systems that only support an eight character file name.
- emit*<filestem>*.def—An export file that contains export entries.
- Makefile—A Makefile for creating a DLL for the new emitter.

For example, the following command creates an emitter class *ReportEmitter* and the name of the emitter is *rep*.

```
newemit ReportEmitter rep
```

The files that are generated are *rep.idl, rep.c, rep.efw, emitrep.c, emitrep.def,* and *Makefile*.

### 9.2.2   The Output Template

The Emitter Framework provides a template facility that allows developers to specify the form of an output file in a readable and maintainable manner. Information about how the output file should look can be placed in a template file. It does not need to be specified in the emitter code. The template file is divided into *sections*. Each section specifies the desired output format for each syntactic unit of the interface definition.

Output templates are stored in files with an *.efw* (stands for Emitter Framework) extension. The **newemit** program generates a generic template file *<filestem>*.efw. This file contains all the standard sections with sample text for each section. This file must be edited so it contains your desired output format.

Figure 9.1 is a partial listing of a generated template file. It contains the sections *classS, attributePrologS, attributeS* and *attributeEpilogS*.

A new section is denoted by a line that starts with the colon. By convention, section names end in capital "S". The section *classS* represents the class section. The section *attributePrologS* represents the prolog for the attribute section. It is only emitted once regardless of how many attributes there are. The section *attributeS* represents the repeating portion. It is repeated once for every attribute. The section *attributeEpilogS* represents the epilog for the attribute section. It is only emitted once regardless of how many attributes there are.

A *symbol* is specified using angle brackets. It is used to represent a corresponding value. The output template above contains the symbols *className, classIDLScopedName, classCScopedName,* etc. When a section is emitted, these symbols are replaced with their actual values. For example, the symbol *class-*

---

[*]The **newemit** program in the SOMobjects Developer Toolkit 2.0 generates the emitter implementation file and the emitter driver program in C. If you install CSD202 or higher, then you can choose to generate a C++ implementation file and emitter driver program.

```
:classS
Section: classS


   className = "<className>"
   classIDLScopedName = "<classIDLScopedName>"
   classCScopedName = "<classCScopedName>"
   classComment = "<-- classComment>"
   classInclude = "<classInclude>"
   classLineNumber = "<classLineNumber>"
   classMods = "<classMods, ...>"
   classMajorVersion = "<classMajorVersion>"
   classMinorVersion = "<classMinorVersion>"
   classReleaseOrder = "<classReleaseOrder, ...>"
   classSourceFile = "<classSourceFile>"
   classSourceFileStem = "<classSourceFileStem>"


:attributePrologS
Section: attributePrologS


:attributeS
Section: attributeS


   attributeDeclarators = "<attributeDeclarators, ...>"
   attributeBaseType = "<attributeBaseType>"
   attributeComment = "<-- attributeComment>"
   attributeLineNumber = "<attributeLineNumber>"
   attributeMods = "<attributeMods, ...>"


:attributeEpilogS
Section: attributeEpilogS
```

**Figure 9.1** Sample template file

*Name* will be replaced by the actual name of the class, and the symbol *classIDL-ScopedName* will be replaced by the scoped name of the class using "::" as delimiters.

The symbols *classMods, ...* and *classReleaseOrder, ...* represent a *list substitution* of symbols. The "..." indicates that *list substitution* is used and the symbol's value must consist of a sequence of items. The character "," is used as the separator character.

The symbols -- *classComment* and -- *attributeComment* represent a *comment substitution* of symbols. When the "--" precedes a symbol name, it indicates that *comment substitution* is used and the symbol's value is emitted in comment form. You can control the style and format of the comment in your emitter program. For example, you can control whether comment uses the C++ style ("//"), or the C style ("/*" and "*/").

Using the *Simple* IDL of Figure 9.2 and the output template of Figure 9.1, the output of Figure 9.3 is produced.

### 9.2.3    The Emitter Implementation

The **newemit** program generates an IDL definition and a default C implementation for your emitter. Your emitter is a subclass of *SOMTEmitC* and overrides the **somtGenerateSections** method. The **somtGenerateSections** method determines which sections of the output template are emitted, and in what order. Typically, you will customize the default implementation of **somtGenerateSections.** The **somtGenerateSections** method is called by the emitter driver program emit<*filestem*>.c, when the emitter is invoked by the SOM compiler.

Figure 9.4 shows the default implementation of **somtGenerateSections** for the emitter class *ReportEmitter.*

The **somtEmit**<*Section*> methods emit a particular section from an emitter's template. For example, the **somtEmitClass** method emits the class section.

The **somtScan**<*Section*> methods iterate through a repeating section and call the section-emitting methods whose names are specified in the **somtScan**<*Section*> method. For example, the **somtScanConstants** method iterates through the constants declarations and emits the *constantS* section for each constant. If a

```
#include <somobj.idl>


interface Simple: SOMObject              // Simple IDL Interface
{
        attribute short a1;              // attribute 1
        attribute long a2;               // attribute 2

        #ifdef __SOMIDL__
        implementation
        {
          releaseorder : _get_a1, _set_a1,
                        _get_a2, _set_a2;
        };
        #endif
};
```

**Figure 9.2** The simple IDL

Section: classS

    className = "Simple"
    classIDLScopedName = "::Simple"
    classCScopedName = "Simple"
    classComment = "// Simple IDL Interface"
    classInclude = "<simple.idl>"
    classLineNumber = "0000003"
    classMods = "releaseorder = _get_a1,_set_a1,_get_a2,_set_a2,
            filestem = simple"
    classMajorVersion = "0"
    classMinorVersion = "0"
    classReleaseOrder = "_get_a1, _set_a1, _get_a2, _set_a2"
    classSourceFile = "simple.idl"
    classSourceFileStem = "simple"

Section: attributePrologS

Section: attributeS

    attributeDeclarators = "a1"
    attributeBaseType = "short"
    attributeComment = "// attribute 1"
    attributeLineNumber = "0000005"
    attributeMods = ""

Section: attributeS

    attributeDeclarators = "a2"
    attributeBaseType = "long"
    attributeComment = "// attribute 2"
    attributeLineNumber = "0000006"
    attributeMods = ""

Section: attributeEpilogS

**Figure 9.3** The output template for Simple

```
SOM_Scope boolean SOMLINK somtGenerateSections(ReportEmitter somSelf)
{
    /* ReportEmitterData *somThis = ReportEmitterGetData(somSelf); */
    SOMTClassEntryC cls = __get_somtTargetClass(somSelf);
    SOMTTemplateOutputC template = __get_somtTemplate(somSelf);
    ReportEmitterMethodDebug("ReportEmitter","somtGenerateSections");


    /*
    * Setup symbols that are common to the whole file
    */
    _somtFileSymbols(somSelf);


    _somtEmitProlog(somSelf);


    if (cls != (SOMTClassEntryC) NULL) {
       _somtScanBases(somSelf,
                         "somtEmitBaseIncludesProlog",
                         "somtEmitBaseIncludes",
                         "somtEmitBaseIncludesEpilog");

       _somtEmitMetaInclude(somSelf);

       _somtEmitClass(somSelf);

       _somtScanBases(somSelf,
                         "somtEmitBaseProlog",
                         "somtEmitBase",
                         "somtEmitBaseEpilog");

       _somtEmitMeta(somSelf);
}
_somtScanConstants(somSelf, "somtEmitConstantProlog",
                "somtEmitConstant", "somtEmitConstantEpilog");

_somtScanTypedefs(somSelf, "somtEmitTypedefProlog",
                "somtEmitTypedef", "somtEmitTypedefEpilog");

_somtScanStructs(somSelf, "somtEmitStructProlog",
                "somtEmitStruct", "somtEmitStructEpilog");

_somtScanUnions(somSelf, "somtEmitUnionProlog",
                "somtEmitUnion", "somtEmitUnionEpilog");
```

**Figure 9.4** The default implementation of somtGenerateSections (continues)

```
        _somtScanEnums(somSelf, "somtEmitEnumProlog",
                        "somtEmitEnum", "somtEmitEnumEpilog");

        if (cls != (SOMTClassEntryC) NULL) {
            _somtScanAttributes(somSelf, "somtEmitAttributeProlog",
                            "somtEmitAttribute", "somtEmitAttributeEpilog");

            _somtScanMethods(somSelf,
                            "somtImplemented",
                            "somtEmitMethodsProlog",
                            "somtEmitMethod",
                            "somtEmitMethodsEpilog",
                            0);

            _somtEmitRelease(somSelf);

            _somtScanPassthru(somSelf, 1,
                            "somtEmitPassthruProlog",
                            "somtEmitPassthru",
                            "somtEmitPassthruEpilog");

            _somtScanPassthru(somSelf, 0,
                            "somtEmitPassthruProlog",
                            "somtEmitPassthru",
                            "somtEmitPassthruEpilog");

            _somtScanData(somSelf,
                            "somtEmitDataProlog",
                            "somtEmitData",
                            "somtEmitDataEpilog");
        }

        if (__get_somtTargetModule(somSelf) != (SOMTModuleEntryC) NULL) {

            _somtScanInterfaces(somSelf, "somtEmitInterfaceProlog",
                            "somtEmitInterface", "somtEmitInterfaceEpilog");

            _somtScanModules(somSelf, "somtEmitModuleProlog",
                            "somtEmitModule", "somtEmitModuleEpilog");
        }

        _somtEmitEpilog(somSelf);

        return (TRUE);
        }
```

**Figure 9.4** continued

*constantPrologS* section is defined, it will be emitted before the first constant. If a *constantEpilogS* section is defined, it will be emitted after the last constant.

The default implementation of **somtGenerateSections** emits the template sections in the following order:

1. Prolog—text before any other sections
2. Base Includes—base (parent) class include statements
3. Meta Includes—metaclass include statements
4. Class—class information
5. Base—base (parent) classes information
6. Meta—metaclass information
7. Constant—user-defined constants
8. Typedef—user-defined types
9. Struct—user-defined structs
10. Union—user-defined unions
11. Enum—user-defined enumerations
12. Attribute—attributes of the class
13. Method—methods of the class
14. Release—release order statement
15. Passthru—passthru statements
16. Data—internal instance variable of the class
17. Interface—interfaces in a module
18. Module—module information
19. Epilog—text after all other sections

You can change the order of these sections, or omit any section not relevant to your emitter.

### 9.2.4    Building the Emitter

The **newemit** program generates a Makefile that you can use to build your emitter. When you invoke NMAKE, the emitter driver program and the emitter C implementation will be compiled and linked to create a DLL for your emitter. The name of the DLL is **emit**<*filestem*>. This DLL should be placed in a directory that can be reached by your LIBPATH statement.

### 9.2.5    Invoking the Emitter

To invoke the emitter, run the SOM compiler using the **-s** option, specifying the name of the emitter. For example, the following command invokes the *rep* emitter on the *test.idl* file.

```
sc -srep test.idl
```

This will produce the file *test.rep* whose format is defined in the output template file *rep.efw*.

The entire development process for an emitter is shown in Figure 9.5.

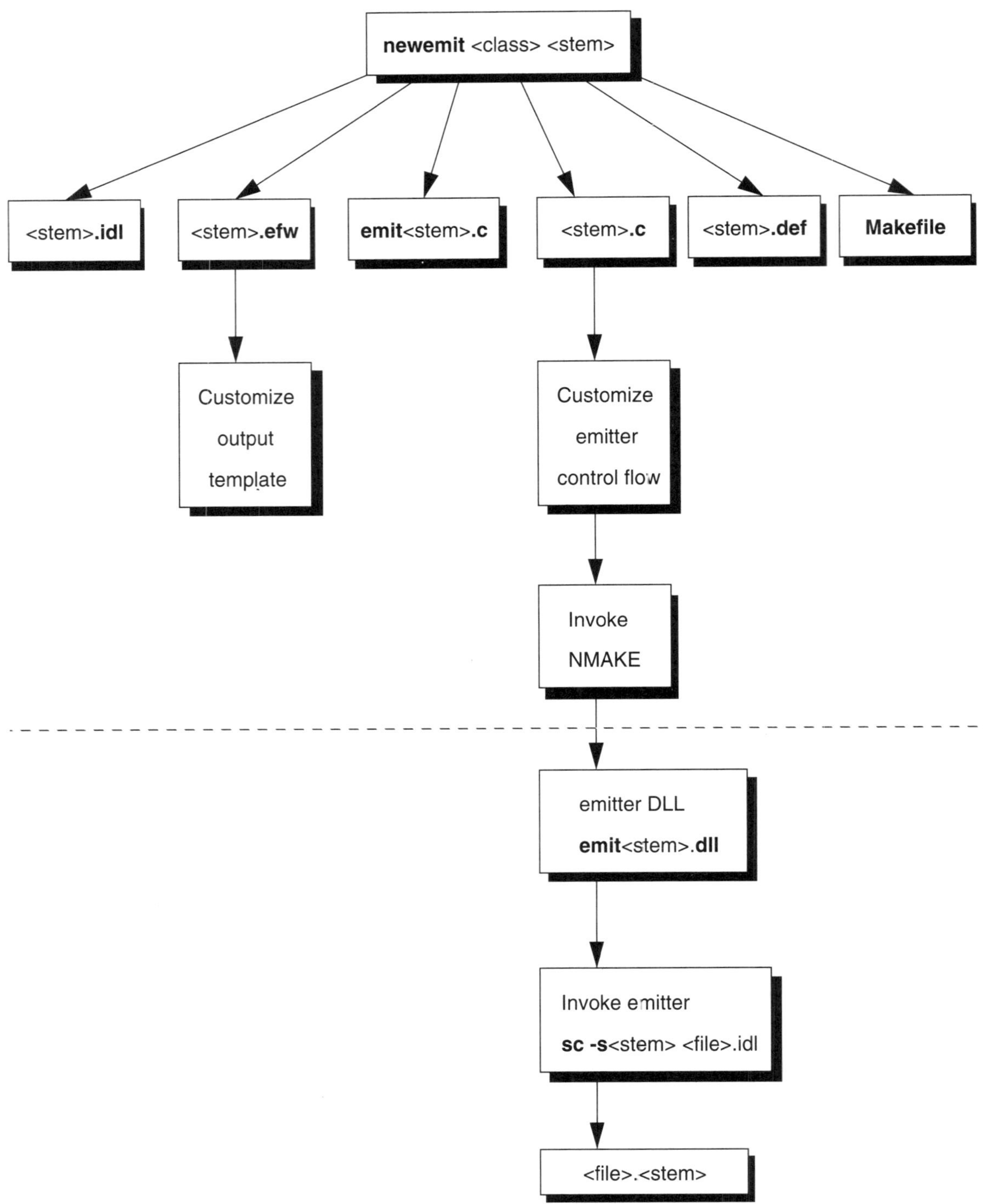


**Figure 9.5** The development process for creating an emitter

## 9.3    EMITTER FRAMEWORK CLASSES

The Emitter Framework consists of a number of classes as shown in Figure 9.6. The *SOMTEmitC* class manages the overall activity of an emitter. All emitters are derived from this class. The *SOMTEmitC* class provides the **somtEmit**<*Section*> and **somtScan**<*Section*> methods for emitting different sections of an output file.

The *SOMTTemplateOutputC* class controls the formatting part of the emitter process by providing a template facility. The template is defined in a file with an *.efw* extension and consists of section names and symbol names. When the emitter is run, the symbols are replaced by the appropriate values. The *SOMTTemplateOutputC* class predefines a set of section and symbol names. It also provides methods where an emitter can define new sections and symbols. We will see an example of this in our Report Emitter.

The *SOMTEntryC* class provides an abstraction for returning information about an IDL interface definition. When the SOM compiler parses an IDL file, it produces an object graph. Each node (entry) in the object graph is derived from some portion of the IDL definition. The *SOMTEntryC* class and its subclasses provide attributes and methods to access the corresponding entry in the object graph. For example, a *SOMTClassEntryC* object represents a complete class interface definition and provides methods for accessing the constants, types, structs, unions, enums, sequences, attributes, and methods defined within an interface statement.

The code fragment in Figure 9.7 shows how you can retrieve the class name and the list of attributes and their types. The **somtTargetClass** attribute returns the target class for the emitter. The *cls* object can then be used to retrieve the class information.

## 9.4    A REPORT EMITTER

In this section, we will build a report emitter. The report emitter produces a report that lists the following information:

- Class name
- Class comment
- Class parent name
- Attribute names and their types
- Method names, their parameters, and return types
- The total number of attributes and methods in an IDL

The format for the output template is shown in Figure 9.8.

Note that the section *summaryS* is not a pre-defined section, and the symbols *totalAttributes* and *totalMethods* are not the standard symbols. We will show how to set the values of these symbols in our emitter.

Invoke the **newemit** program using the following command:

```
newemit ReportEmitter rep
```

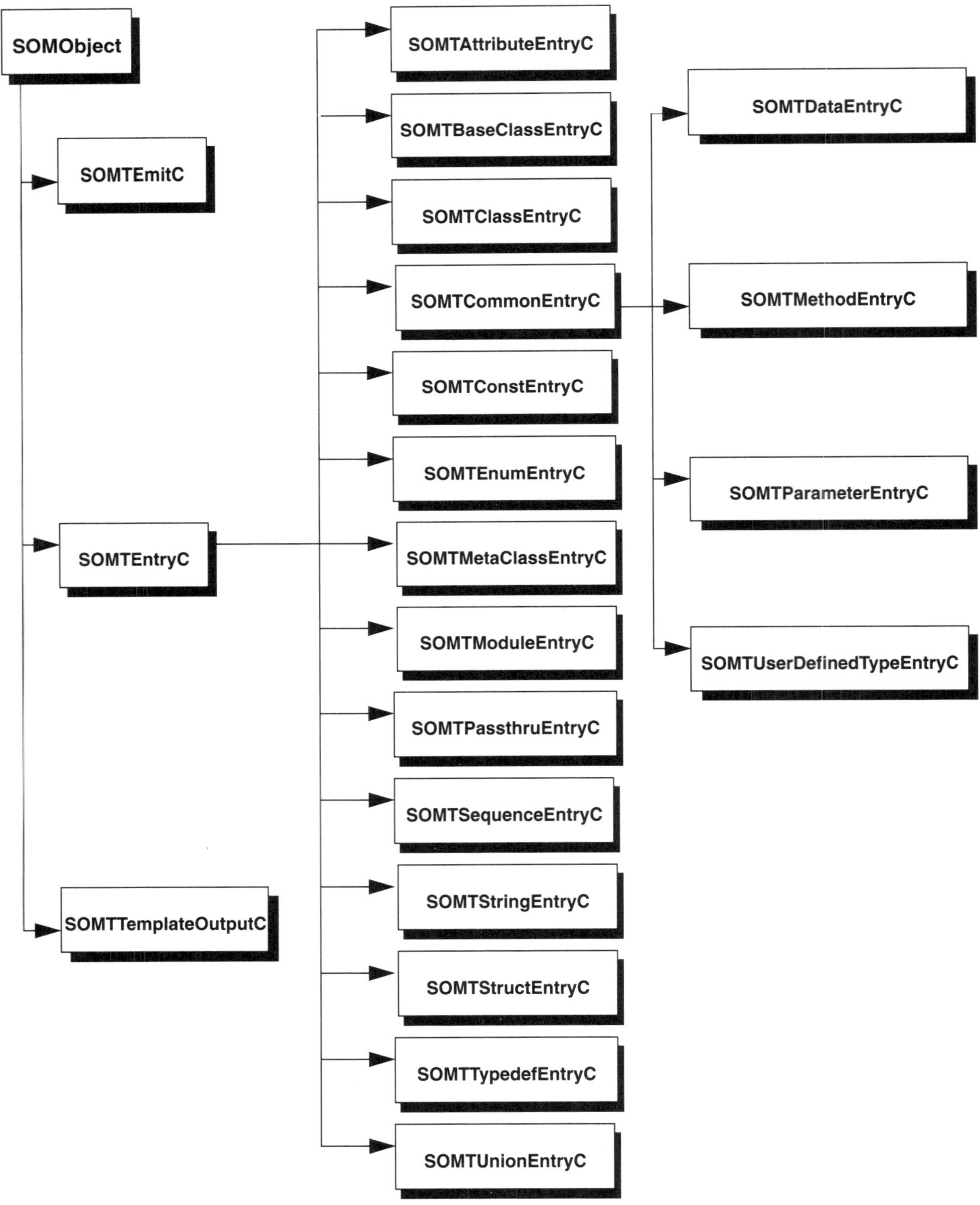


**Figure 9.6** Emitter Framework class hierarchy

```
SOMTClassEntryC     cls = __get_somtTargetClass(emitter);
SOMTAttributeEntryC attrb;
SOMTDataEntryC      myEntry;
SOMTEntryC          attrType;


printf("Class Name: %s\n", __get_somtEntryName(cls) );

for ( attrb = _somtGetFirstAttribute(cls); attrb;
    attrb = _somtGetNextAttribute(cls) )
{
   // Handles the case where there is a list of declarators for an attribute type.
   // For example: attribute short a1, a2, a3;
   for ( myEntry = _somtGetFirstAttributeDeclarator(attrb); myEntry;
        myEntry = _somtGetNextAttributeDeclarator(attrb) )
   {
      printf("Attribute Name: %s ", __get_somtEntryName(myEntry) );
   }


   attrType = __get_somtAttribType(attrb);
   printf( "Attribute Type %s\n", __get_somtEntryName(attrType) );
}
```

**Figure 9.7** Example to show how to use the Emitter Framework classes

This generates the file *rep.efw*. Edit this file so that its format is the same as the output template given in Figure 9.8.

The file *rep.idl* contains the IDL definition for *ReportEmitter*. We will add the following to this file:

- **somtEmitMethod**—this method is redefined so that it can count the number of methods the emitter emits.
- **somtEmitAttribute**—this method is redefined so that it can count the number of attributes the emitter emits.
- **somInit**—this method is redefined to initialize instance variables.

The changes that are made to the IDL are shown in Figure 9.9 in bold.

The file *rep.c* contains the C implementation for the *ReportEmitter*. We modify the default implementation of **somtGenerateSections** so that it only generates the sections that we need in our output template. We also add the implementation for **somtEmitMethod, somtEmitAttribute**, and **somInit**. The modified *rep.c* appears in Figure 9.10.

Notice how we use the **somtSetSymbolCopyBoth** method to set the values of the symbols *totalAttributes* and *totalMethods*. The **somtOutputSection** method is then used to output the *summaryS* section.

```
:classS
 Report on class <className>

======================================================
? Description: <classComment>
IDL source file: <classSourceFile>
Parent Name: <baseName>


:attributePrologS
 Attribute Definitions

======================================================
:attributeS
<attributeDeclarators, ...> <attributeBaseType>
:attributeEpilogS


:methodsPrologS
 Method Definitions

======================================================
:methodsS
<methodType> <methodName> <methodIDLParamList, ...>
:methodsEpilogS


:summaryS
 Summary

======================================================
Total number of attributes: <totalAttributes>
Total number of methods: <totalMethods>
```

**Figure 9.8** The output template for our report

The emitter can then be built by invoking NMAKE. This creates the DLL *emitrep.dll*.

### 9.4.1    Invoking the Report Emitter

Make sure the file *emitrep.dll* is placed in a directory that is specified on your LIBPATH. Also make sure the output template *rep.efw* is placed in a directory that is specified by the environment variable SMINCLUDE. For example, the following setting will cause the SOM compiler to search the current directory and then the SOM include directory for the output template:

```
set SMINCLUDE=.;%SOMBASE%\INCLUDE
```

```
        #ifndef ReportEmitter_idl
        #define ReportEmitter_idl

        #include <scemit.idl>
        interface ReportEmitter : SOMTEmitC
        {
              #ifdef __SOMIDL__
              implementation
              {
                //# Class Modifiers
                callstyle = oidl;

                //# Method Modifiers
                somtGenerateSections: override;

                somtEmitMethod: override;
                somtEmitAttribute: override;
                somInit: override;

                short numOfAttributes;
                short numOfMethods;
              };
              #endif /* __SOMIDL__ */
        };

        #endif /* ReportEmitter_idl */
```

**Figure 9.9**  The ReportEmitter IDL


The *test.idl* in Figure 9.11 is provided as a test case.

To run the report emitter on *test.idl*, invoke the SOM compiler using the **-s** option.

```
        sc -srep test.idl
```

This produces the file *test.rep* listed in Figure 9.12.

```c
/*
 * File: rep.c
 * Author: SOMObjects Emitter Framework.
 * Contents: Generic framework implementation for ReportEmitter.
 * Date: Mon Jan 3 18:24:38 1994.
 */

#define ReportEmitter_Class_Source
#include <rep.ih>
#include <stdio.h>

SOM_Scope boolean SOMLINK somtGenerateSections(ReportEmitter somSelf)
{
    ReportEmitterData *somThis = ReportEmitterGetData(somSelf);
    char buf[50];

    SOMTClassEntryC cls = __get_somtTargetClass(somSelf);
    SOMTTemplateOutputC template = __get_somtTemplate(somSelf);
    ReportEmitterMethodDebug("ReportEmitter","somtGenerateSections");


    /*
     * Setup symbols that are common to the whole file
     */
    _somtFileSymbols(somSelf);

    if (cls != (SOMTClassEntryC) NULL) {
      _somtScanBases(somSelf,
                        "somtEmitBaseProlog",
                        "somtEmitBase",
                        "somtEmitBaseEpilog");
      _somtEmitClass(somSelf);

      _somtScanAttributes(somSelf, "somtEmitAttributeProlog",
                            "somtEmitAttribute", "somtEmitAttributeEpilog");

      _somtScanMethods(somSelf,
                        "somtImplemented",
                        "somtEmitMethodsProlog",
                        "somtEmitMethod",
                        "somtEmitMethodsEpilog",
                        0);
```

**Figure 9.10** The ReportEmitter class implementation (continues)

```
            sprintf(buf, "%d", _numOfAttributes);
            _somtSetSymbolCopyBoth(template, "totalAttributes", buf);

            sprintf(buf, "%d", _numOfMethods);
            _somtSetSymbolCopyBoth(template, "totalMethods", buf);

            _somtOutputSection(template, "summaryS");
        }

        return (TRUE);
}

SOM_Scope void SOMLINK somtEmitMethod(ReportEmitter somSelf,
                                      SOMTMethodEntryC entry)
{
    ReportEmitterData *somThis = ReportEmitterGetData(somSelf);
    SOMTTemplateOutputC template = __get_somtTemplate(somSelf);

    ReportEmitterMethodDebug("ReportEmitter","somtEmitMethod");

    ReportEmitter_parent_SOMTEmitC_somtEmitMethod(somSelf, entry);
    _numOfMethods++;
}

SOM_Scope void SOMLINK somtEmitAttribute(ReportEmitter somSelf,
                                         SOMTAttributeEntryC att)
{
    ReportEmitterData *somThis = ReportEmitterGetData(somSelf);
    ReportEmitterMethodDebug("ReportEmitter","somtEmitAttribute");

    ReportEmitter_parent_SOMTEmitC_somtEmitAttribute(somSelf, att);
    _numOfAttributes++;
}

SOM_Scope void SOMLINK somInit(ReportEmitter somSelf)
{
    ReportEmitterData *somThis = ReportEmitterGetData(somSelf);
    ReportEmitterMethodDebug("ReportEmitter","somInit");

    ReportEmitter_parent_SOMTEmitC_somInit(somSelf);

    _numOfAttributes = 0;
    _numOfMethods = 0;
}
```

**Figure 9.10** continued

```
#include <somobj.idl>

interface Test: SOMObject
{
      const unsigned short MAXSIZE = 50;
      union Foo switch (long)
      {
        case 1: long x;
        case 2: float y;
        default: char z;
      };

      attribute Foo myfoo;
      attribute double mydouble;
      attribute any anyvalue;
      attribute sequence<long,MAXSIZE> longList;

      void add(in string name);
      string query(in short index, inout octet aByte);
      long print(out boolean status);

      #ifdef __SOMIDL__
      implementation
      {
        releaseorder : _get_myfoo, _set_myfoo,
                    _get_mydouble, _set_mydouble,
                    _get_anyvalue, _set_anyvalue,
                    _get_longList, _set_longList,
                    add, query, print;
      };
      #endif
};
```

**Figure 9.11** An IDL to illustrate the report emitter

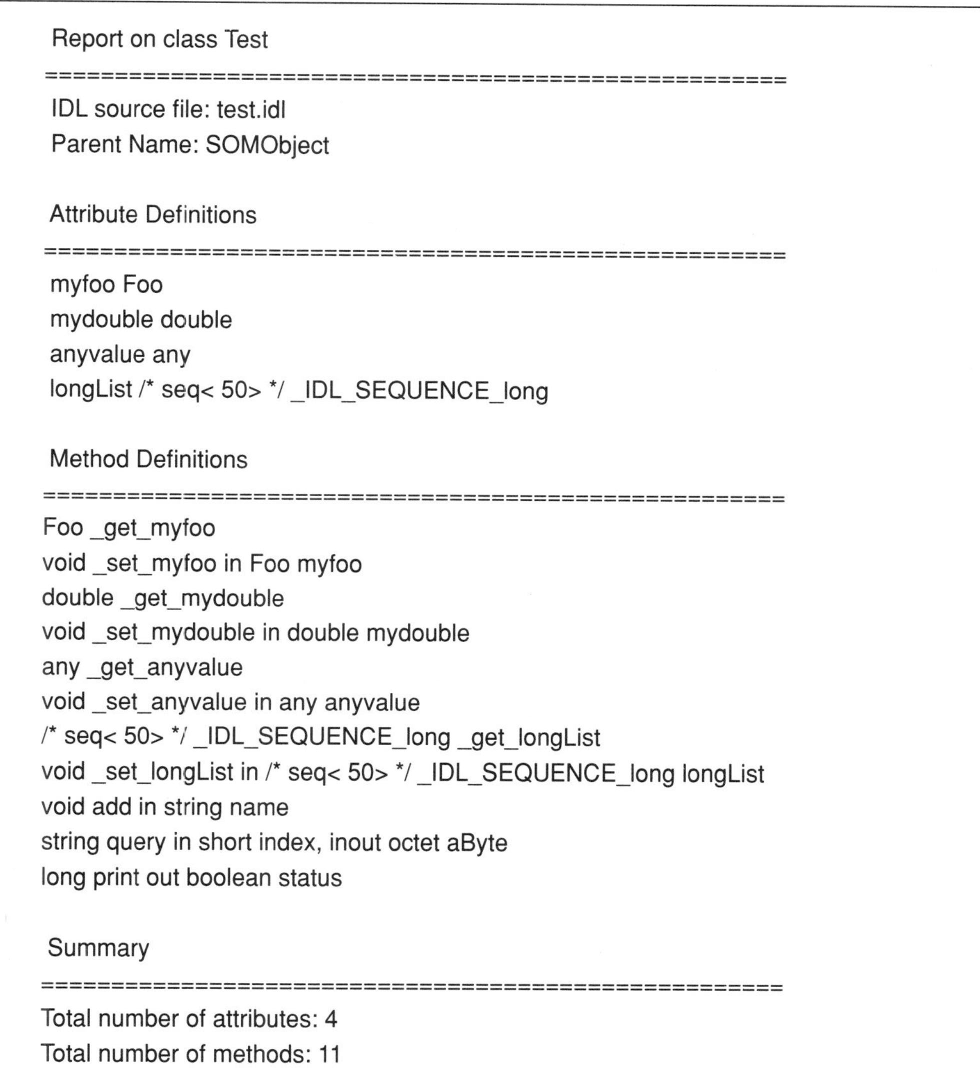

```
   Report on class Test
   ===========================================================
   IDL source file: test.idl
   Parent Name: SOMObject

   Attribute Definitions
   ===========================================================
   myfoo Foo
   mydouble double
   anyvalue any
   longList /* seq< 50> */ _IDL_SEQUENCE_long

   Method Definitions
   ===========================================================
   Foo _get_myfoo
   void _set_myfoo in Foo myfoo
   double _get_mydouble
   void _set_mydouble in double mydouble
   any _get_anyvalue
   void _set_anyvalue in any anyvalue
   /* seq< 50> */ _IDL_SEQUENCE_long _get_longList
   void _set_longList in /* seq< 50> */ _IDL_SEQUENCE_long longList
   void add in string name
   string query in short index, inout octet aByte
   long print out boolean status

   Summary
   ===========================================================
   Total number of attributes: 4
   Total number of methods: 11
```

**Figure 9.12** Output from the report emitter

# 10

# Future Directions

SOM, with its set of Frameworks, provides the underlying facilities for building object-oriented applications in a language-neutral manner. However, this is only the beginning. SOM is envisioned as a "software bus" that links operating systems and compilers. Software components can be plugged into this bus and have access to resources located anywhere on the network.

To allow distributed applications to be built across multiple platforms, IBM is working on porting SOM to different systems including Windows, Apple System 7, MVS, OS/400, and Hewlett-Packard Unix. The SOMobject Developer Toolkit for Windows has been recently announced and will be available in the summer of 1994.

There will be new versions of SOM. It will continue to comply with CORBA as it evolves. It will also provide the following object services, which are being defined and standarized by OMG.

- Naming: provides the ability to attach textual names to object references.
- Event Notification: provides notification of asynchronous events.
- Life Cycle: defines services and conventions for creating, deleting, copying, and moving objects.
- Persistence: provides common interfaces to make all, or part of an object state persistent.

In addition, IBM is pursuing relationships with different vendors to integrate SOM into their environment. The following provides a summary of the announcements by different companies to incorporate SOM into various product offerings. This is an area of intense activity. We expect a number of other SOM related announcements in the coming months.

## 10.1   IBM AND HEWLETT-PACKARD ANNOUNCEMENT

IBM's Personal Software Division (PSP) has announced an agreement with Hewlett-Packard (HP) to integrate IBM and HP object technologies into a common framework for distributed computing. This framework will provide the infrastructure needed to support the creation, management, and use of object-oriented applications in a heterogeneous, distributed systems environment.

The companies will integrate IBM's System Object Model (SOM) and HP's Distributed Object Management Facility (DOMF), with extensions for distribution (DSOM), into a robust enabling framework for the implementation of IBM and HP distributed object services, applications, and development tools. This will provide developers, systems administrators, and end-users with language-neutral, enterprise-wide, heterogeneous support for building, managing, and using distributed object-oriented applications that inter-operate across multiple platforms—initially HPs and IBMs.

HP's DOMF and IBM's SOM/DSOM are implementations of the OMG's Common Object Request Broker Architecture (CORBA) standard that provides location-transparent access to distributed objects. HP's DOMF provides access to distributed objects by utilizing the Open Software Foundation's (OSF) Distributed Computing Environment (DCE) technology. IBM's SOM and DSOM provides access to distributed objects by utilizing workgroup-based sockets. Together, these technologies will provide workgroup and enterprise-wide access to distributed objects.

The first IBM/HP object-framework products will be available across the HP 9000 Series 700 and Series 800 PA-RISC-based platform of workstations and business servers, and across IBM's range of OS/2-based PCs and AIX/6000 workstations. Availability is planned for 1994.

The IBM/HP technology will fully comply with the CORBA specification and provide significant additional capabilities not available today. The OMG's Interface Definition Language (IDL) will be supported as the standard for all objects created in the IBM/HP environment.


## 10.2   Digitalk ANNOUNCEMENT

Digitalk, the developer of Smalltalk/V and PARTS, has licensed SOM and workstation DSOM for OS/2 and AIX with plans to incorporate the technology in a future release of Digitalk products. Smalltalk/V is a leading pure object-oriented programming language with more than 150,000 users. PARTS (Parts Assembly and Reuse Tool Set) Workbench for OS/2 and Windows is a client/server integration framework that enables rapid visual application development from prefabricated software components, including CICS, COBOL, and all popular databases. PARTS delivers the benefit of objects without the complexity in an interactive visual environment.

Jim Anderson, chairman of Digitalk, said, "Digitalk is committed to cross-platform, cross-language object interaction. IBM's licensing of SOM technology to

Digitalk benefits our mutual customers by providing a single source for the premier object-oriented language, and the industry standard for cross-language object communication. With SOM, Smalltalk/V, and C++ objects are interchangeable, so a wide range of Smalltalk/V and C++ class libraries are available to our customers."

## 10.3   ParcPlace SYSTEMS ANNOUNCEMENT

ParcPlace Systems has announced plans to integrate SOM and workstation DSOM into ParcPlace's VisualWorks Smalltalk client/server development environment. The support of SOM, and workstation DSOM, will enable Smalltalk application developers to easily access objects developed in C++ or any other language that supports the SOM and workstation DSOM specification. VisualWorks is a powerful application development environment for corporate developers to create graphical, client/server applications that are instantly portable across PC, Macintosh, and Unix platforms. VisualWorks includes a graphical user interface builder, hierarchical, relational and object-oriented database access capabilities, reuse application framework, instant cross-platform portability, and the Smalltalk language.

Richard Dym, vice-chairman of marketing for ParcPlace, said, "ParcPlace is pleased to be working with IBM to enhance the opportunities for object-oriented application development. The integration of VisualWorks with SOM and DSOM enhances the best object-oriented client/server development tool for corporate IS groups, enabling them to leverage existing application investments and increase development productivity."

## 10.4   WATCOM ANNOUNCEMENT

WATCOM has announced plans to integrate SOM and workstation DSOM into the WATCOM's C/C++ compiler, VX*REXX visual development environment, and PC-based client/server SQL database products. WATCOM plans to offer fundamental benefits to its customers by providing tools to create reusable software components that can be assembled to create business solutions in a distributed, heterogeneous computing environment.

Ian McPhee, president of WATCOM, said, "We intend to use SOM and DSOM to amplify the competitive advantage offered by WATCOM's application development tools. The SOM technology promises to deliver a flexible and efficient binary standard for object interfaces which, with SOM enabled tools, will let developers and users realize greater benefits from object-oriented software engineering."

## 10.5   OBJECTIVE: INC. ANNOUNCEMENT

Objective: Inc. has licensed SOM and workstation DSOM with the intent of releasing, in 1994, a MacroScope interface layer that provides a generic message interface to any object created with SOM and DSOM. The interface will enable developers to send messages to invoke any SOM/DSOM created facility. The integration of SOM/DSOM into MacroScope produces the only fully-proven rapid development environment that is CORBA compliant.

Bernadette Reiter, president of Objective: Inc., said, "The real significance of IBM's SOM/DSOM being integrated with MacroScope is that business and organizations will immediately be able to start reaping the benefits of object technology. They can have practical business solutions built in time frames they never thought possible. At the same time, they can exploit to the fullest their existing investments in hardware and software, and the most flexible options for future migration."

## 10.6   DirectToSOM

MetaWare announced at the Fall COMDEX' 93 in Las Vegas it has started beta shipments of its High C/C++ compilers for IBM AIX/6000 and OS/2 2.1 that include DirectToSOM support for IBM's SOM and workstation DSOM. DirectToSOM permits software developers to create SOM binaries by compiling standard C++ source code. Developers can move existing C++ code to SOM by recompiling all of the supporting components are included. Thereafter, recompiling will be needed only when source code changes are made.

Bennett Watson, president of MetaWare, said, "We believe that SOM is an important step in advancing C++ as a commercially-viable language. Reusable software components, a key promise of object-oriented methodology, is fulfilled by SOM. MetaWare and IBM have worked closely together to define DirectToSOM support for C++ compilers. MetaWare's High C/C++ for OS/2 2.1 and for IBM AIX/6000 systems are the first compilers to implement the DirectToSOM feature."

IBM has also announced that it will support native SOM and workstation DSOM in its C Set++ compilers starting in the first half of 1994.

## 10.7   VisualAge ANNOUNCEMENT

IBM's VisualAge is an integrated application development environment designed for a client-server, mission-critical, line of business applications through visual programming and construction-from-components technologies. Using popular relational databases, VisualAge enables customers to develop client/server database applications.

IBM has announced plan for VisualAge to support SOM and workstation DSOM on OS/2 during the first half of 1994.

## 10.8   SUMMARY

This chapter concludes the book and gives you an idea on where SOM is going. If you would like to find out more, or to order the SOMobjects Developer Toolkit, call 1 800 3-IBM-OS2.

# References


*IBM SOMobjects Developer Toolkit Users Guide,* Version 2.0.

*IBM SOMobjects Developer Toolkit Programmers Reference Manual,* Version 2.0.

*IBM SOMobjects Developer Toolkit Emitter Framework Guide and Reference,* Version 2.0.

*IBM SOMobjects Developer Toolkit Collection Classes Reference Manual,* Version 2.0.

*IBM SOMobjects Developer Toolkit Installation / Configuration Guide,* Version 2.0.

*IBM SOMobjects Workstation Enabler Installation / Configuration Guide,* Version 2.0.

*IBM SOMobjects Workgroup Enabler Installation / Configuration Guide,* Version 2.0.

Lajoie, Josee. 1993. *The new language extensions.* C++ Report, 5(6):47-52.

Meyers, Scott. 1992. *Effective C++.* Massachusetts. Addison-Wesley.

*Object Management Architecture Guide,* Revision 2.0, Second Edition, September 1, 1992, OMG TC Document 92.11.1.

*IBM User Interface Class Library User's Guide.* An IBM Red Book.

*The Common Object Request Broker: Architecture and Specification,* OMG Document Number 91.12.1, Revision 1.1.

Sessions Roger. 1992. *Class Construction in C and C++: Object Oriented Programming Fundamentals.* New Jersey. Prentice-Hall.

Stroustrup, Bjarne and Dmitry Lenkov. Run-time type identification for C++. *C++ Report.* 4(3):32-42.

# Index